Paul Wadsworth

India
Stories From The Banyan Tree

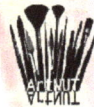

Stories From The Banyan Tree

Copyright © Paul Wadsworth 2022

The right of Paul Wadsworth to be identified as the author of this work has been asserted in accordance with sections 77 and 78 of the Copyright Design and Patent Act 1988.

For further information about the book email: paulwads@btinternet.com
Website: www.paulwadsworth.co.uk

Published by ArtNut, imprint of MAPublisher (Penzance)
Published in UK, July 2022
Email: mapublisher@yahoo.com, Website: www.mapublisher.org.uk

ISBN-13: 978-1-910499-81-8

All rights reserved. No part of this publication may be reproduced, stored in a retrieval system, or transmitted, in any form or by any means, electronic, mechanical, photocopying, recording, public performances or otherwise, without prior written permission of the copyright holder, except for brief quotations embodied in critical articles or reviews.

Book & Cover design and layout by Mayar Akash
Cover artwork: Paul Wadsworth
Typeset: Time New Roman

Paper printed on is FSC Certified, lead free, acid free, buffered paper made from wood-based pulp. Our paper meets the ISO 9706 standard for permanent paper. As such, paper will last several hundred years when stored.

Contents

Title: Tiger tiger burning bright	6
Introduction	7
India - Stories From The Banyan Tree	8
Oil Paintings	9
Title: Bring home the catch	9
Title: Butterfly in your hand	10
Title: The Kerala market sellers	11
Title: An eagle flew by the lake	12
Title: Bathing in blue water	13
Title: Blue dress falling leaves	14
Title: Breathing nature	15
Title: By the Indian Ocean	16
Title: Camillia tree	17
Title: Carpet weaver	18
Title: Carpet weavers	19
Title: Chai	20
Title: Cooking fire	21
Title: Dancing in the garden	22
Title: Dreamer	23
Title: Elephant in the mango tree	24
Title: Festival balloon seller	25
Title: Festival day	26
Title: Figure in white	27
Title: Fishing net	28
Title: Fishing on the blue river	29
Title: Warm air	30
Title: Flying over India	31
Title: Forest home	32
Title: Forest lovers	33
Title: Forest lovers	34
Title: Fruit picker	35
Title: Full moon swimmer	36
Title: Fun fair	37
Title: Hampi sunrise	38
Title: Harem	39
Title: Hidden within nature	40
Title: Home from school	41
Title: In the night garden	42
Title: Indian Bazaar	43
Title: Kerala life and bauty	44
Title: Moonlit swimmer	45
Title: Kerala's beauty	46
Title: Life around a small red temple	47
Title: Living by the sea	48
Title: Love shack	49
Title: Lovers	50
Title: Meditation	51
Title: Monkey temple	52
Title: Monsoon water	53
Title: Moonlight water	54
Title: Natures garden	55
Title: Night ocean	56
Title: Old Goa	57
Title: Orange Garden	58
Title: Orange sunshine	59
Title: Paddling through the sound of birds	60
Title: Picking mangos	61
Title: Picking the fruits	62
Title: Pilgrimage	63
Title: Pink city	64
Title: Drifting in a small boat	65
Title: Pink temple	66

Title: Pleasure garden	67
Title: Pleasure garden 2	67
Title: Pretty in pink	68
Title: Rainbow doorway	69
Title: Rajasthan gypsy dancer	70
Title: Rajasthan gypsy dancer 2	71
Title: Red dress	72
Title: Red river shore	73
Title: Red umbrellas	74
Title: River journey	75
Title: Sweet isolation	76
Title: River swimmer	77
Title: River takes you	78
Title: Round boat river	79
Title: Sacred water	80
Title: She lives by the beach	81
Title: Silent air	82
Title: Silent colour	83
Title: Silent lake	84
Title: Sitting in the rose garden	85
Title: Sleeping by the lake	86
Title: Small pink temple	87
Title: Small yellow temple	88
Title: Standing by the sacred river	89
Title: Stories from the banyan tree	90
Title: Sun umbrellas	91
Title: Sunlit path	92
Title: Sunset	93
Title: Sunshine	94
Title: Swimmer and blue bird	95
Title: Tantric dancers	96
Title: Tea pickers	97
Title: Temple cow	98
Title: Stream reflection	99
Title: Temple lake dancers	100
Title: Temple meeting	101
Title: The angels have a party	102
Title: The colour balloon seller	103
Title: The colour garden	104
Title: The elephant friend	105
Title: The fish seller	106
Title: The magic flute player	107
Title: The magician and the sacred cow	108
Title: The musician and his cow	109
Title: The pink dancer	110
Title: The red Rajasthan dancer	111
Title: The Taylor shop	112
Title: The water garden	113
Title: Three men in a boat	114
Title: Together in a forest of colour	115
Title: Touching god	116
Title: Tranquility	117
Title: Travellers by sea	118
Title: Travelling together	119
Title: Under the banyan tree	120
Title: Under the waterfall	121
Title: Waiting	122
Title: Walking home after the festival	123
Title: Walking to the waterfall	124
Title: Water carriers	125
Title: Waterfall	126
Title: White butterfly	127
Title: Yellow desert	128

Title: Yellow sari	129
Title: Pink forest swimmer	130
Acrylic on paper	131
Title: Pink Ambassador	131
Title: Surf up	131
Title: A beautiful conversation	132
Title: Beach below the orange cliff	133
Title: Fisherman	134
Title: Forest cow	135
Title: Golden Island	136
Title: Home by the sea	137
Title: Morning walk	138
Title: Red forest	139
Title: Sun swimmers	140
Title: Wood collector	141
Watercolours	142
Title: Hauling the nets, Kerala	142
Title: Kerala fishermen	143
Title: Pilgrimage	143
Title: Pushkar walk	144
Title: Sacred swim	144
CV	145

Stories From The Banyan Tree

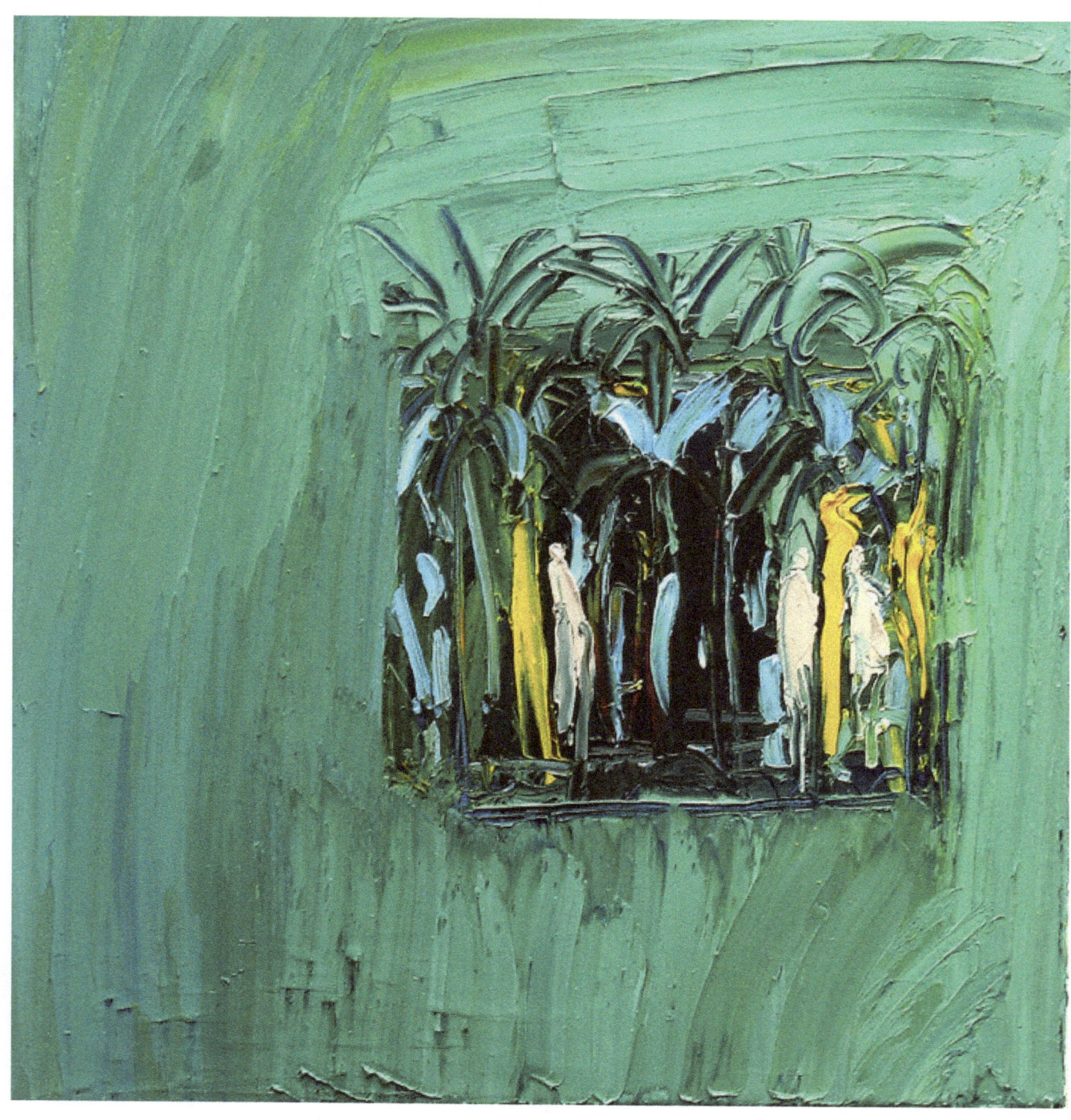

Title: Tiger tiger burning bright
Size: 61x61cm

Introduction

A Paul Wadsworth painting hangs in our living room – a shard of sunlight leaping up from a Cornish moor, a bright streak of yellow bursting from an earthy Celtic landscape. The painting changes during the day; as the light shifts around it the image seems to dance, a bold swathe of dark green coming in and out of focus, the clouds in the sky billowing and rearranging. Sometimes I can see figures moving along the ridgeway at the point where the land meets the sky. At other times, I just see an explosion of colour.

The paintings which emerge from Paul's time in India amplify that sense of colour leaping from the canvas - the rich textures of verdant foliage, the humid warmth of the air, the dripping fullness of the trees. Water is a recurrent element, reflecting and intensifying the life which throngs through the paintings. And just as these images are vibrant with adventure and personal narrative, so they are peopled with figures who emerge from the landscape to tell their own stories; working, walking, worshipping, dancing. At times the paintings burst the confines of their own canvasses, affixed to larger boards which allow them to continue expanding, shrines at the centre of a world which is fruitful and multiplying.

There is nothing 'touristy' here; this is the work of someone who has immersed himself in these landscapes, succumbed to them, become intoxicated by them. They are overwhelmingly positive and life-affirming. A painting of trees over water shimmers and shifts, the colours constantly rearranging themselves, reflections moving as if still fluid. I think that's what I love most about Paul's work – the sense that each painting is still growing, still evolving, still finding its own story. I could look at them for hours, days, years. I am sure you will feel the same.

Mark Kermode

India - Stories from the Banyan tree

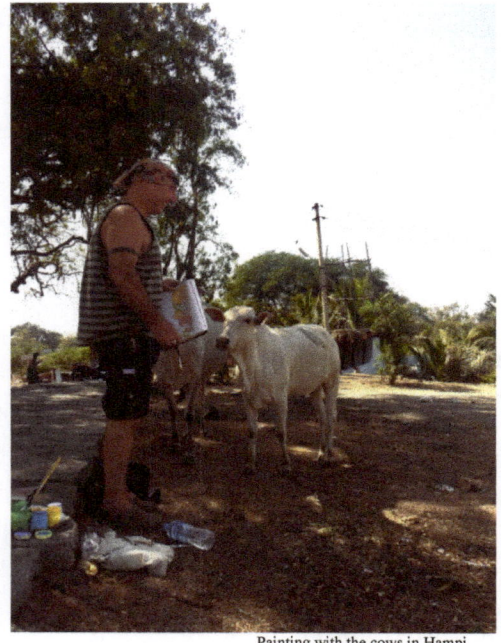
Painting with the cows in Hampi

Ever since my early twenties I wanted to visit and explore the magical place of Banyan trees, Temples, deities, colour, architecture, festivities, Tigers, Monkeys and Elephants. These are just a few offerings that tell the story of India.

For seventeen years I painted and travelled extensively in the United Arab Emirates and Oman showing works in Dubai and Muscat but over the last 6 years my travels have taken me to the amazingly colourful India.

My first trip took me to the west coast of Goa.

For one month I spent time travelling by moped, taxis , boats and buses exploring the amazing diversity of landscape and culture. Carrying a sketchbook, acrylics and water colours I started to make my first impressions of India on paper.

Multicoloured temples and white churches sit amongst the palm trees that run alongside the rivers splitting the landscape. Everywhere you looked would be some colour. The ladies saris, the decorated cow, the musician playing for money or the bustling markets selling flowers.

Subsequent trips took me to the temples of Rajasthan and to the tropical forests and tea fields of Kerala.

I try to find the power of storytelling in a painting and in India I found it in abundance.

Over these times I have worked on many sketches and smaller location based works. These were the beginnings and memories for paintings to come.

Once home I start work on much larger canvases with oils and the stories begin. Each painting gradually finding its own way and revealing parts of the personnel journeys that I intend to continue over the years to come.

Paul Wadsworth

Oil paintings

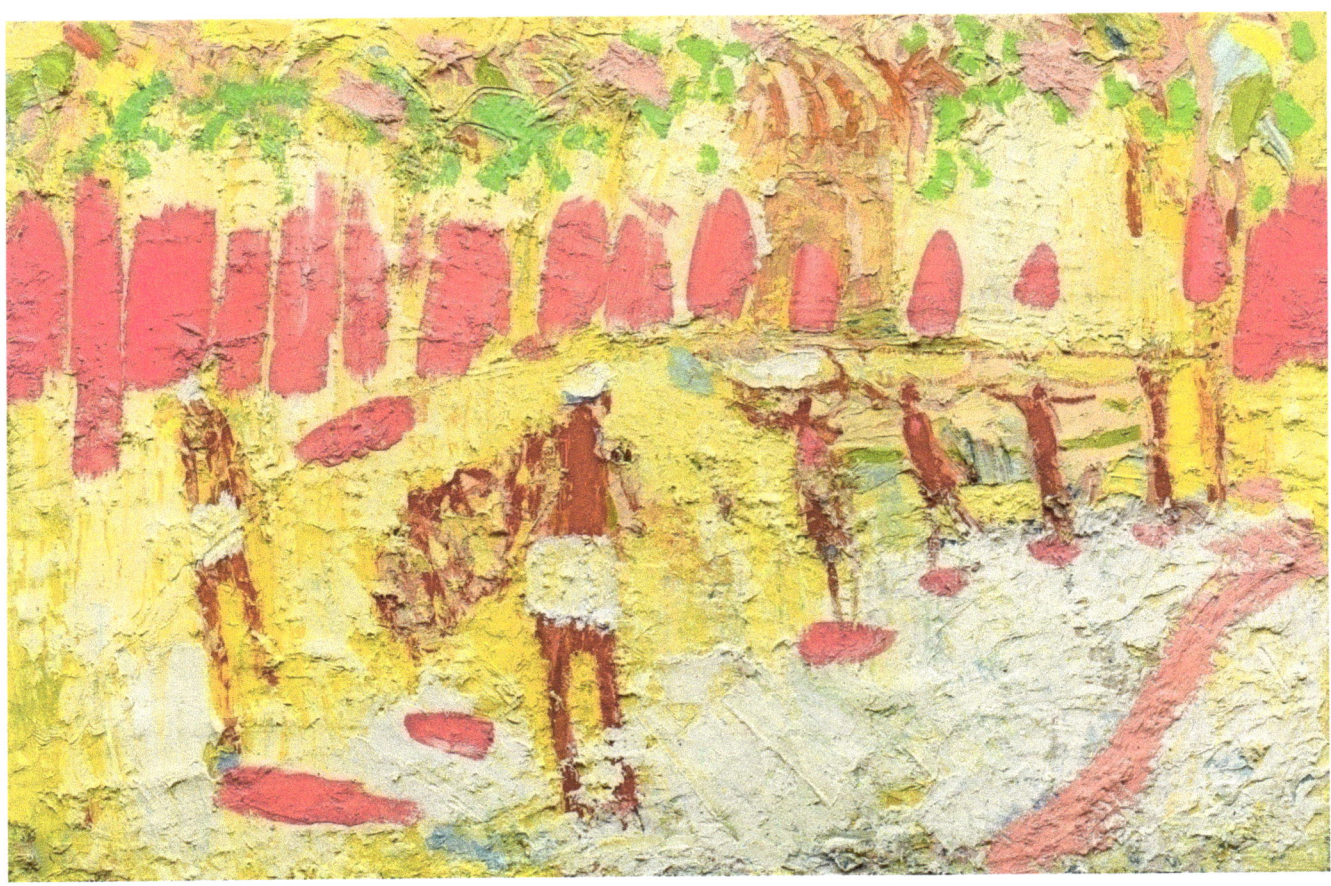

Title: Bring home the catch

Size: 70x90cm

Stories From The Banyan Tree

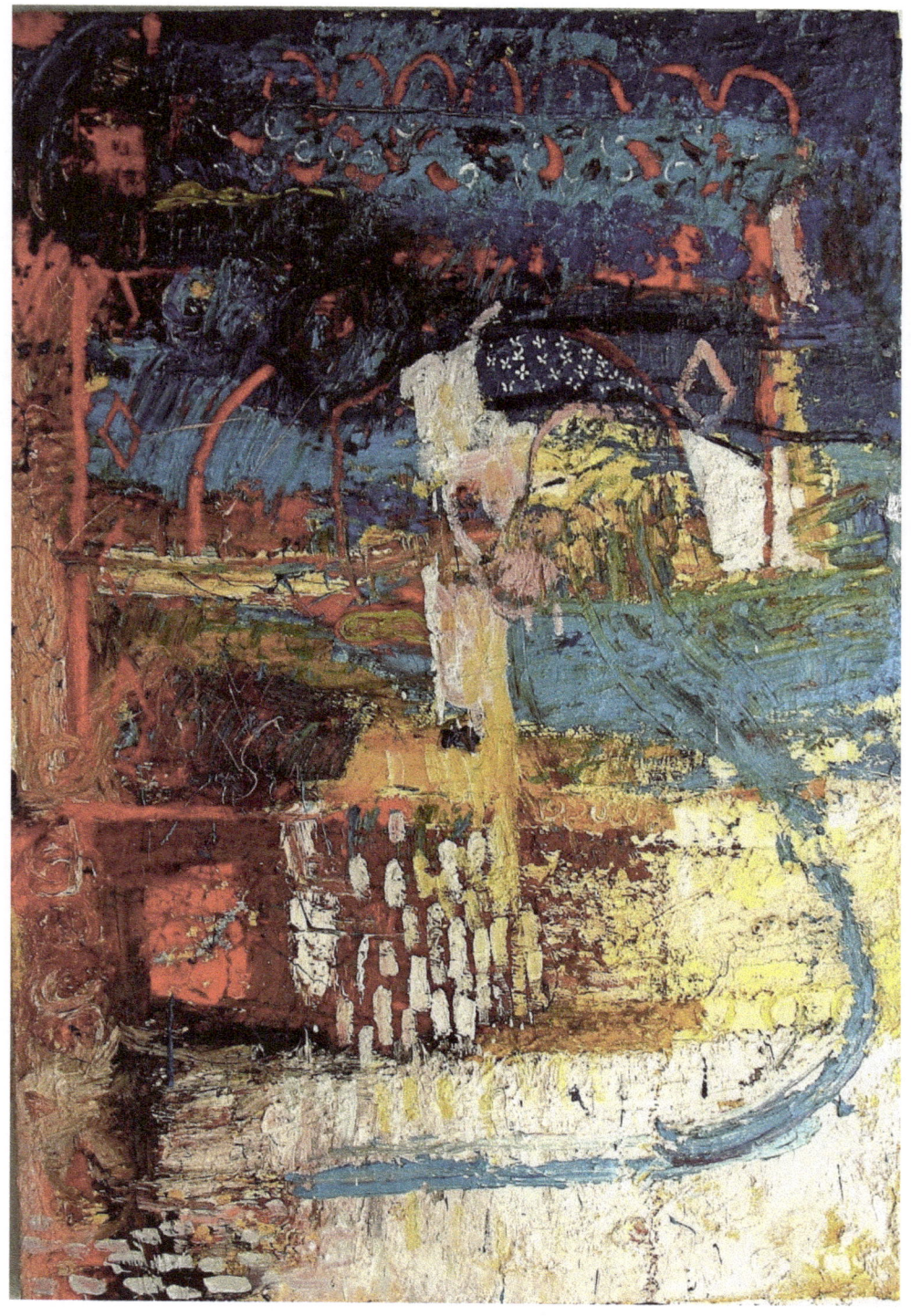

Title: Butterfly in your hand
Size: 181x121cm

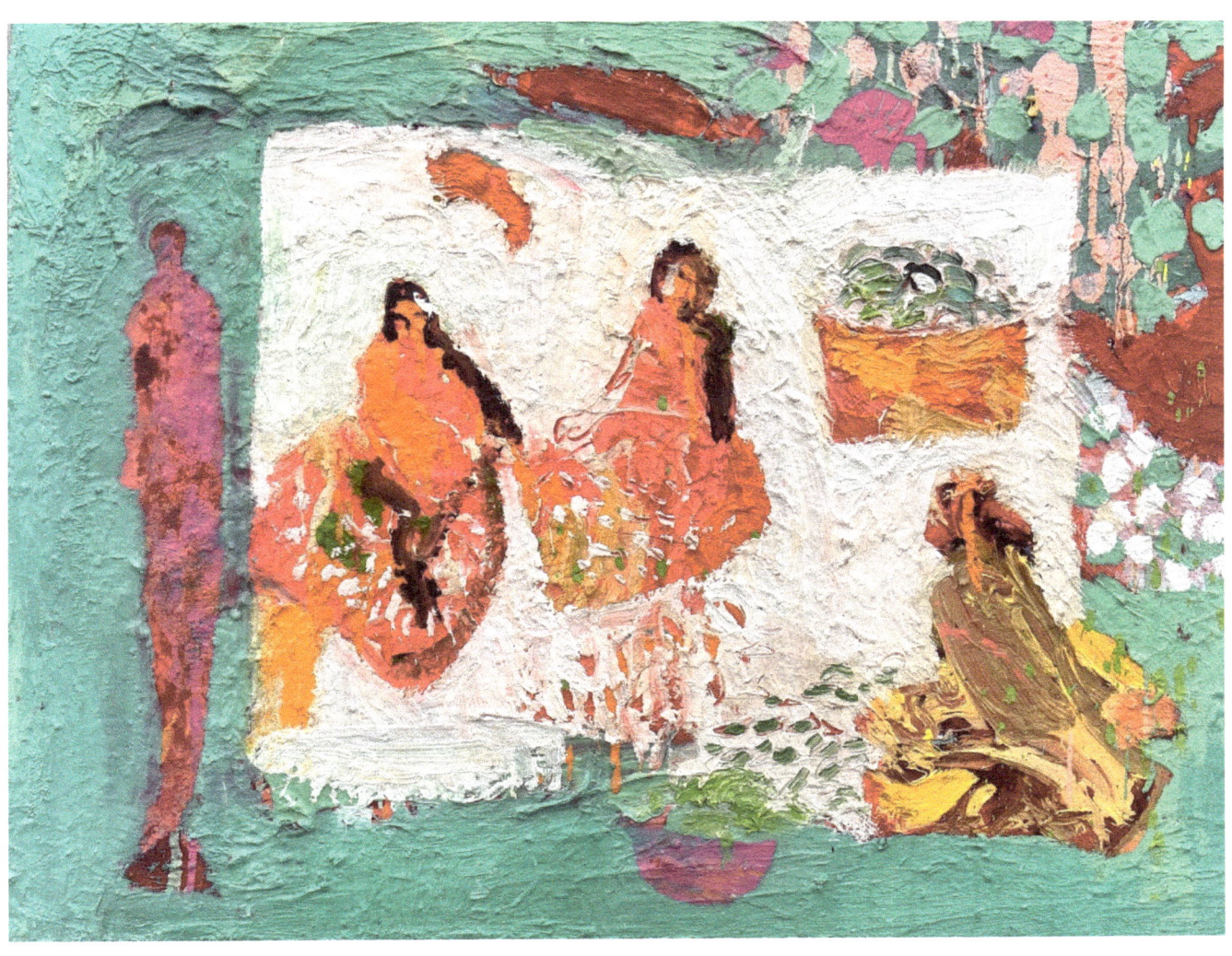

Title: The Kerala market sellers

Size: 102x82cm

Stories From The Banyan Tree

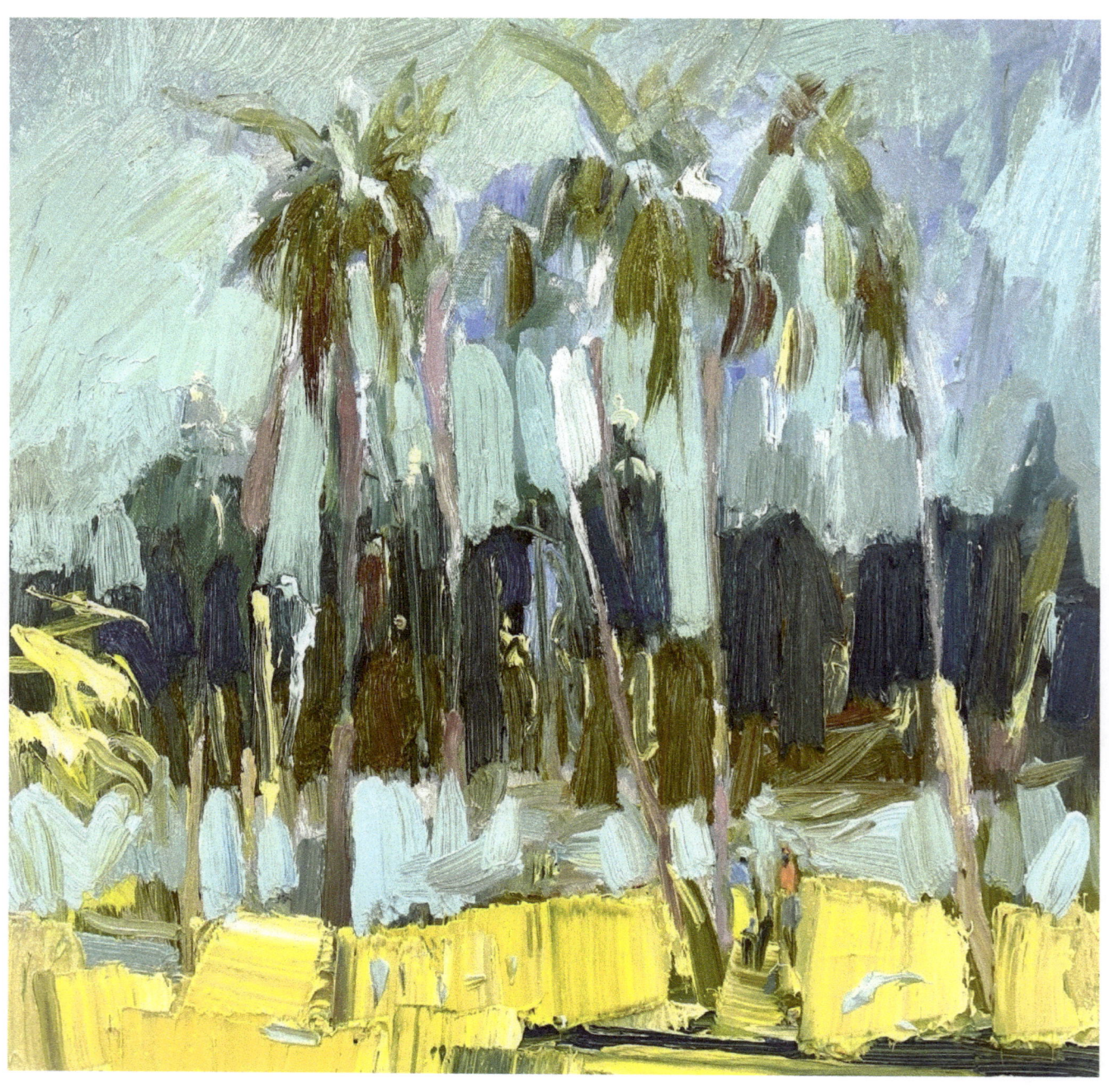

Title: An eagle flew by the lake
Size: 60x60cm

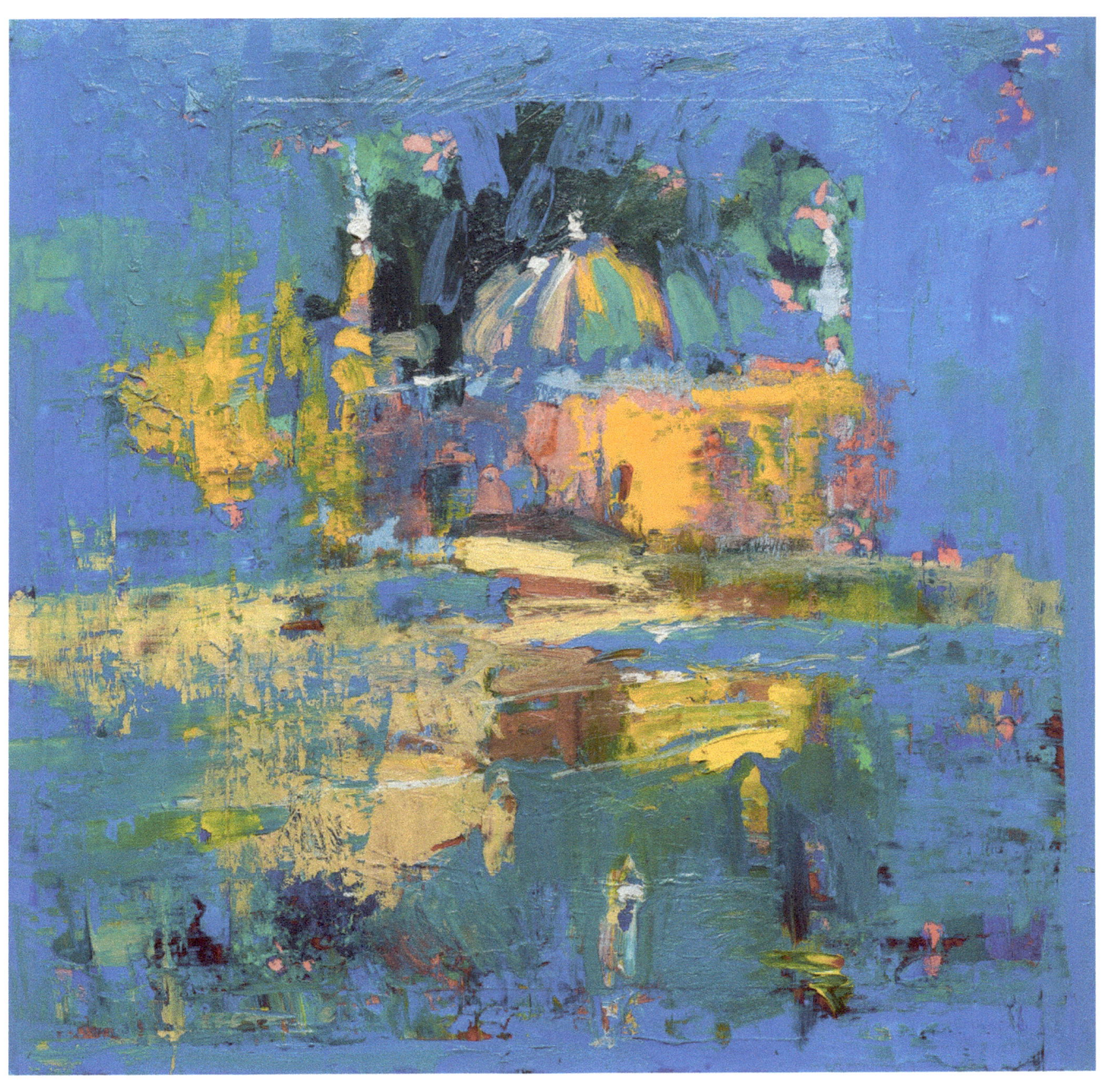

Title: Bathing in blue water

Size: 120x120cm

Stories From The Banyan Tree

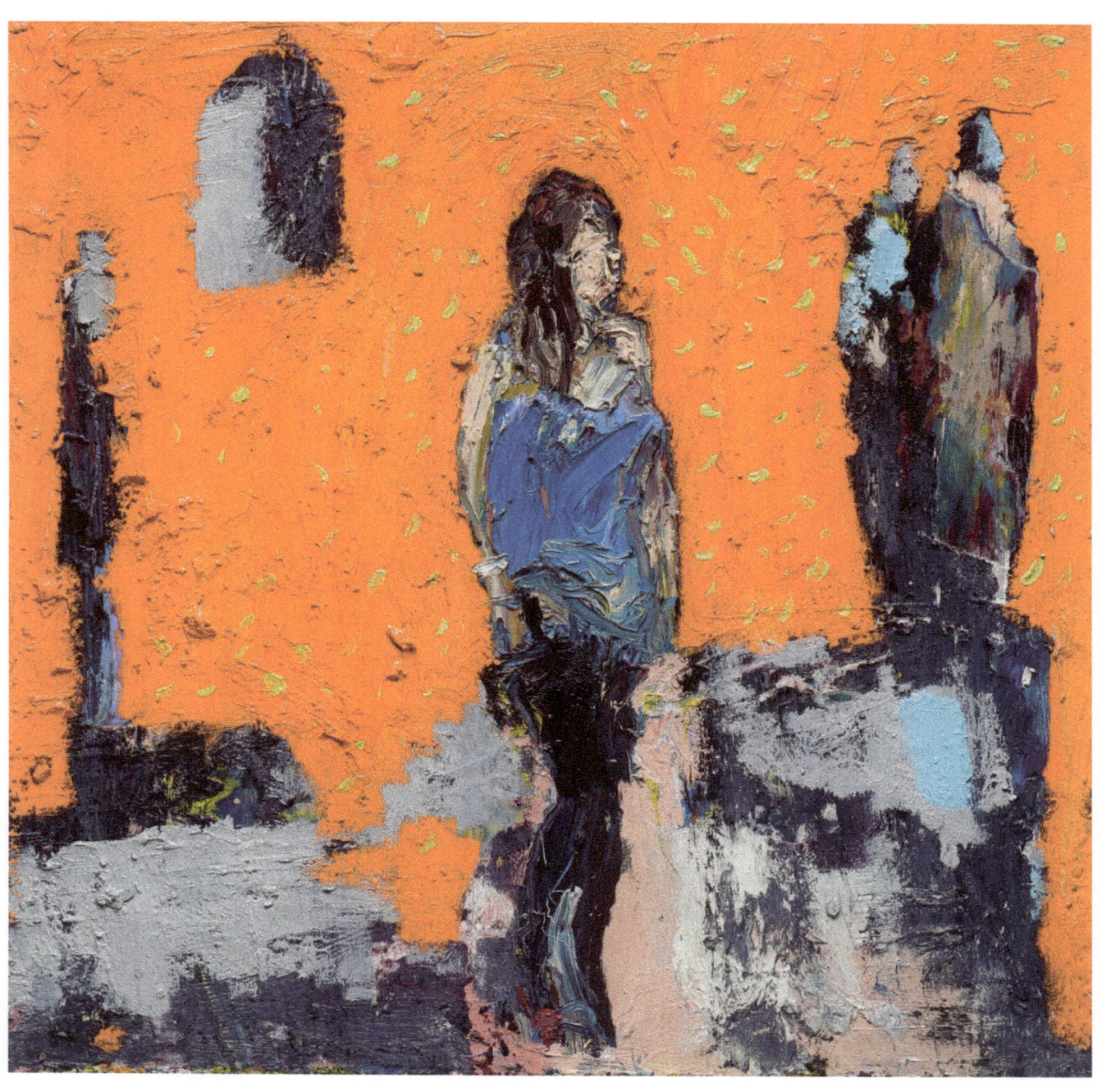

Title: Blue dress falling leaves
Size: 60x60cm

Paul Wadsworth

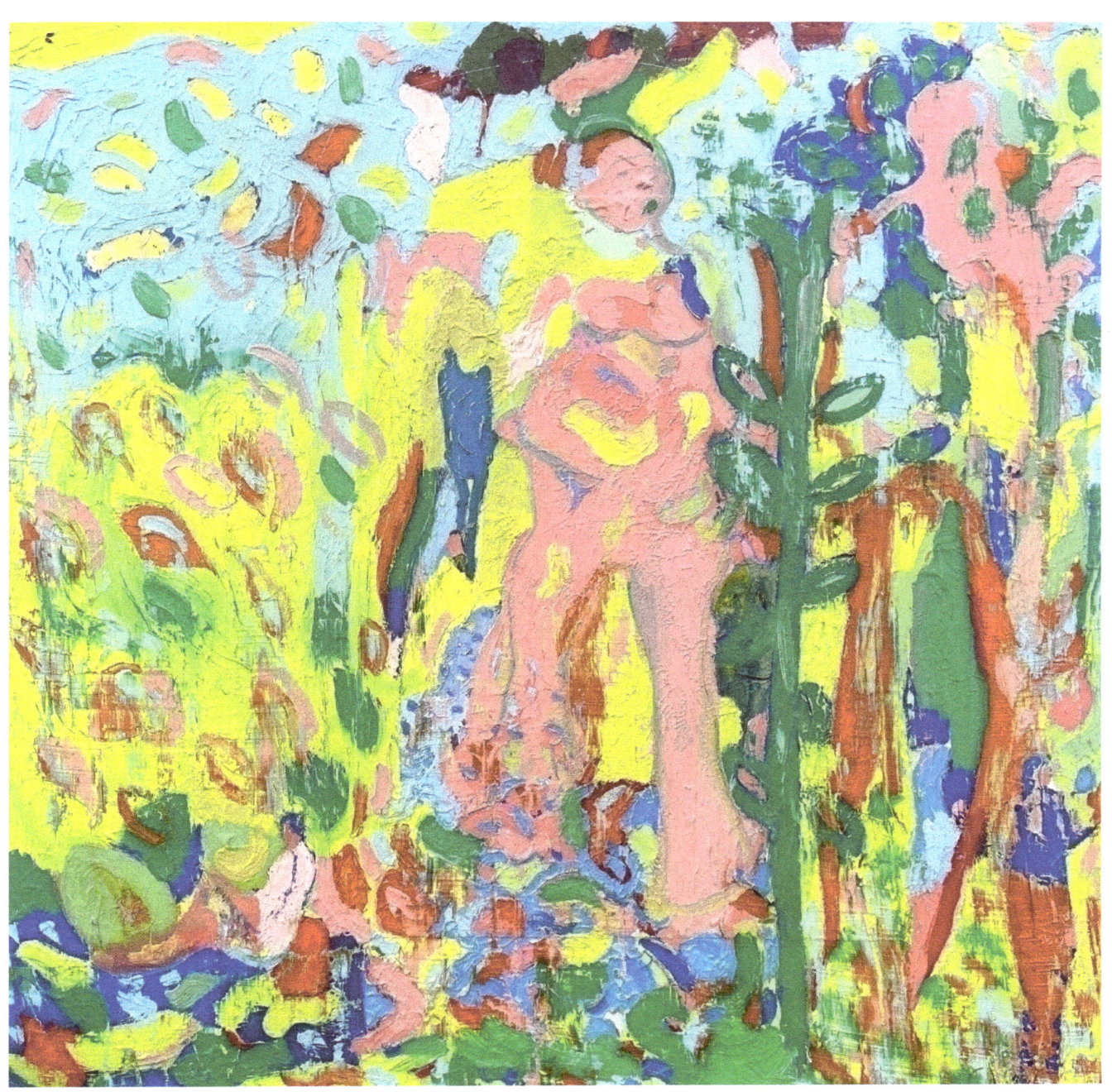

Title: Breathing nature
Size: 140x140cm

Stories From The Banyan Tree

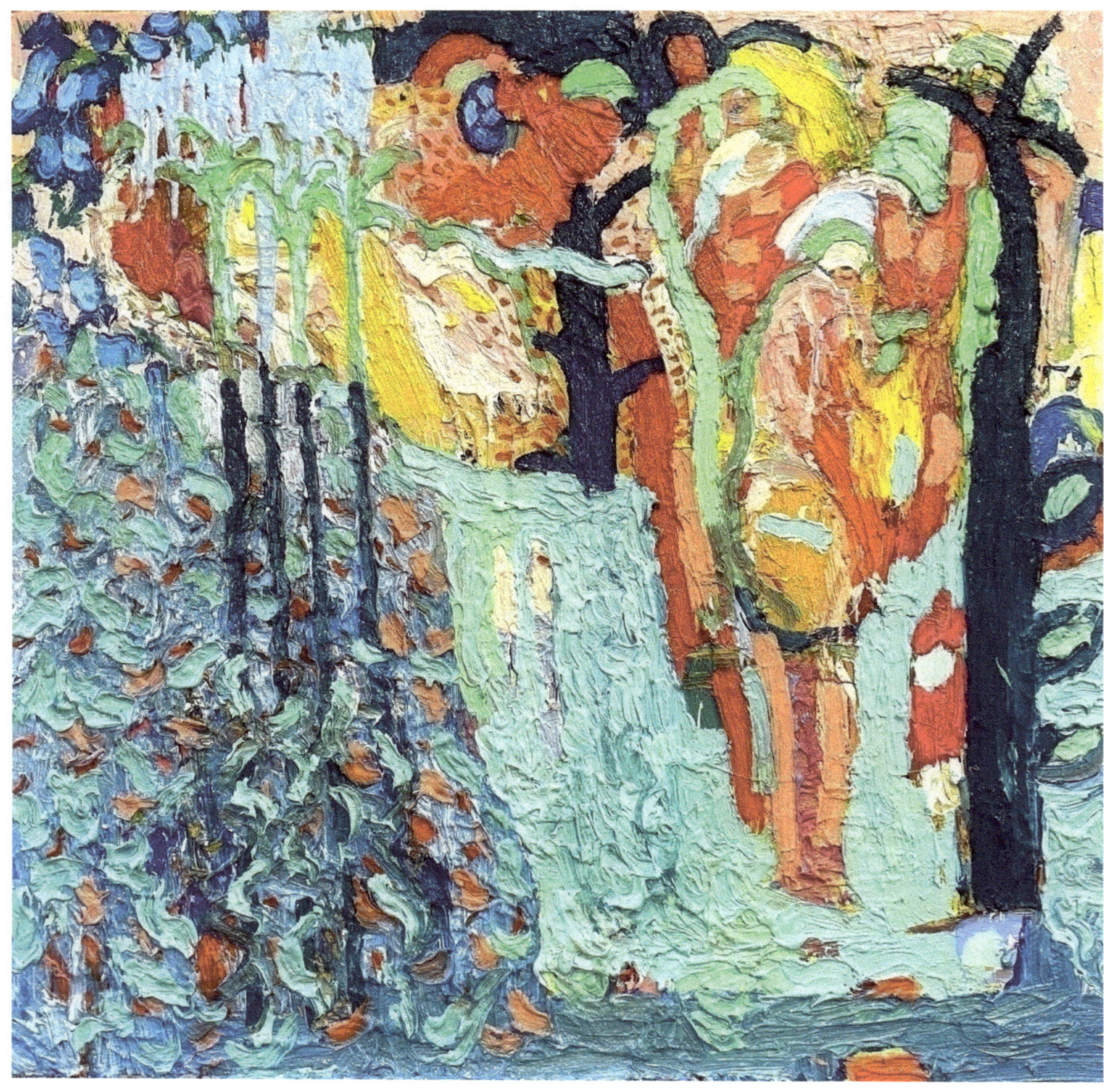

Title: By the Indian Ocean
Size: 120x120cm

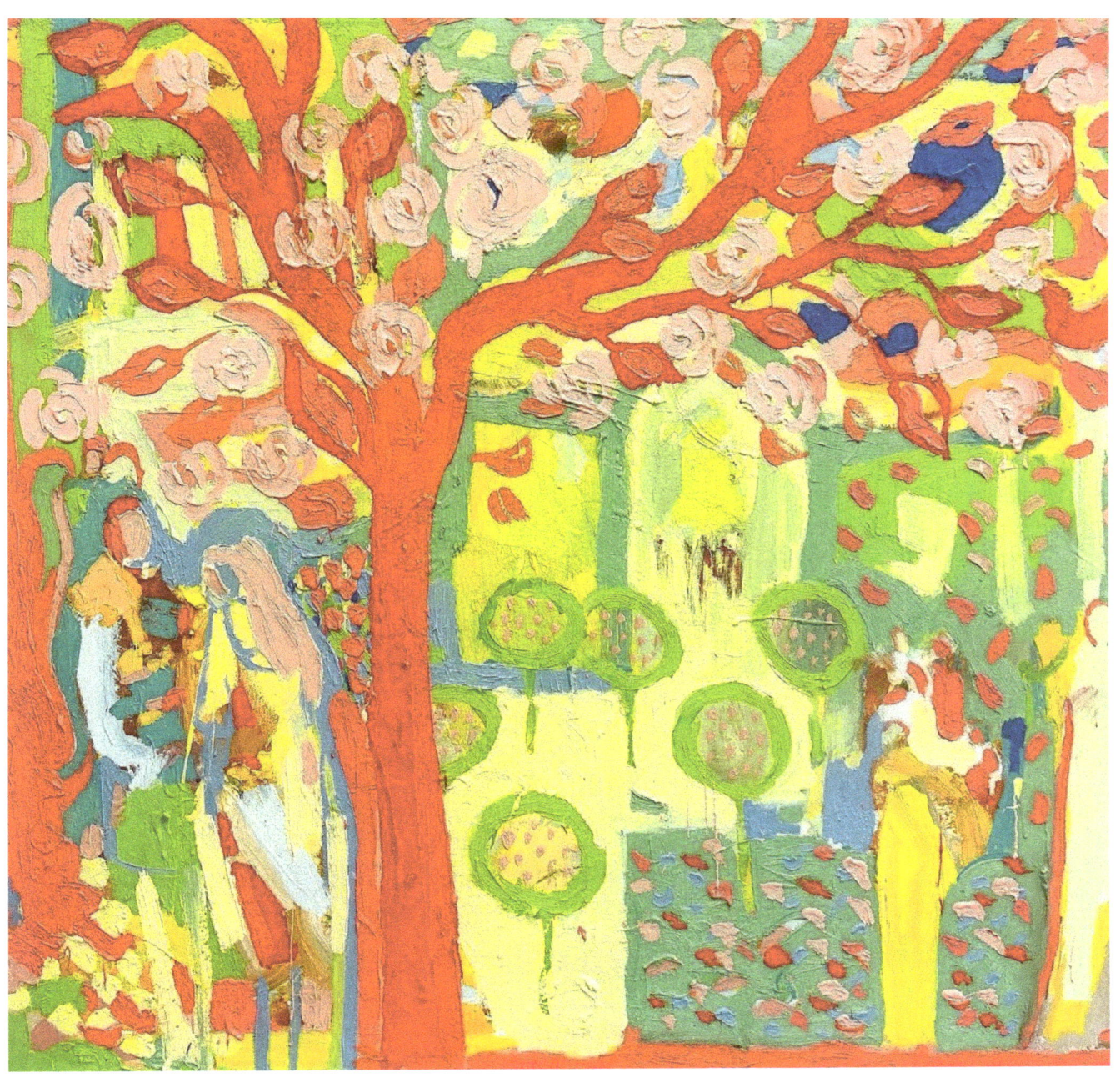

Title: Camillia tree

Size: 140x140cm

Stories From The Banyan Tree

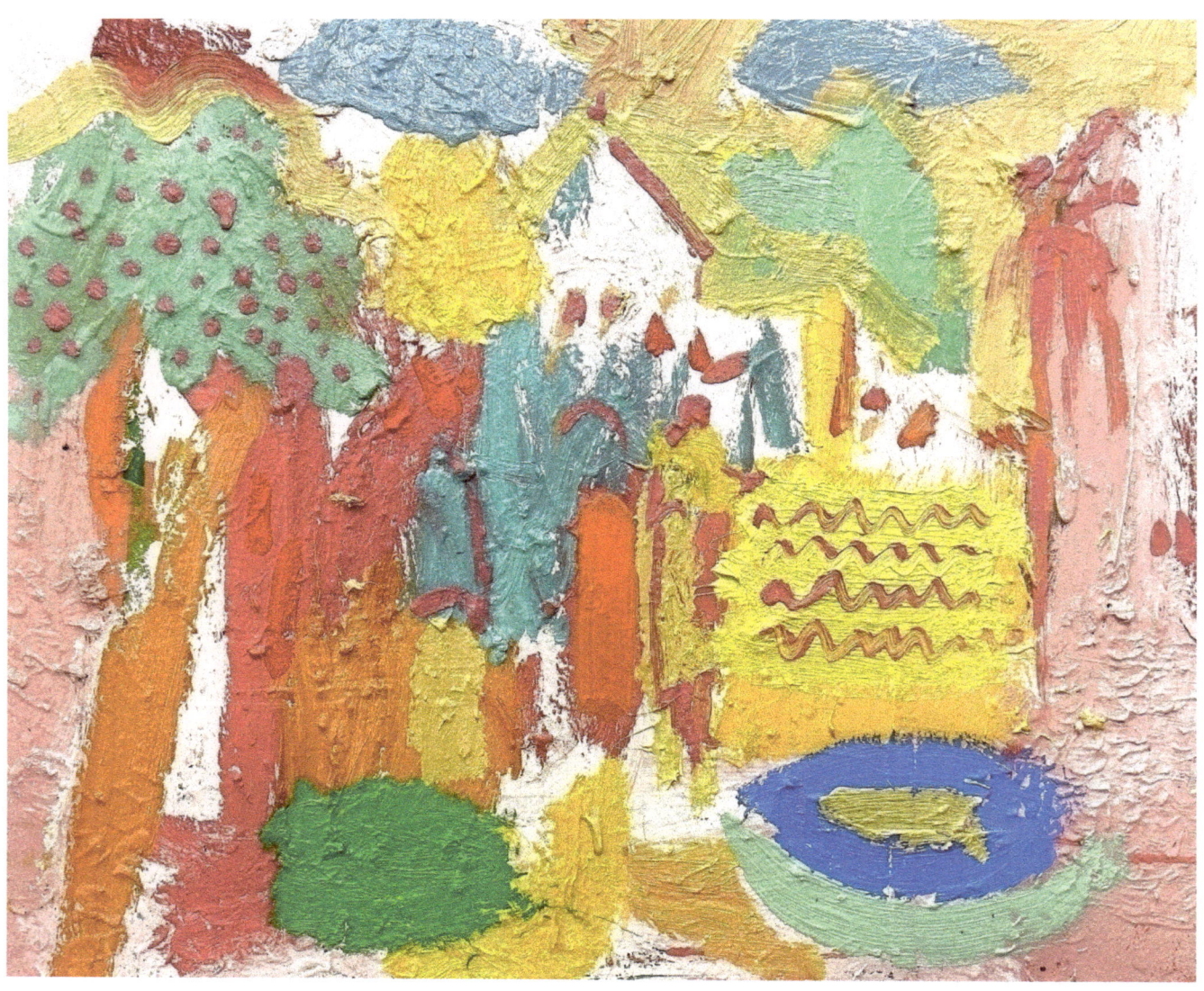

Title: Carpet weaver
Size: 63x77cm

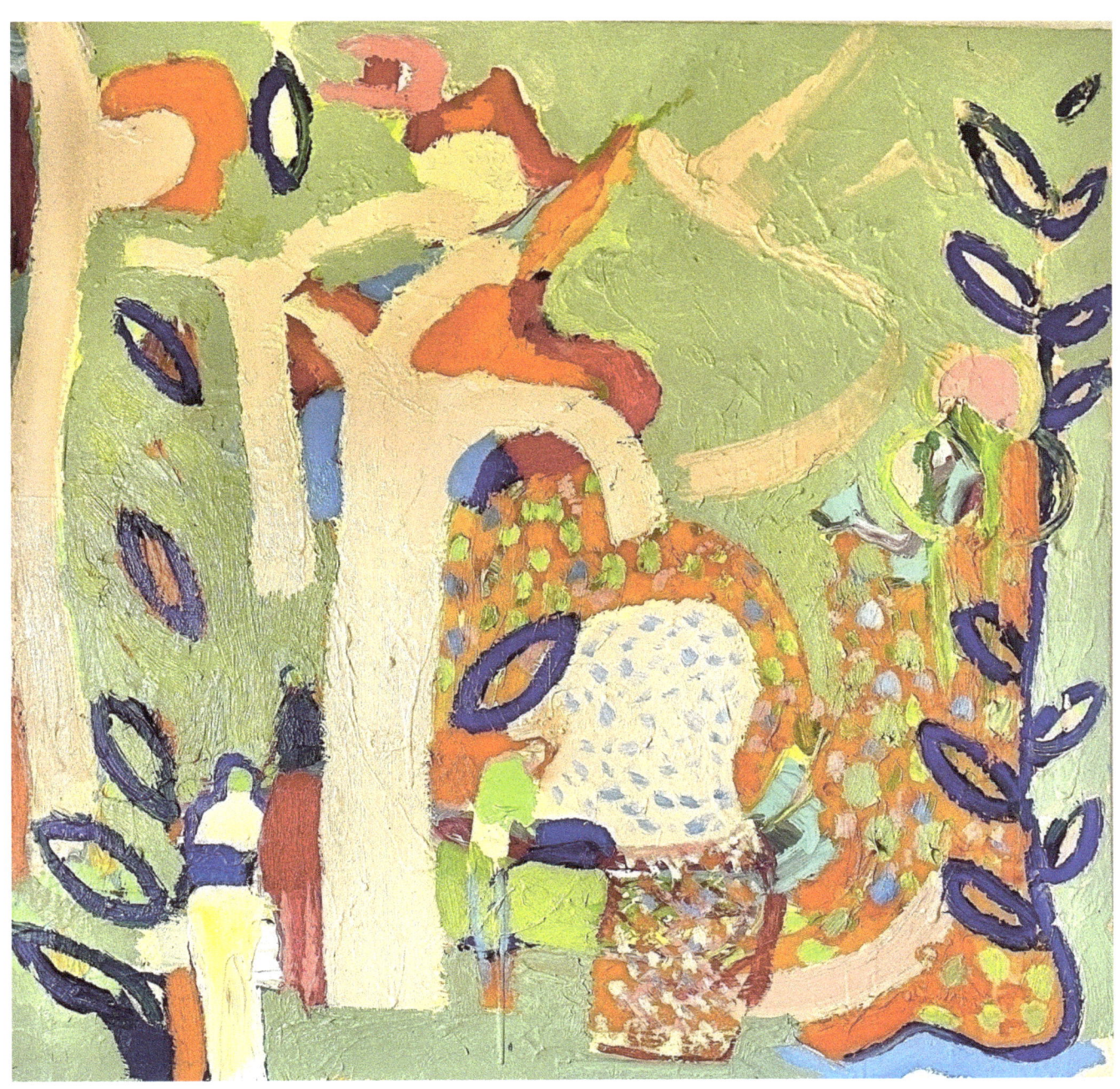

Title: Carpet weavers

Size: 120x120cm

Stories From The Banyan Tree

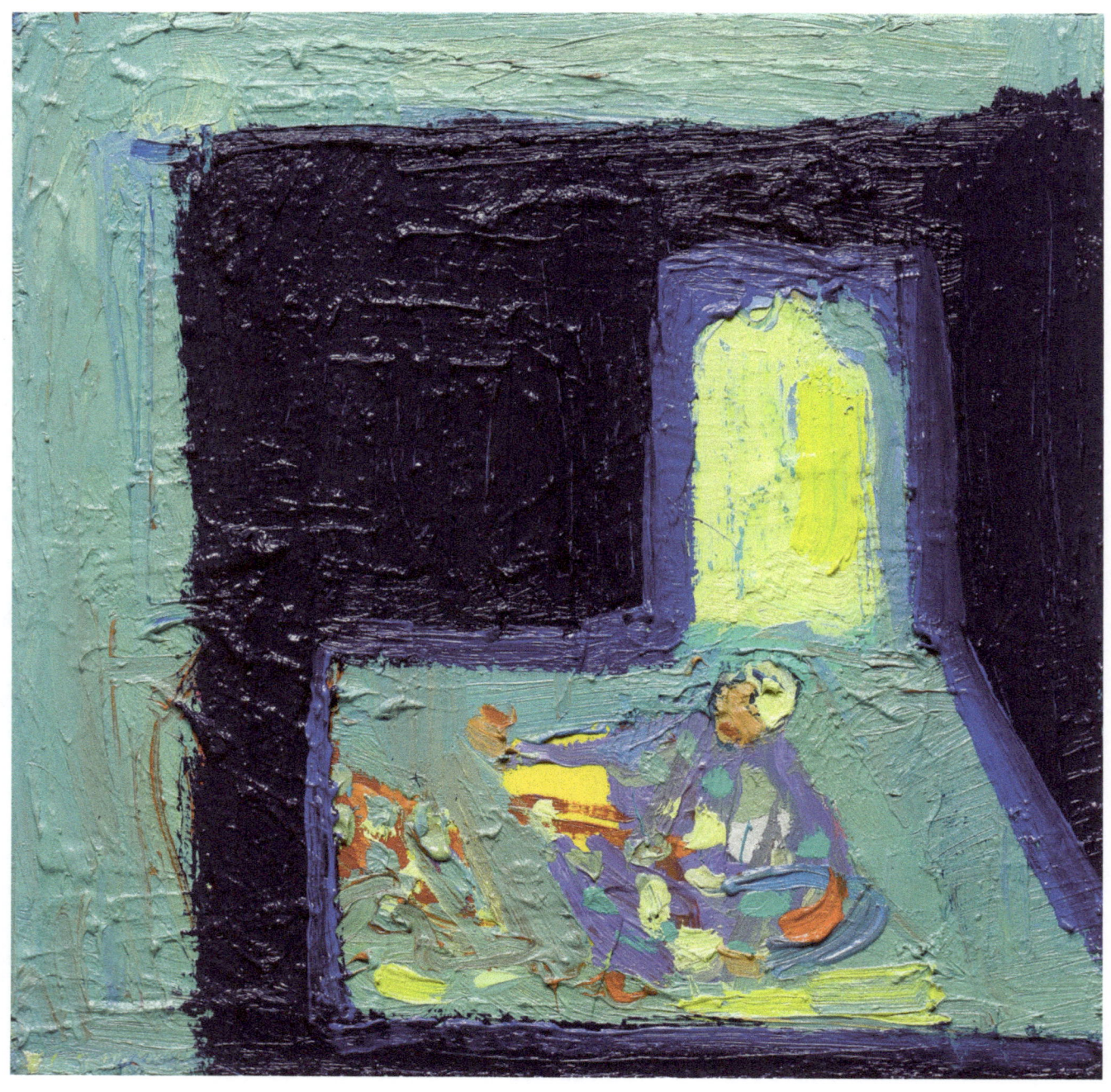

Title: Chai
Size: 50x50cm

Paul Wadsworth

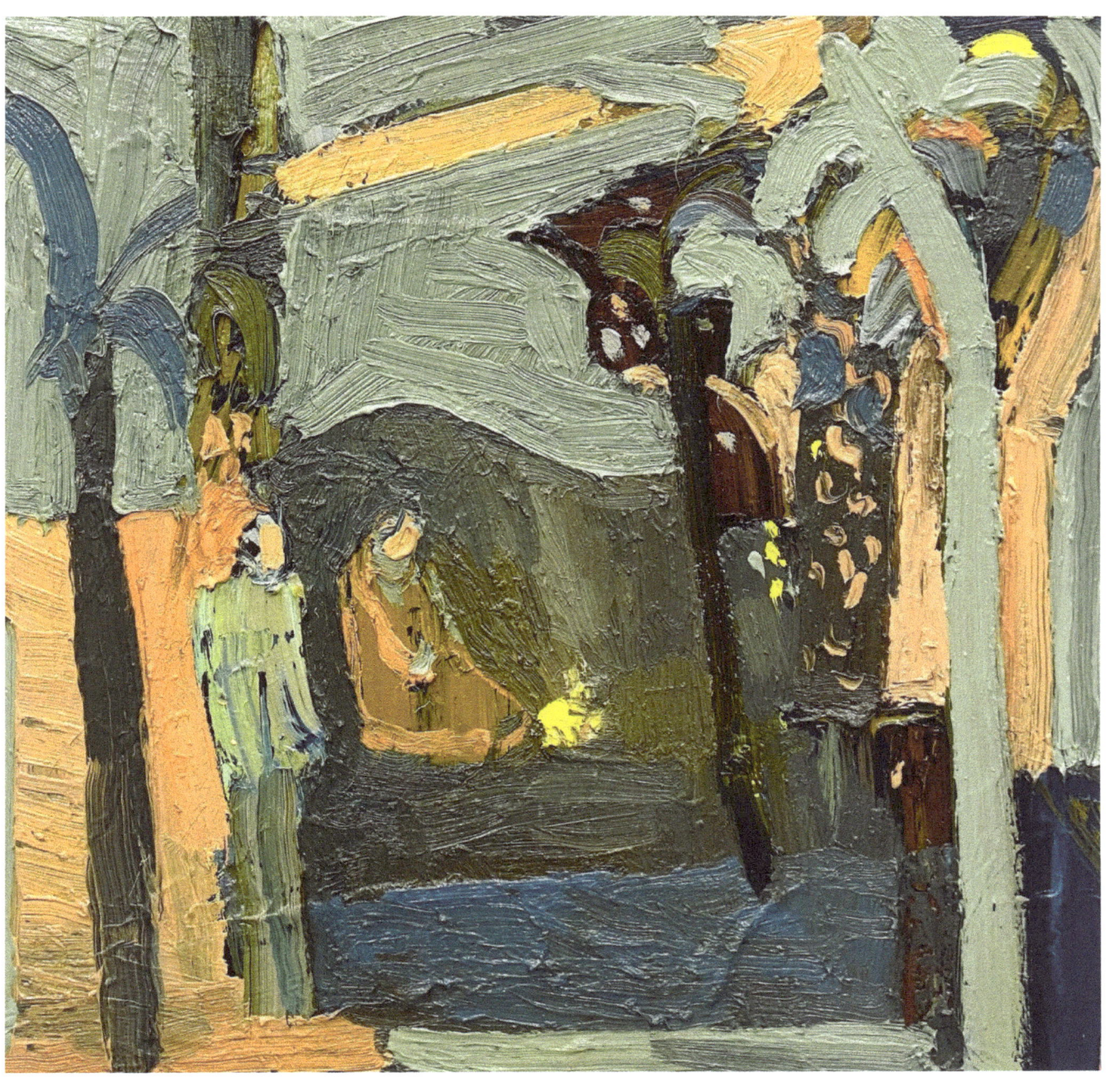

Title: Cooking fire

Size: 60x60cm

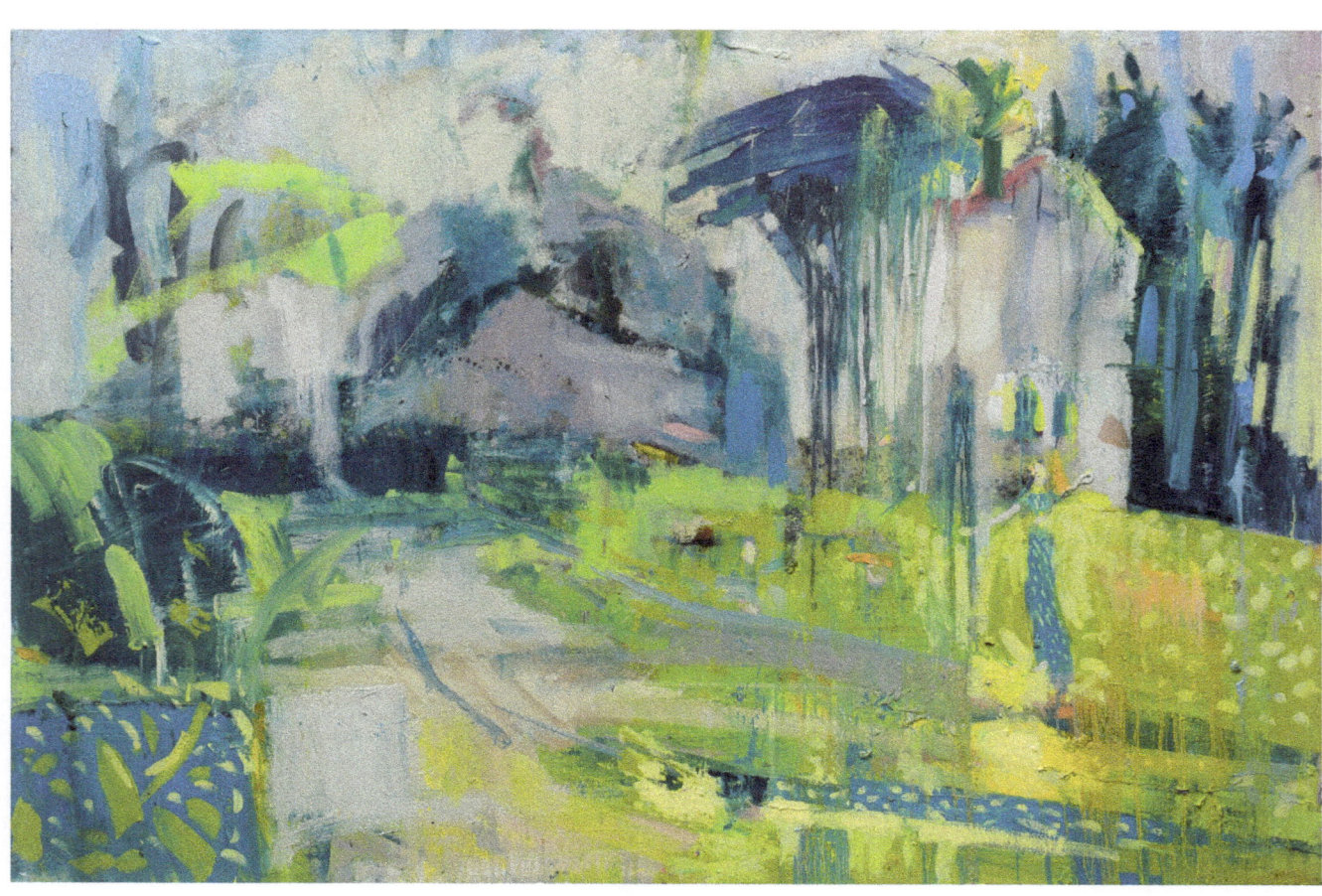

Title: Dancing in the garden
Size: 120x180cm

Paul Wadsworth

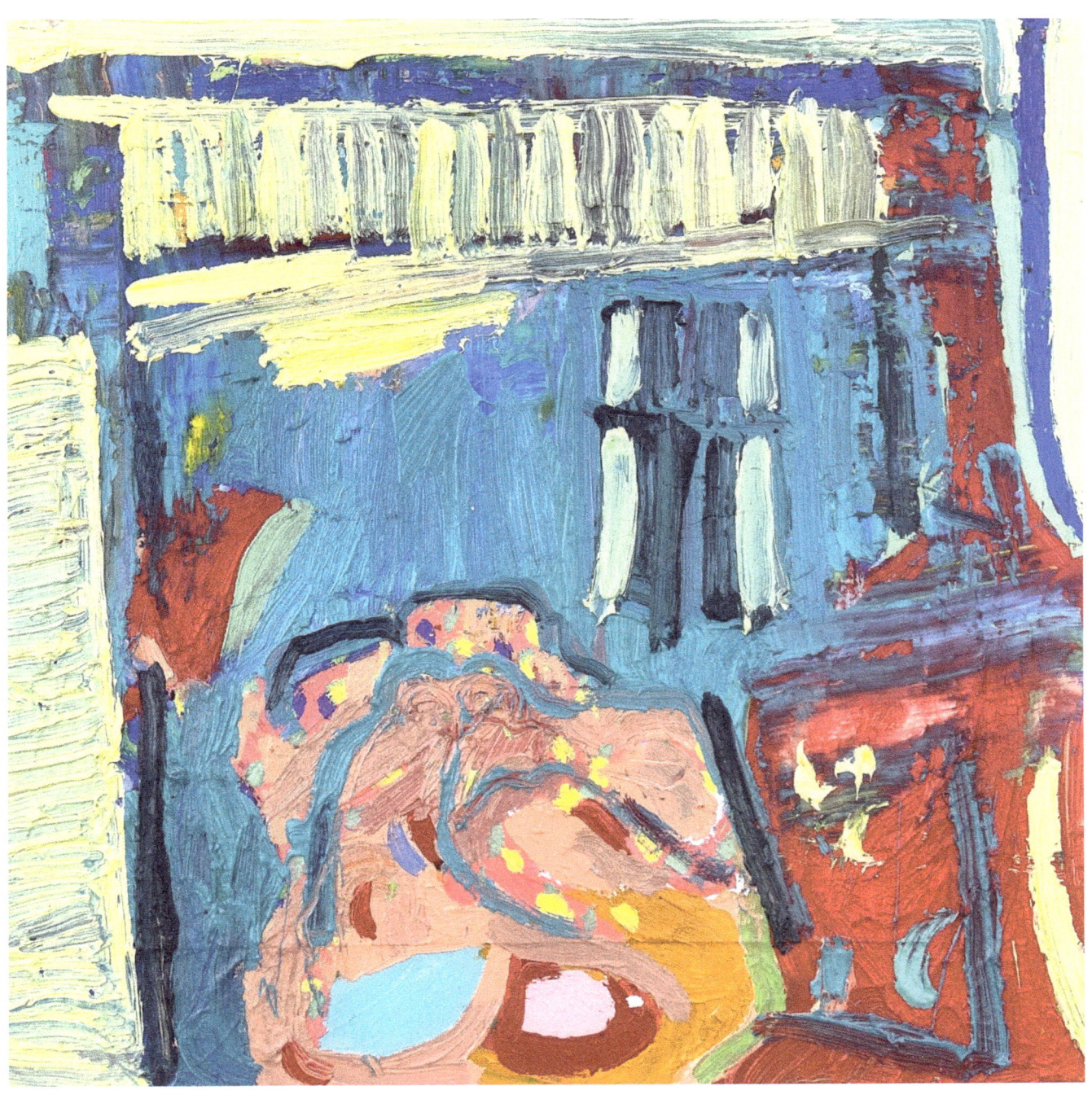

Title: Dreamer
Size: 70x70cm

Stories From The Banyan Tree

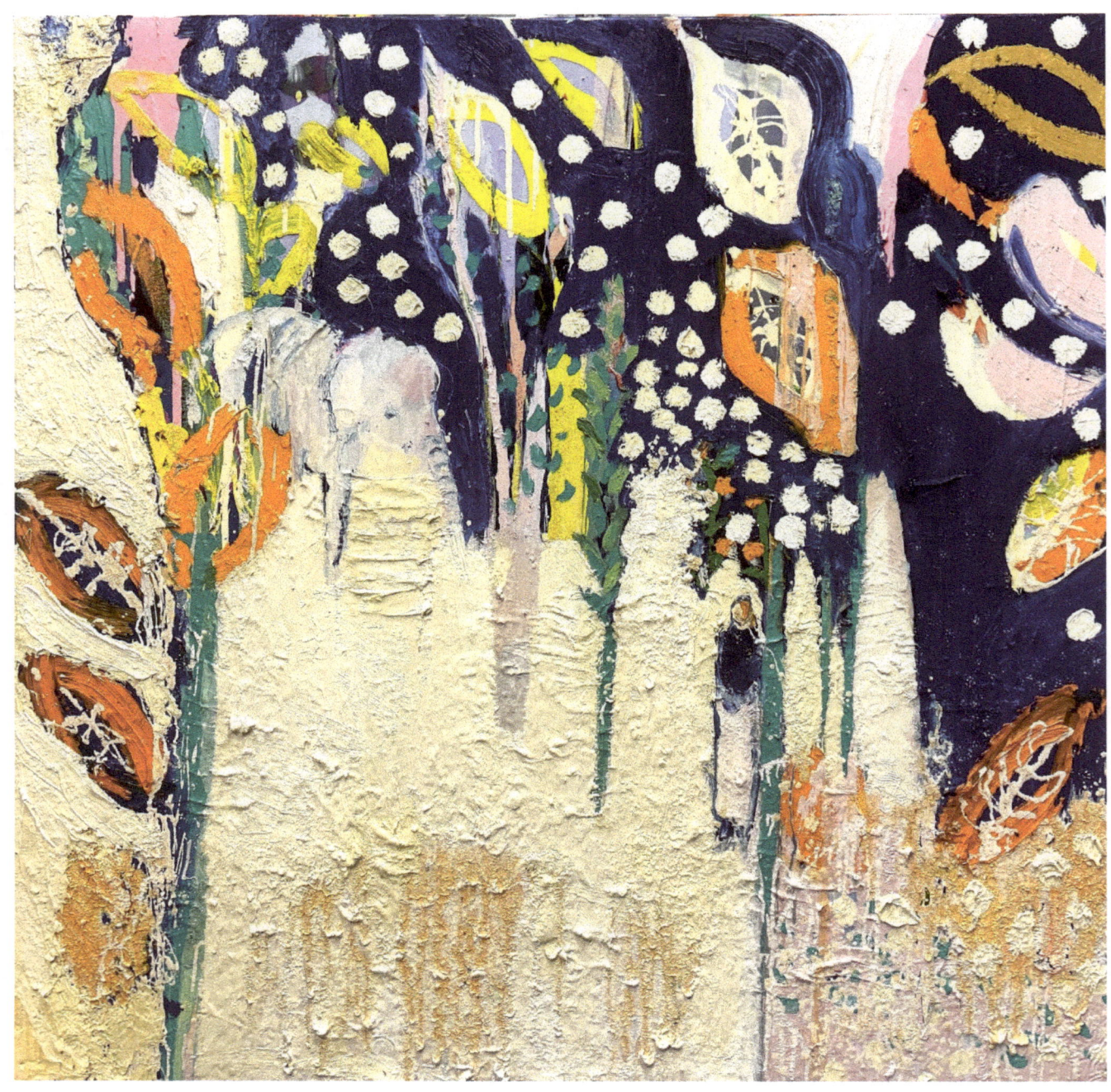

Title: Elephant in the mango tree

Size: 120x120cm

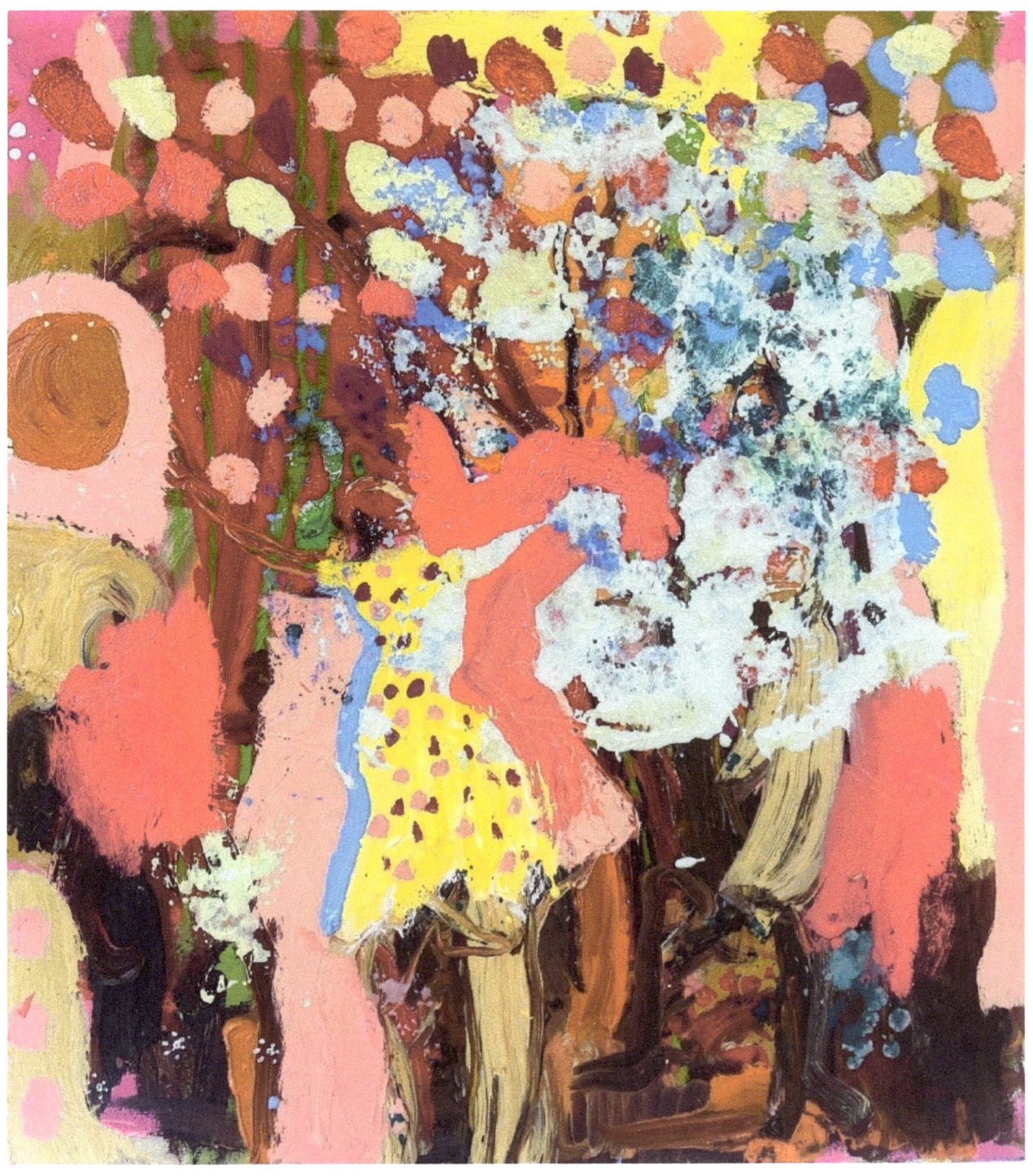

Title: Festival balloon seller
Size: 70x60cm

Stories From The Banyan Tree

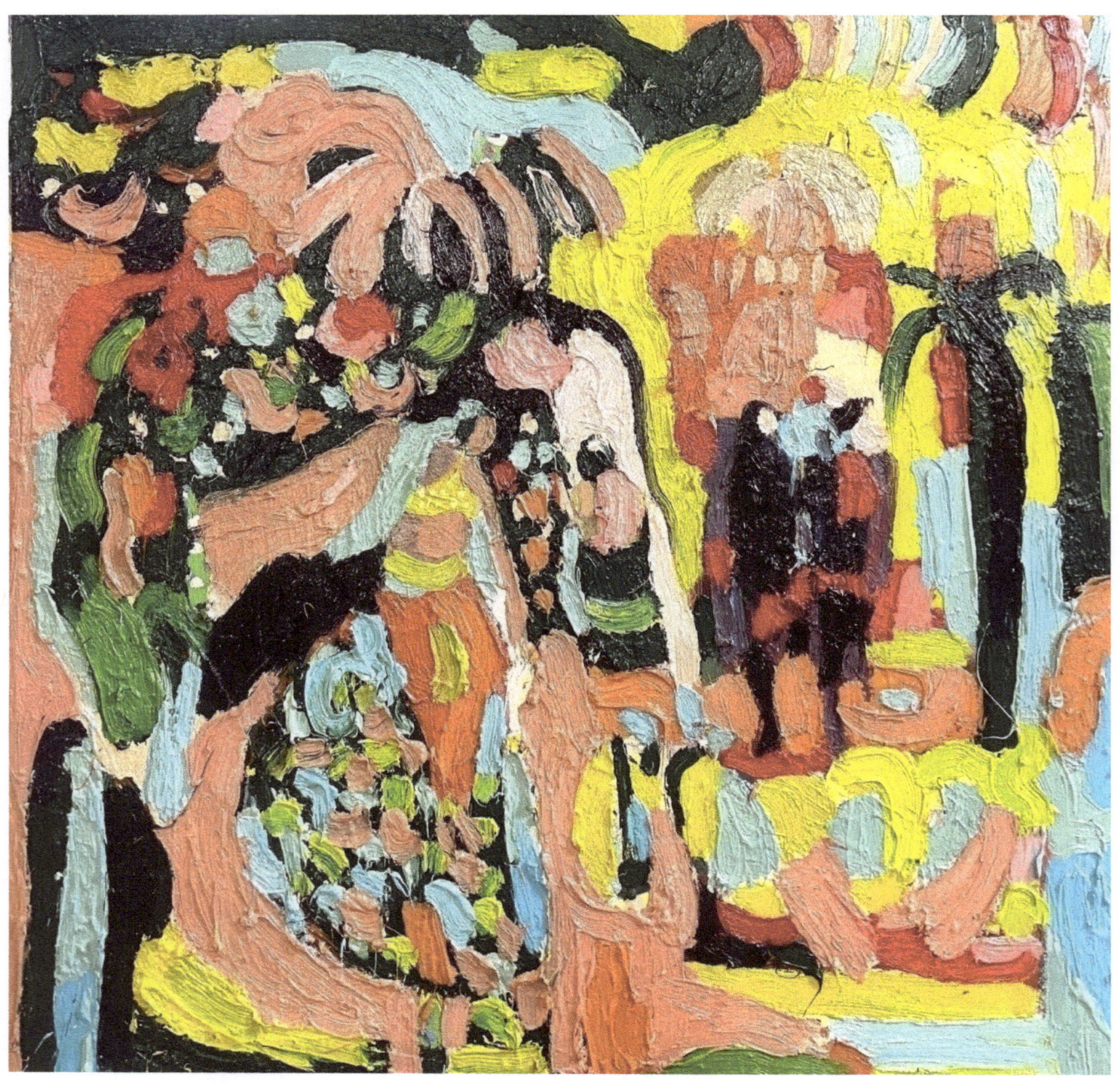

Title: Festival day

Size: 90x90cm

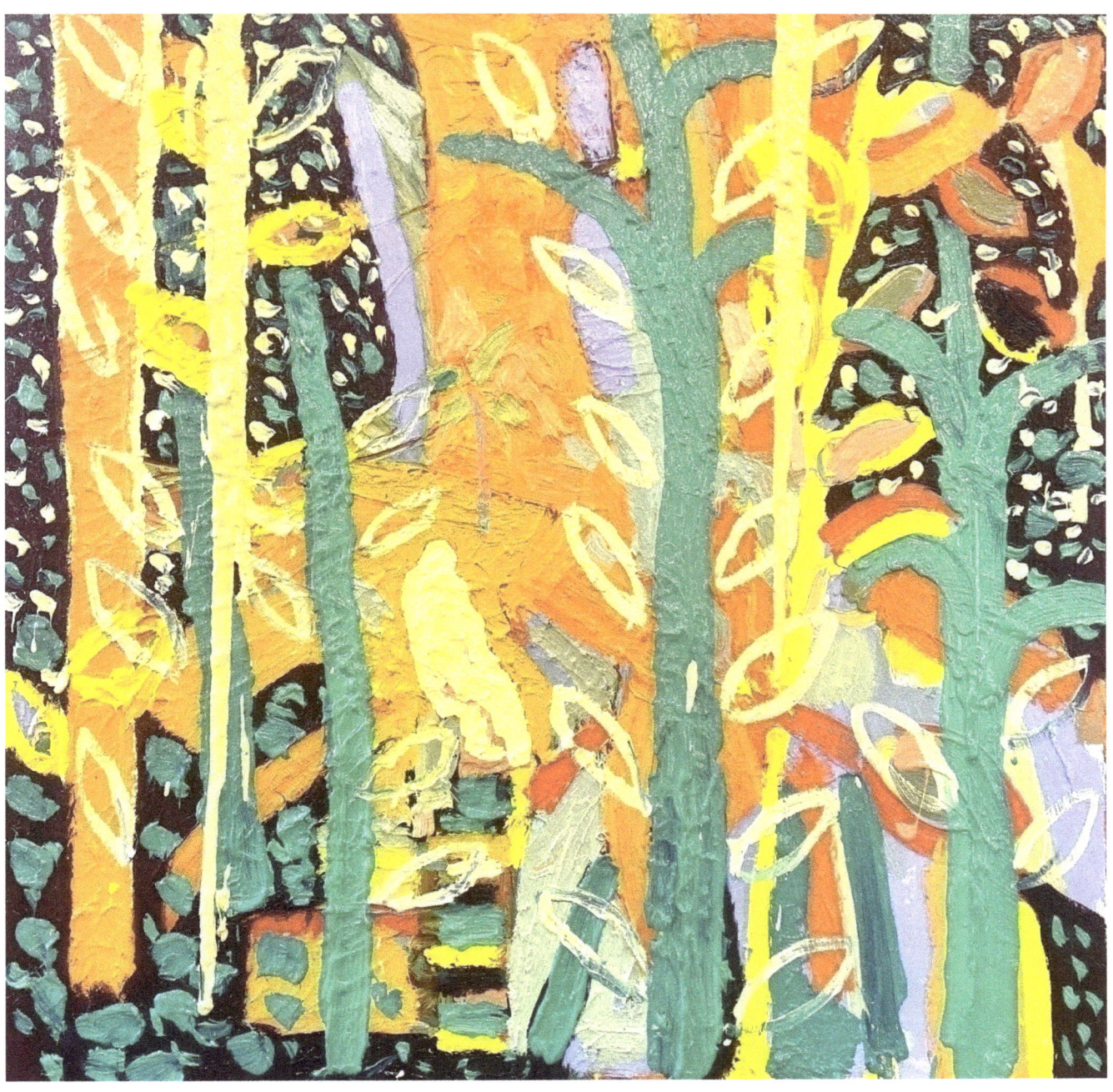

Title: Figure in white

Size: 90x90cm

Stories From The Banyan Tree

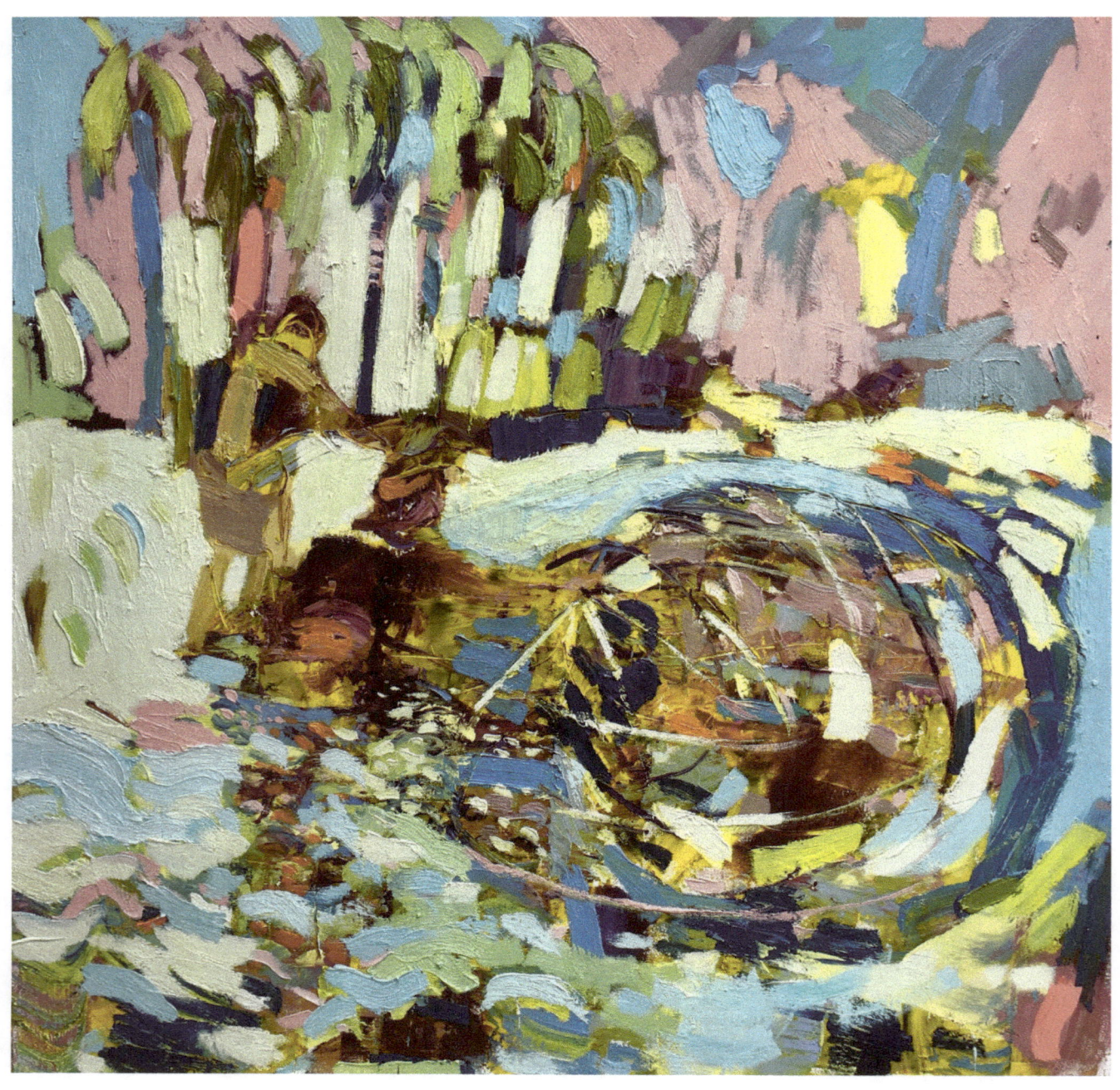

Title: Fishing net
Size: 120x120cm

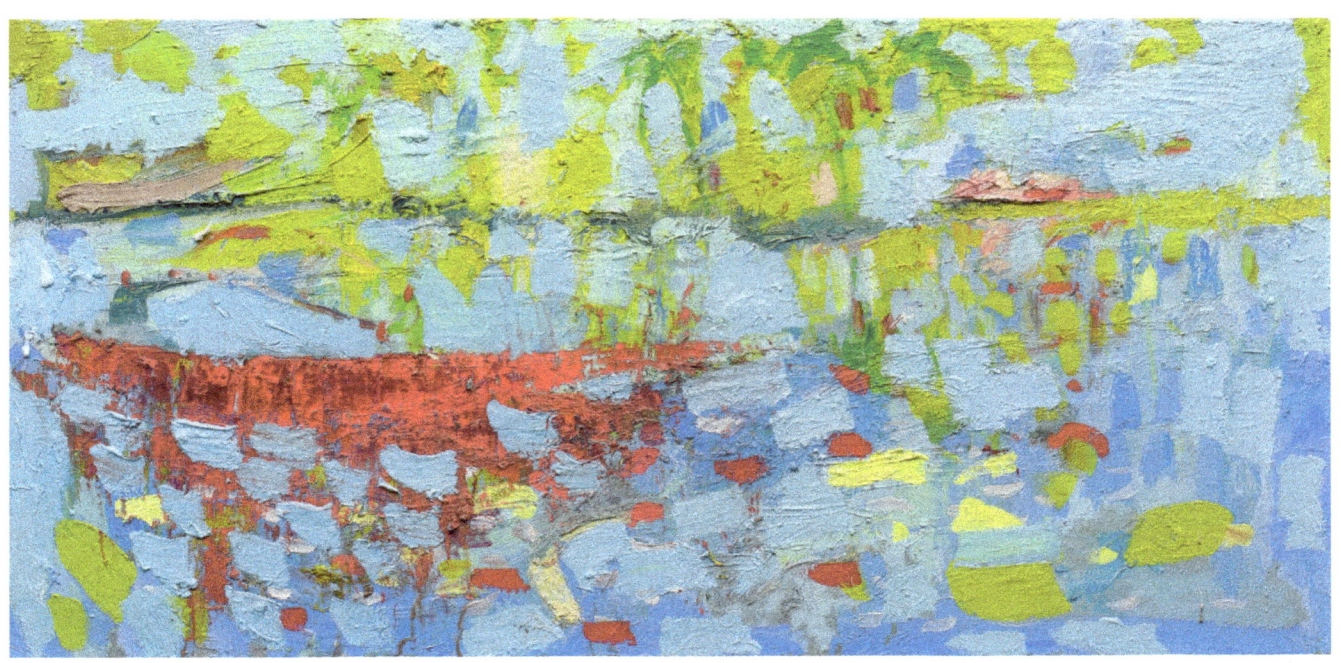

Title: Fishing on the blue river

Size: 60x90cm

Stories From The Banyan Tree

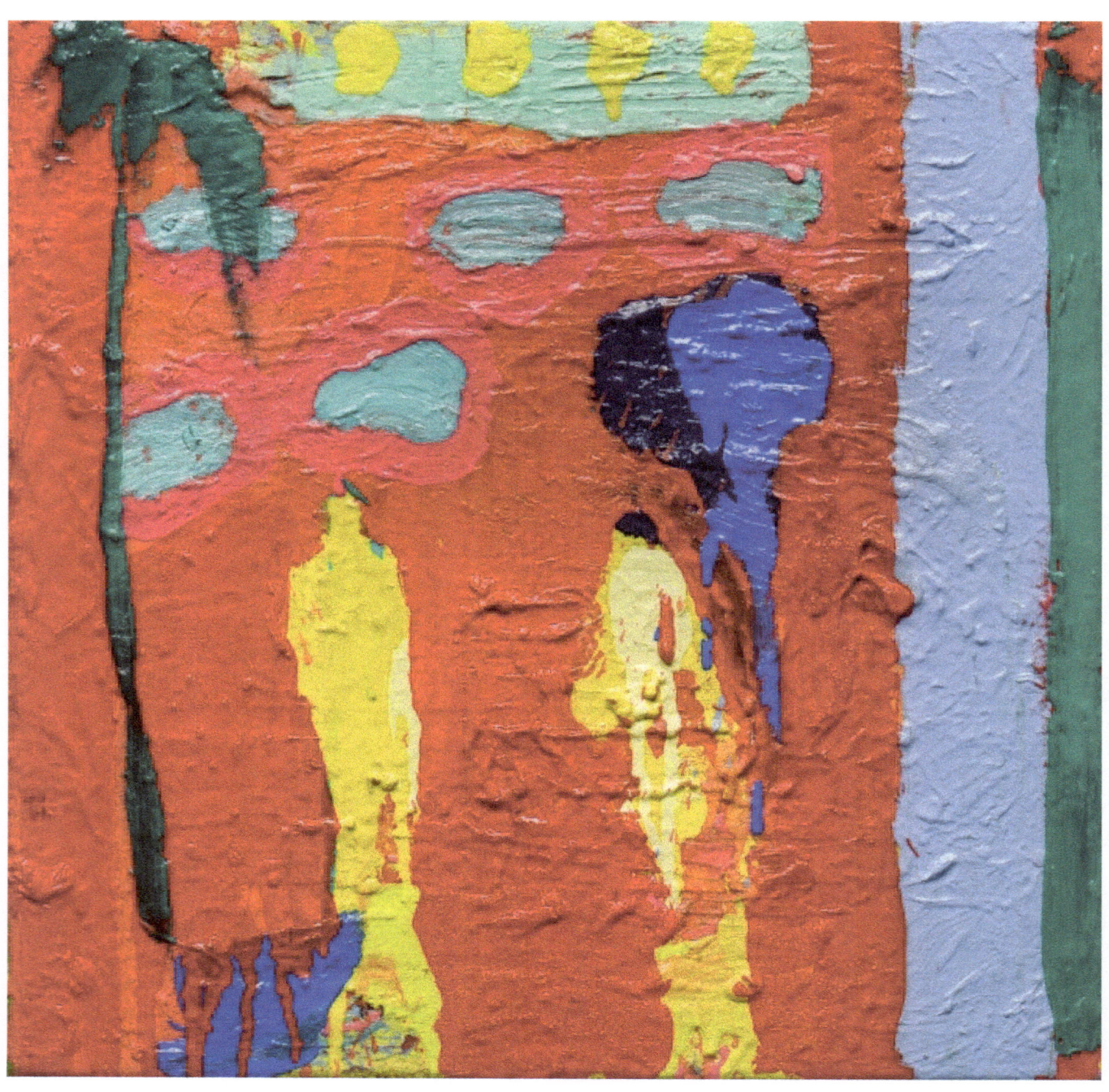

Title: Warm air

Size: 40x40cm

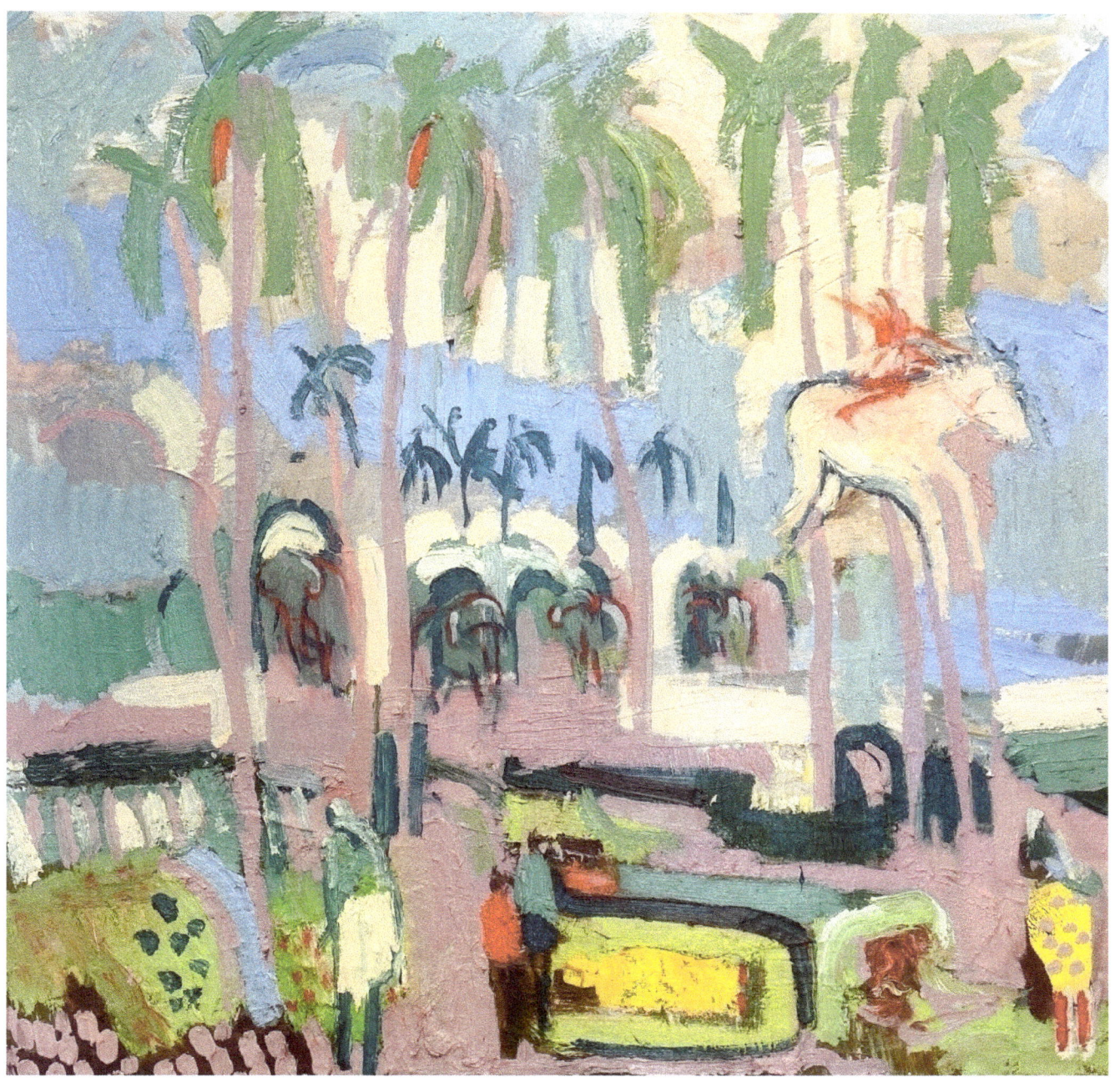

Title: Flying over India

Size: 120x120cm

Stories From The Banyan Tree

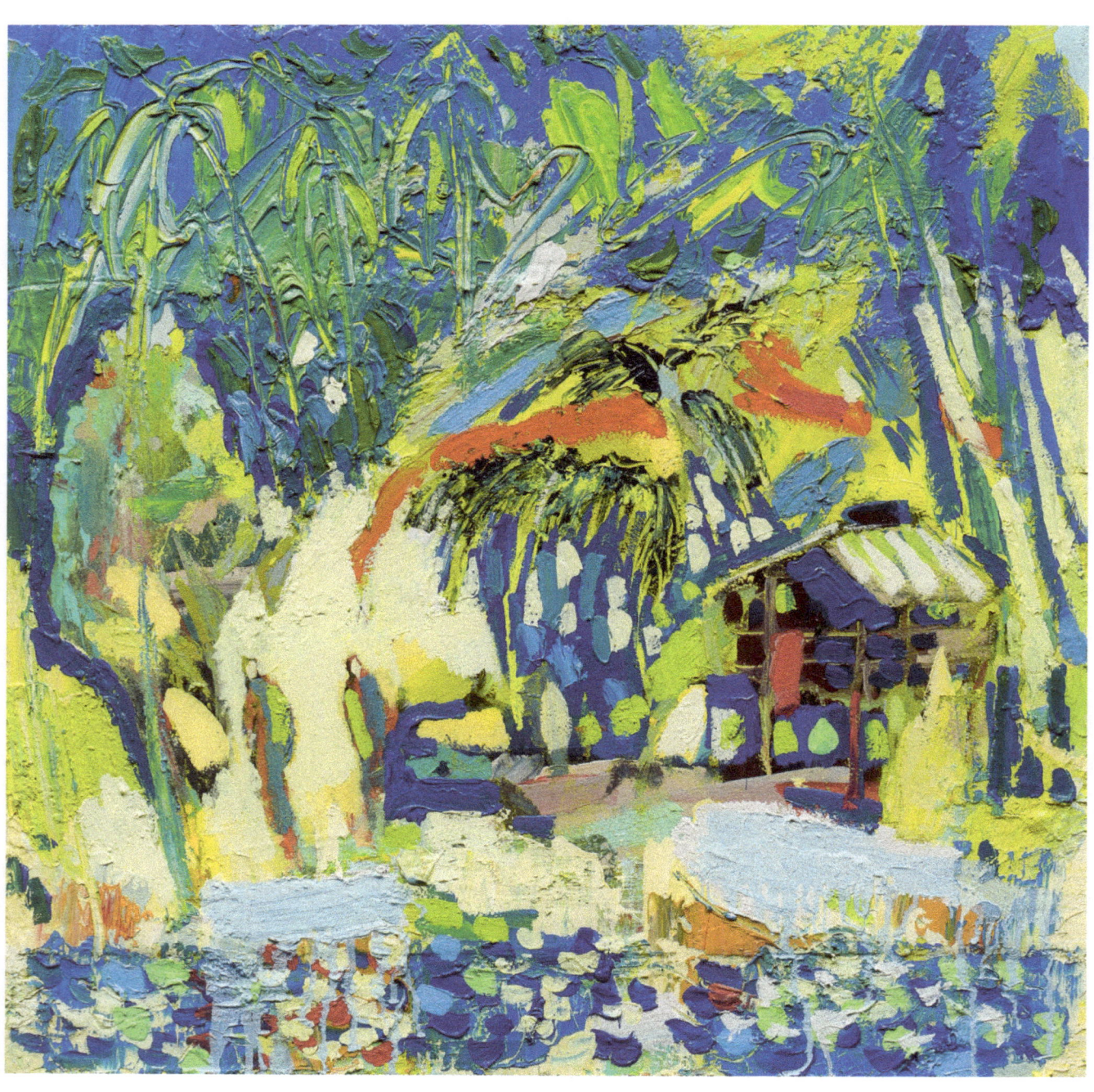

Title: Forest home
Size: 60x60cm

Paul Wadsworth

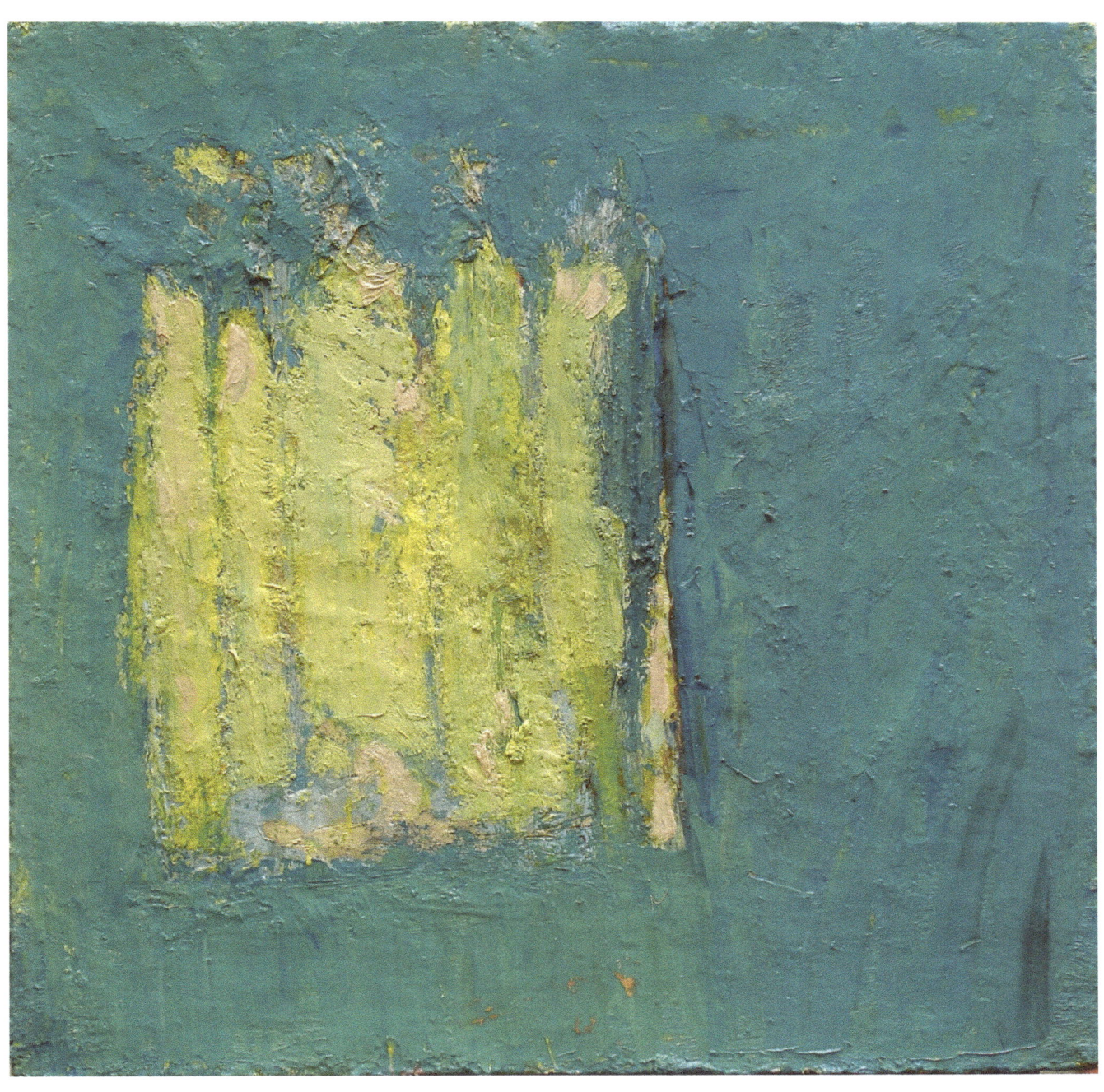

Title: Forest lovers

Size: 70x70cm

Stories From The Banyan Tree

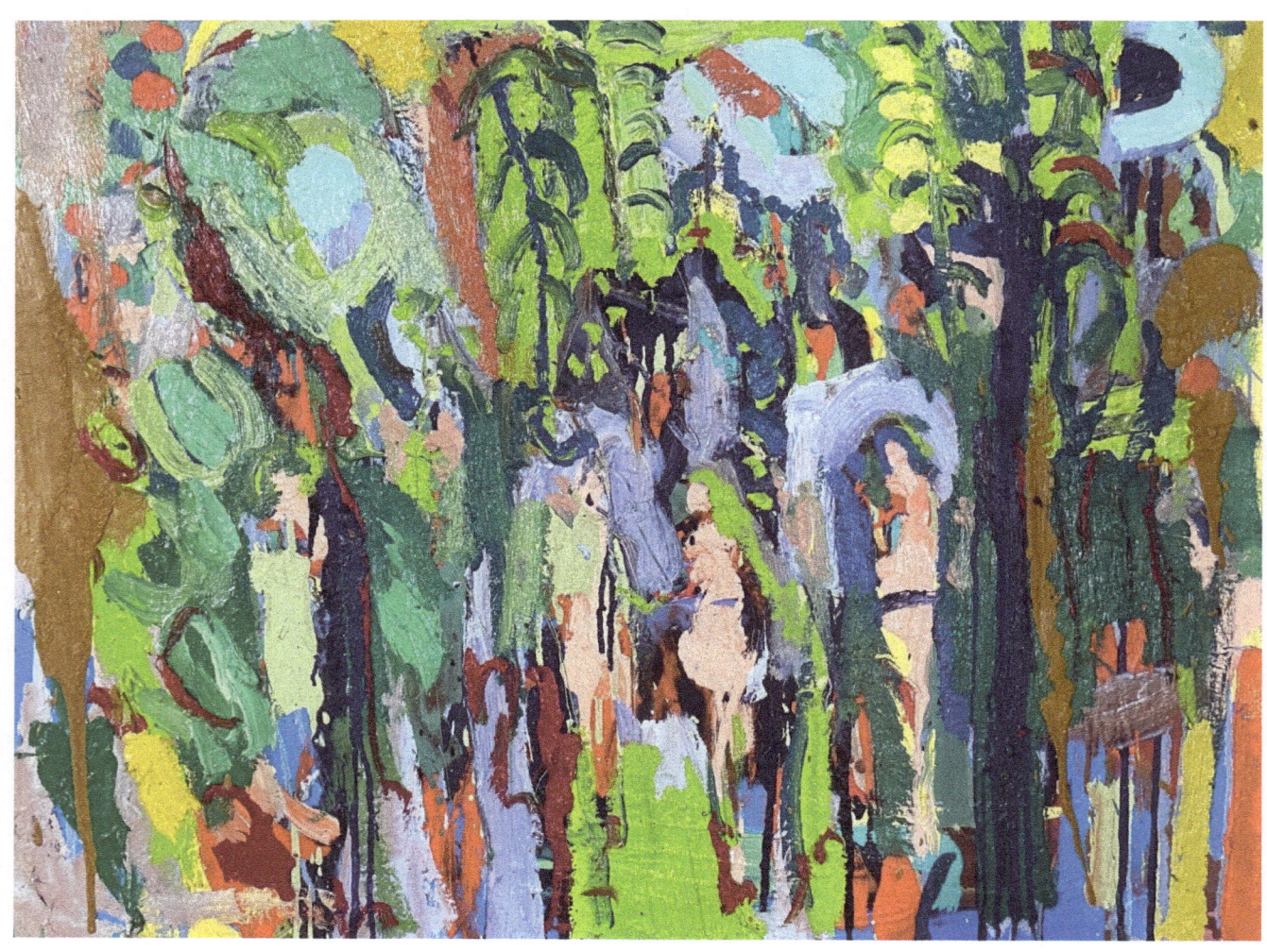

Title: Forest lovers
Size: 80x100cm

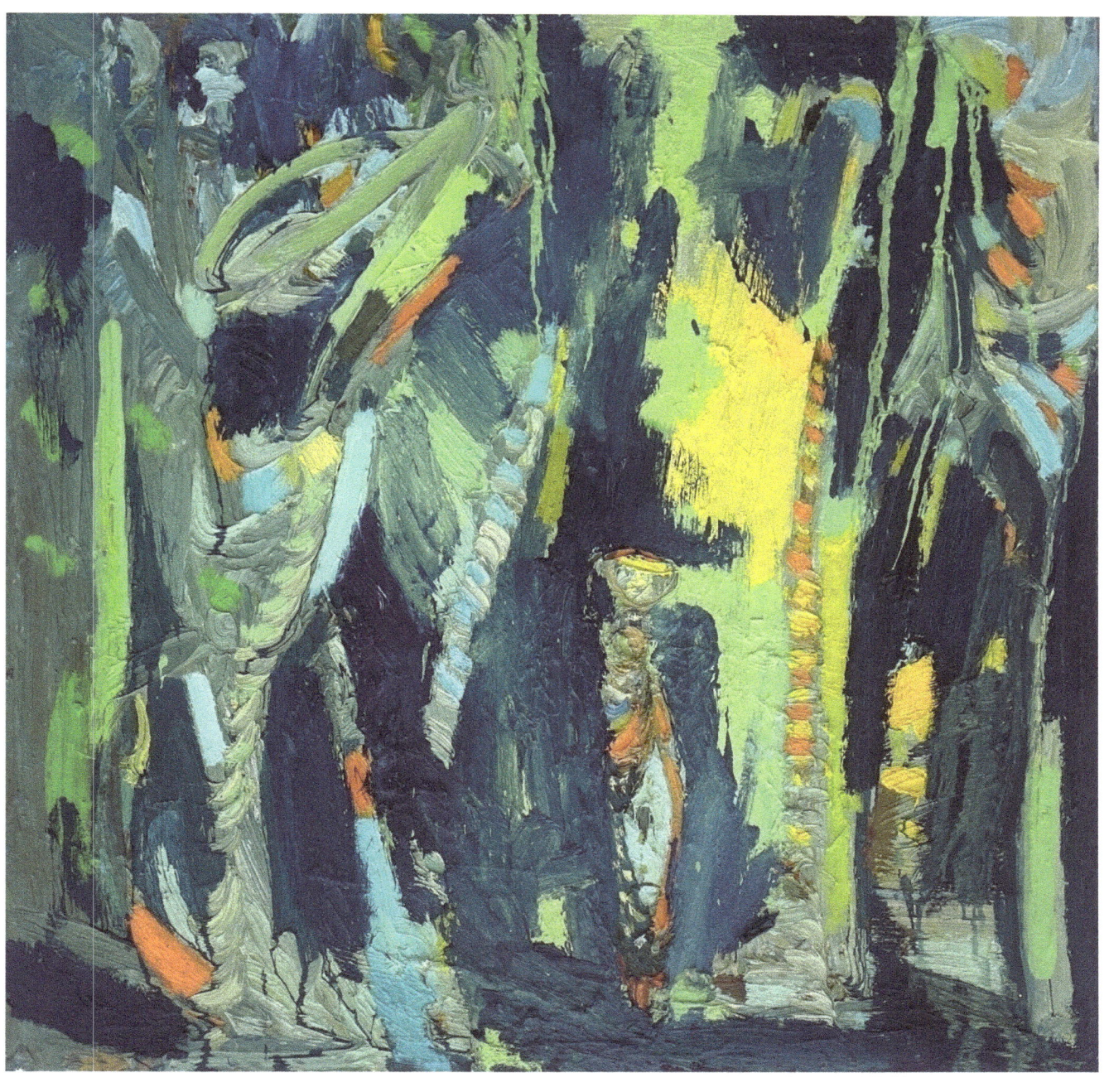

Title: Fruit picker
Size: 100x100cm

Stories From The Banyan Tree

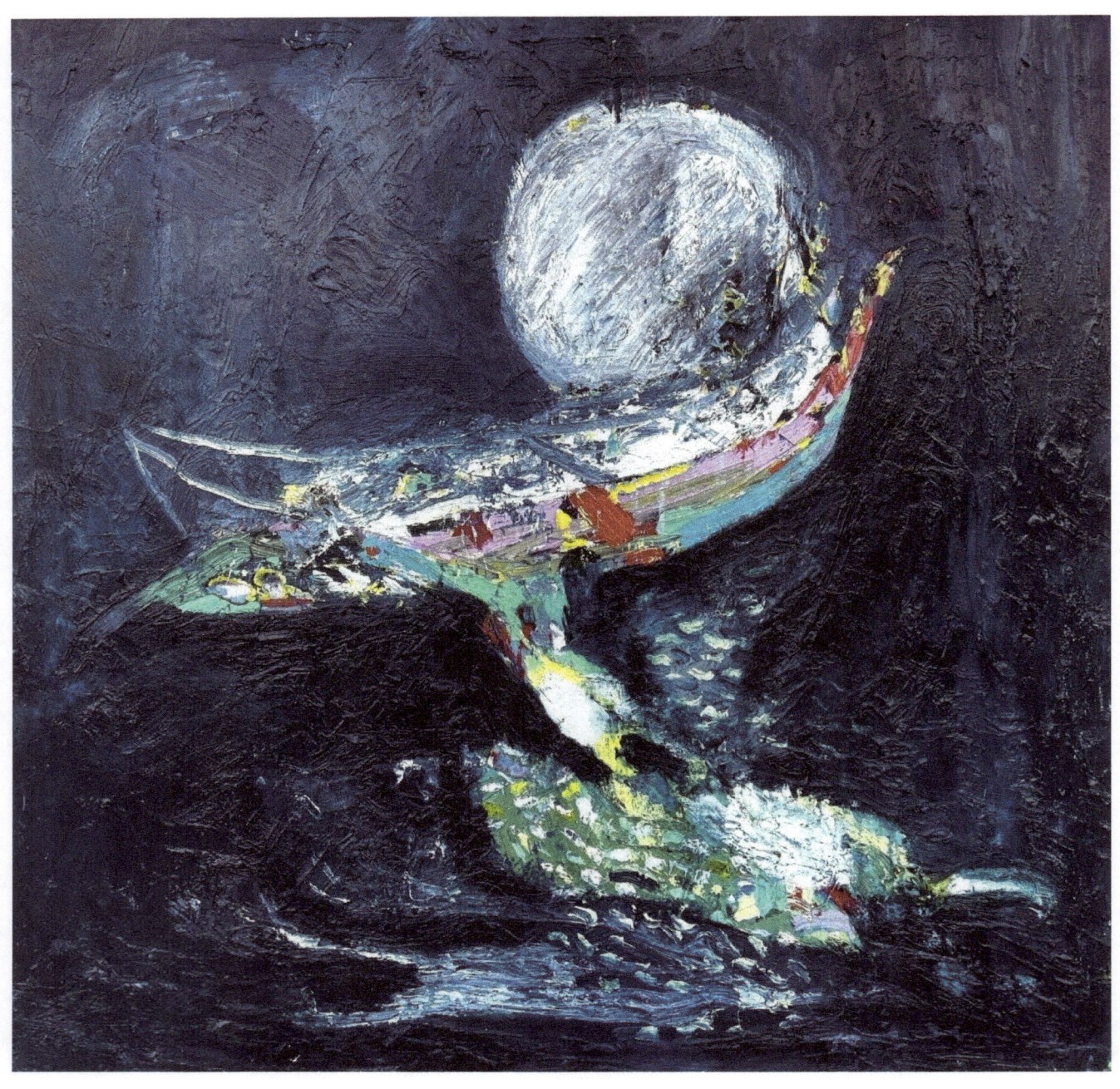

Title: Full moon swimmer

Size: 100x100cm

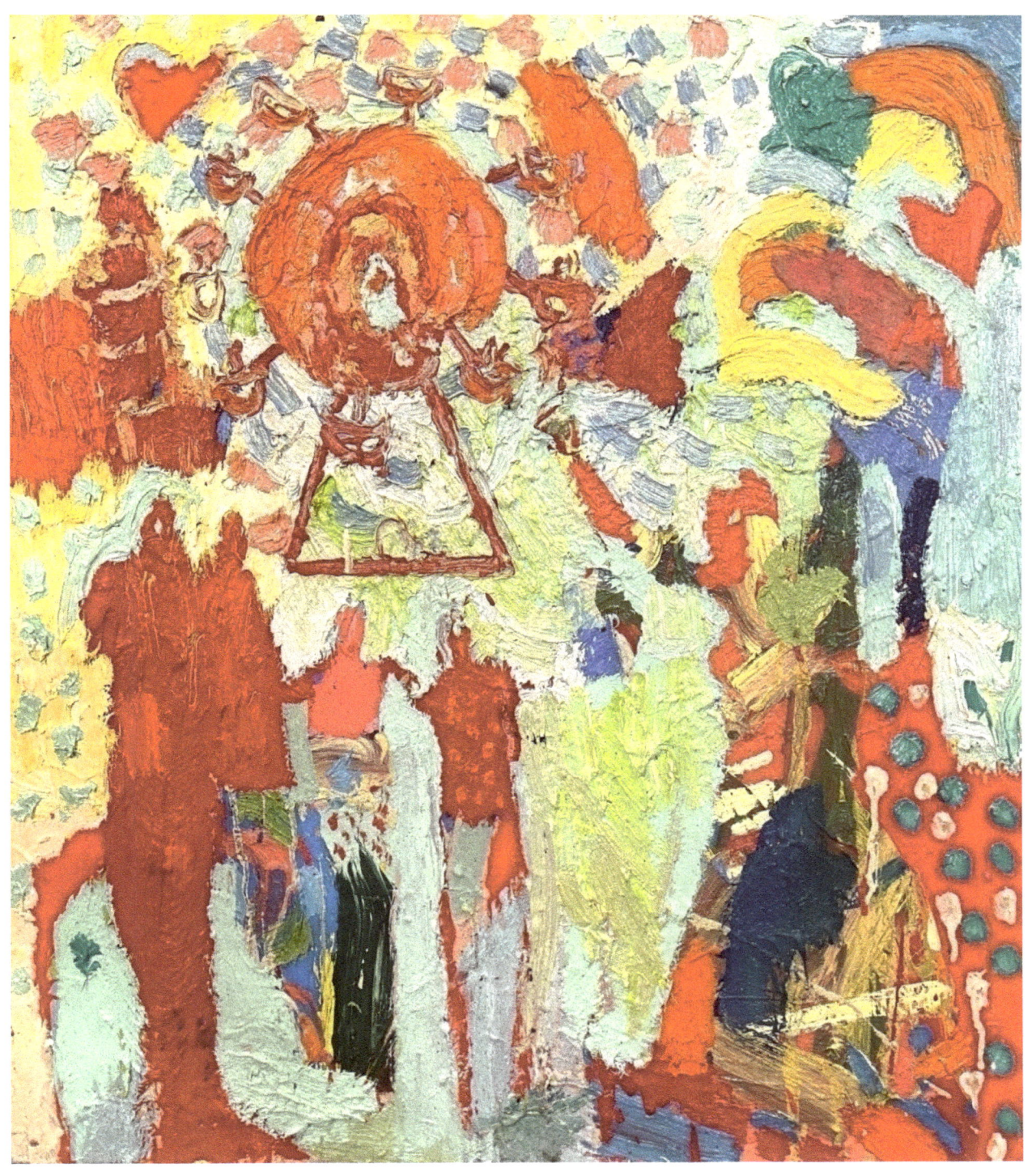

Title: Fun fair

Size: 77x63cm

Stories From The Banyan Tree

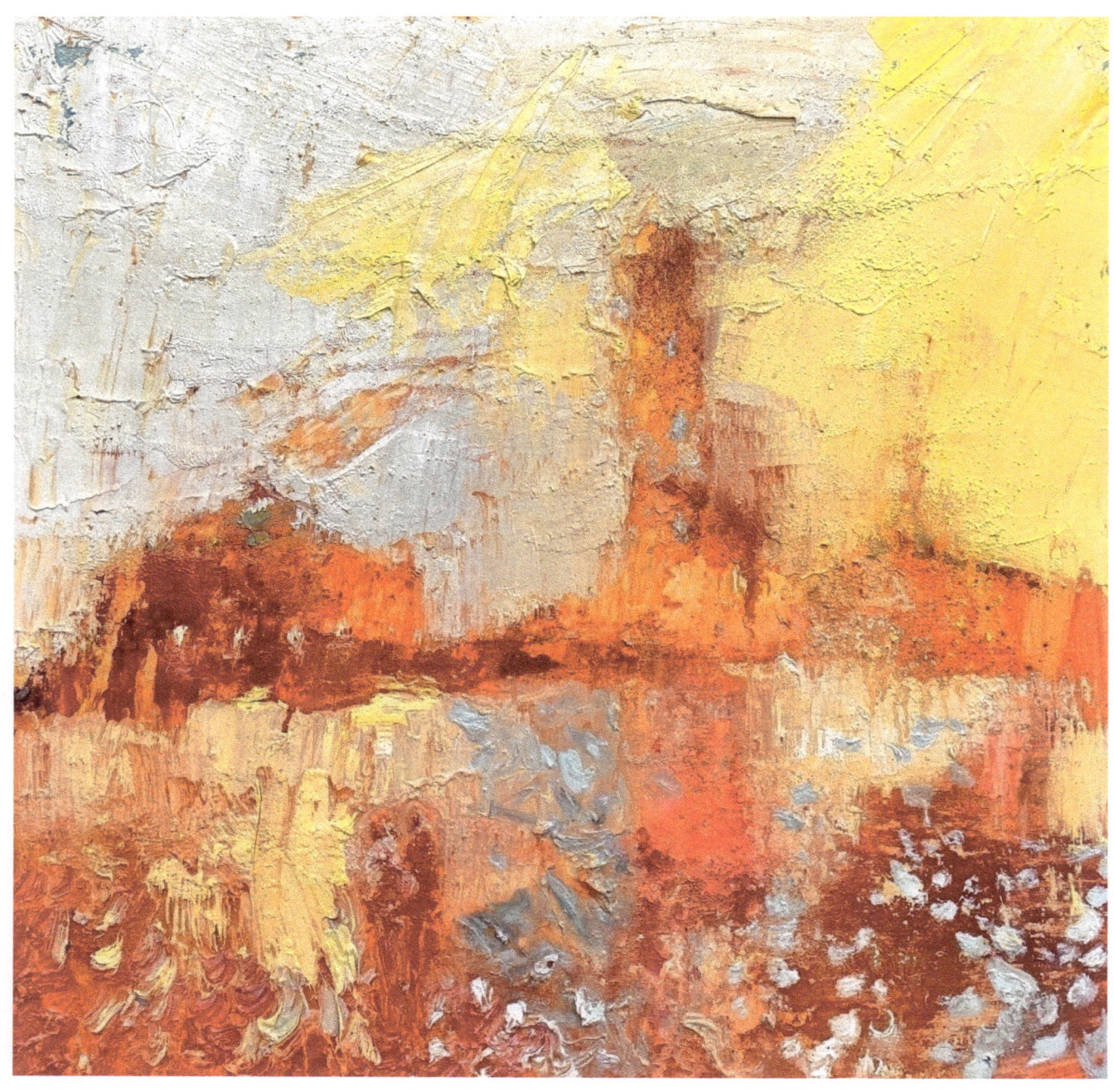

Title: Hampi sunrise

Size: 50x50cm

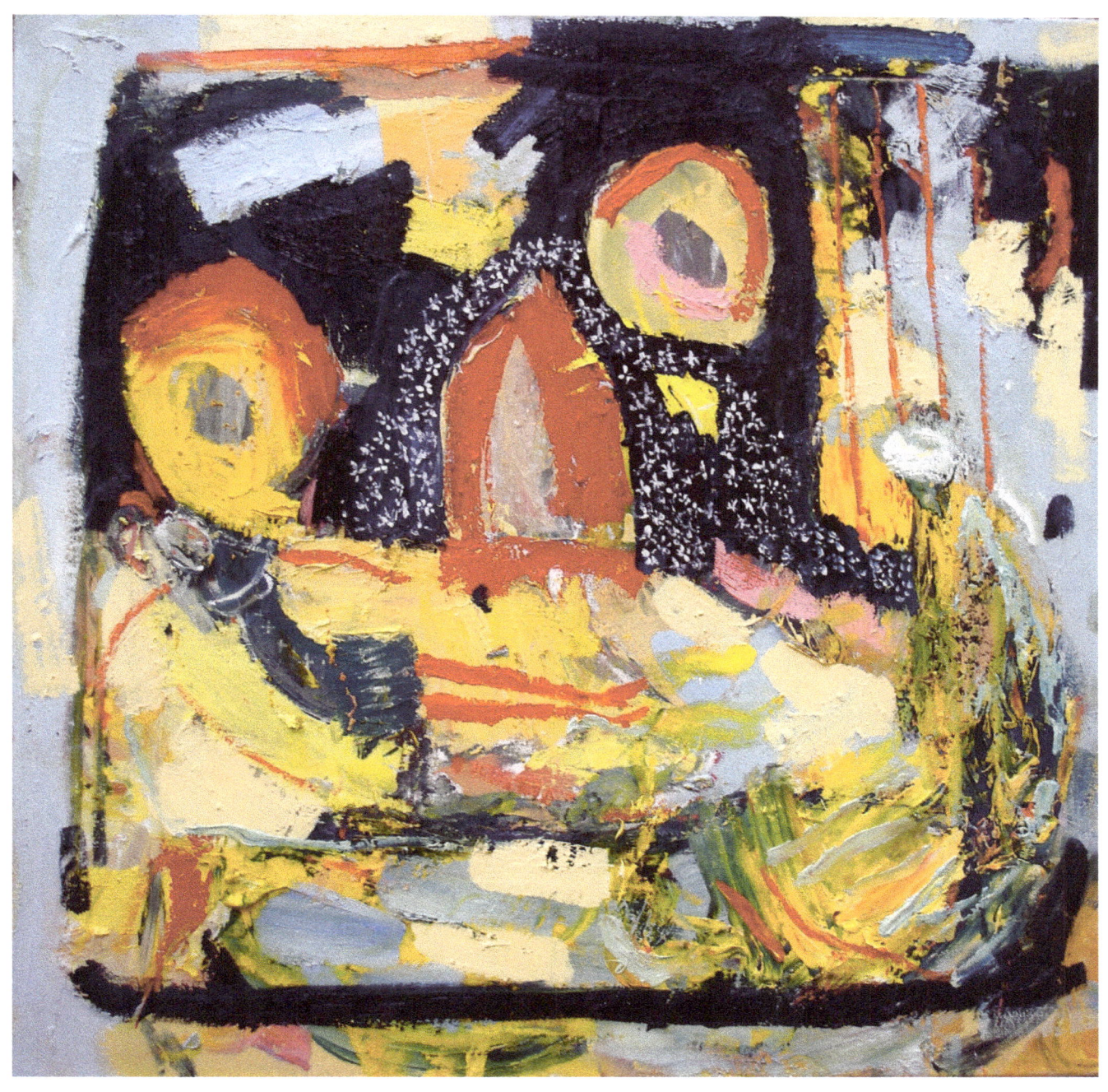

Title: Harem

Size: 90x90cm

Stories From The Banyan Tree

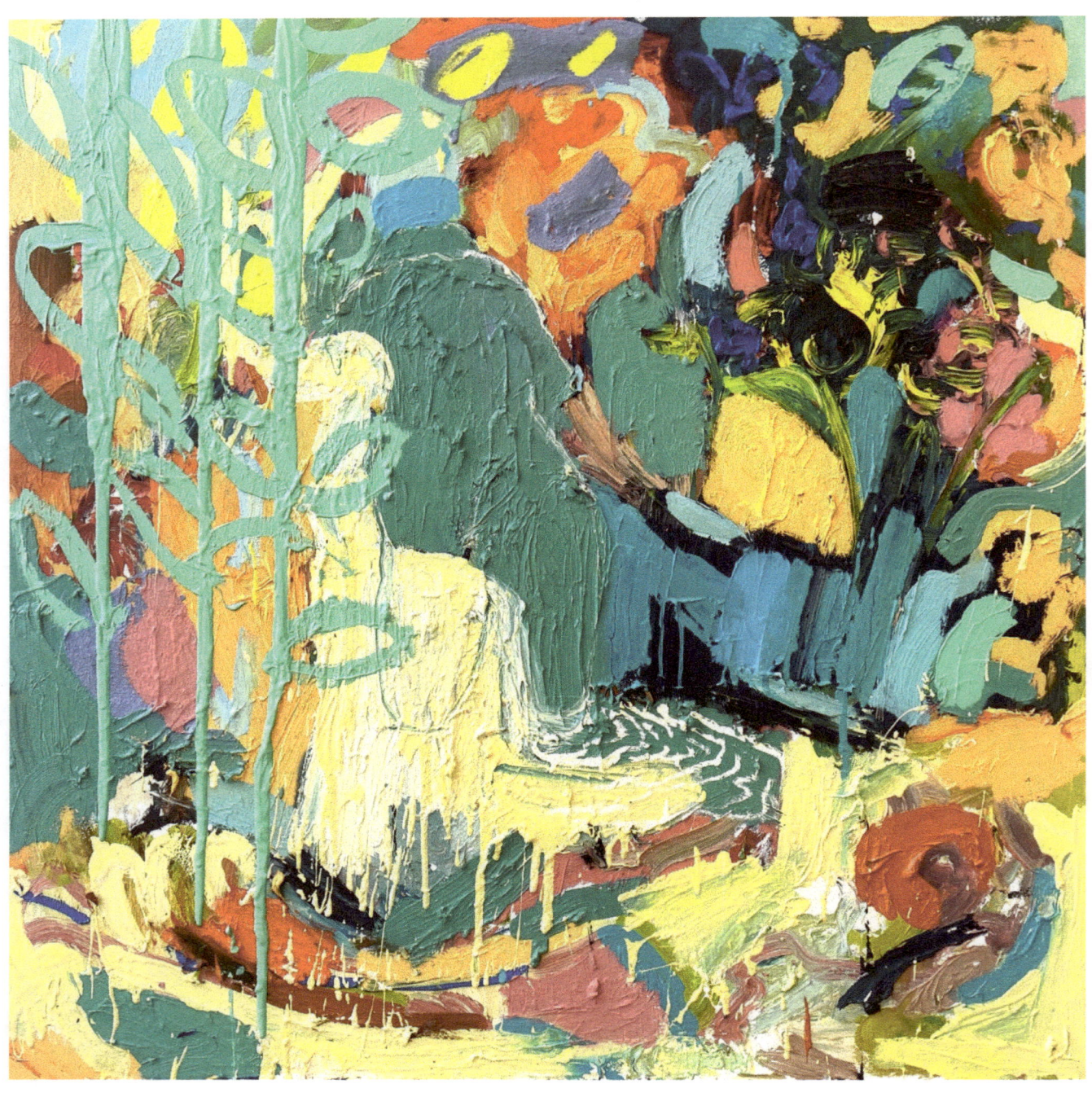

Title: Hidden within nature
Size: 120x5120cm

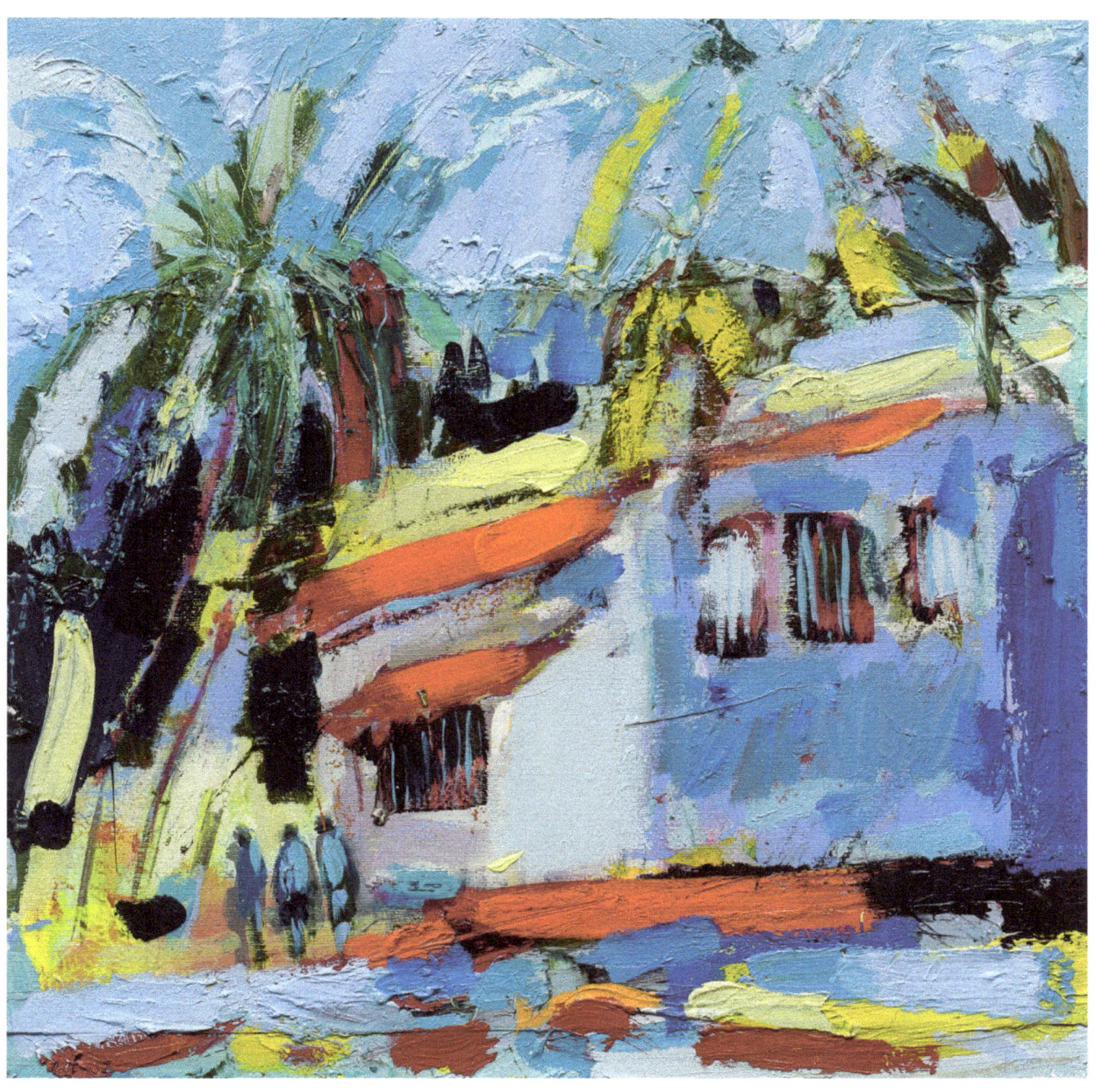

Title: Home from school

Size: 60x60cm

Stories From The Banyan Tree

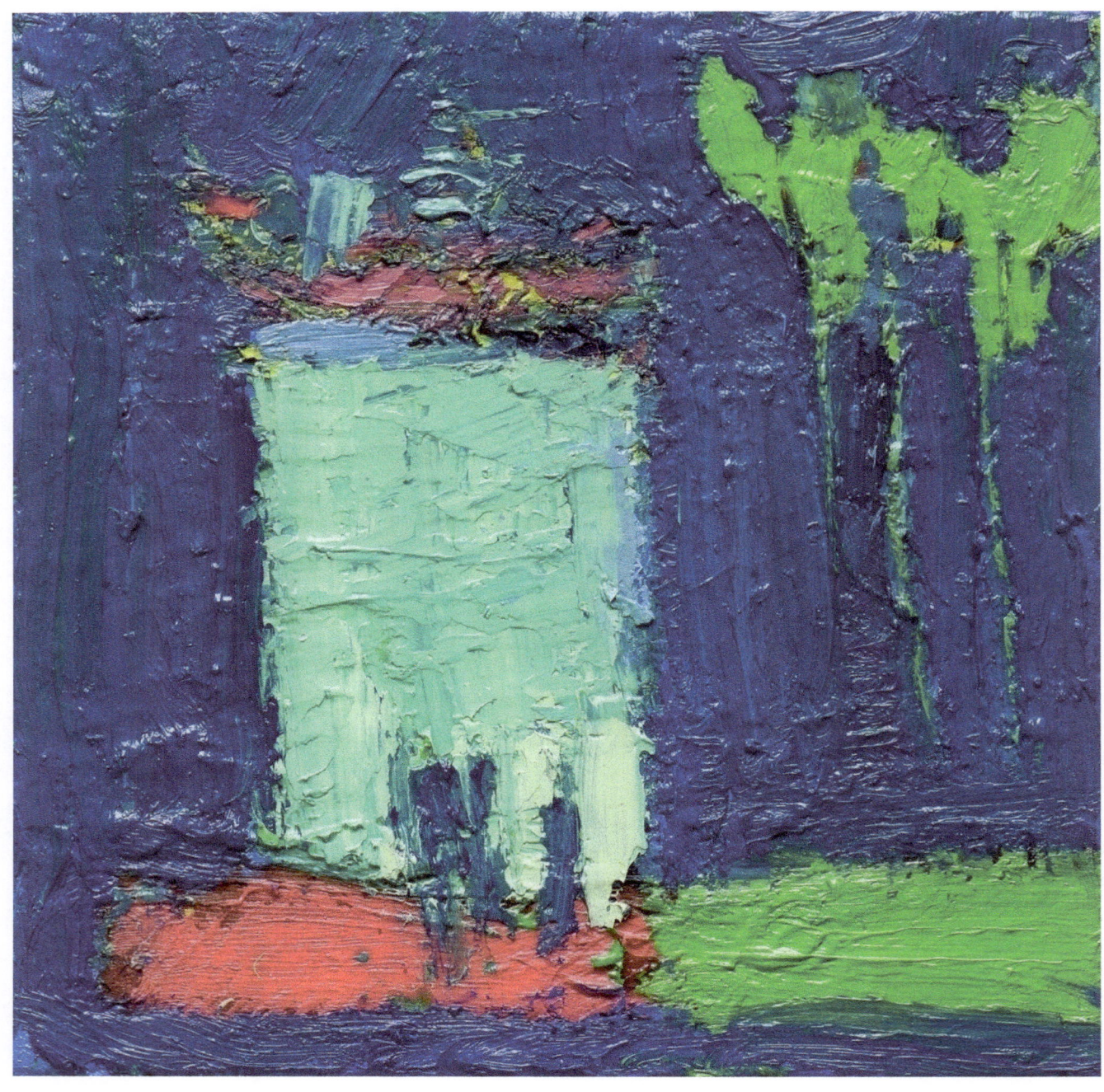

Title: In the night garden
Size: 40x40cm

Paul Wadsworth

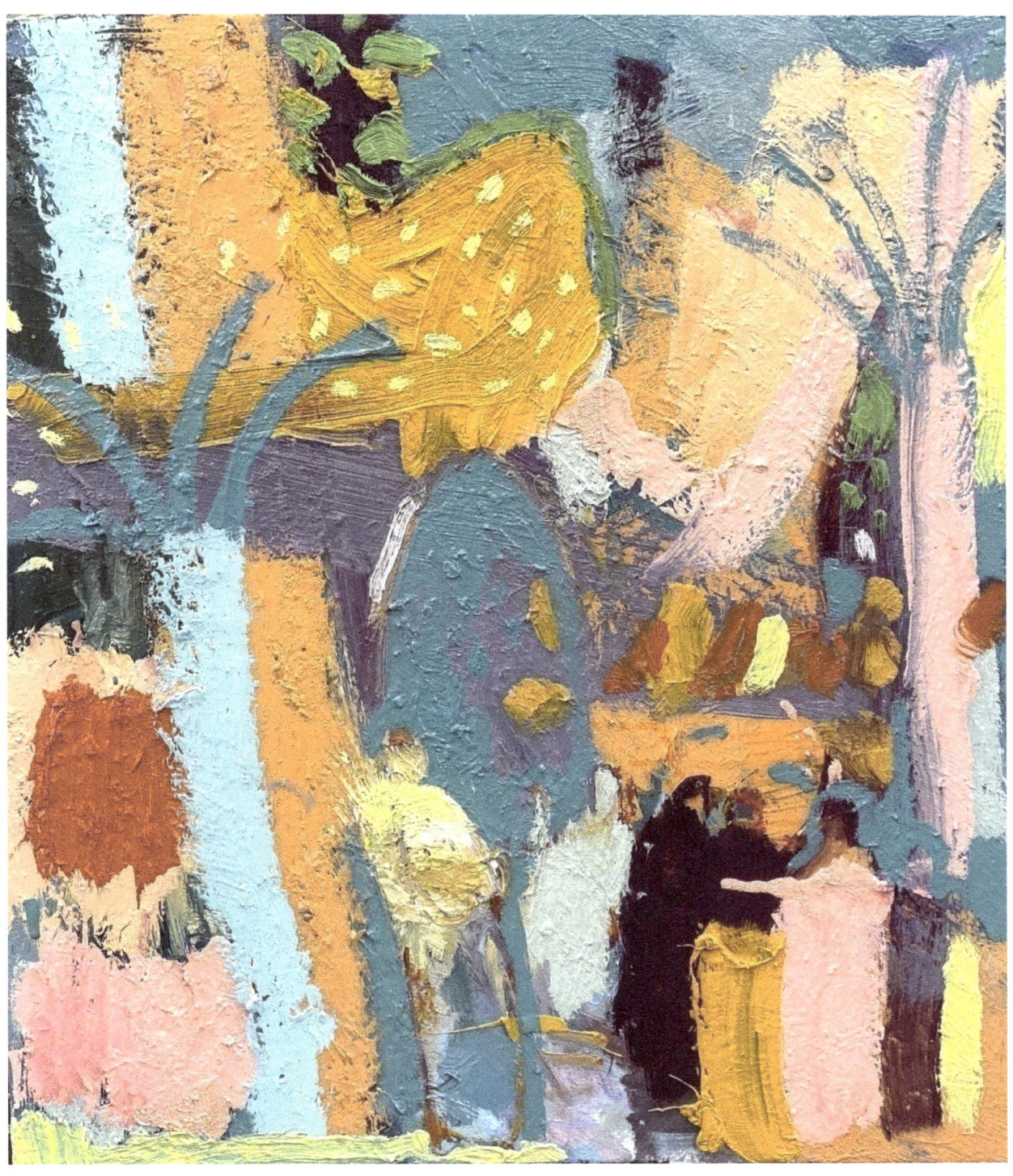

Title: Indian Bazaar
Size: 70x60cm

Stories From The Banyan Tree

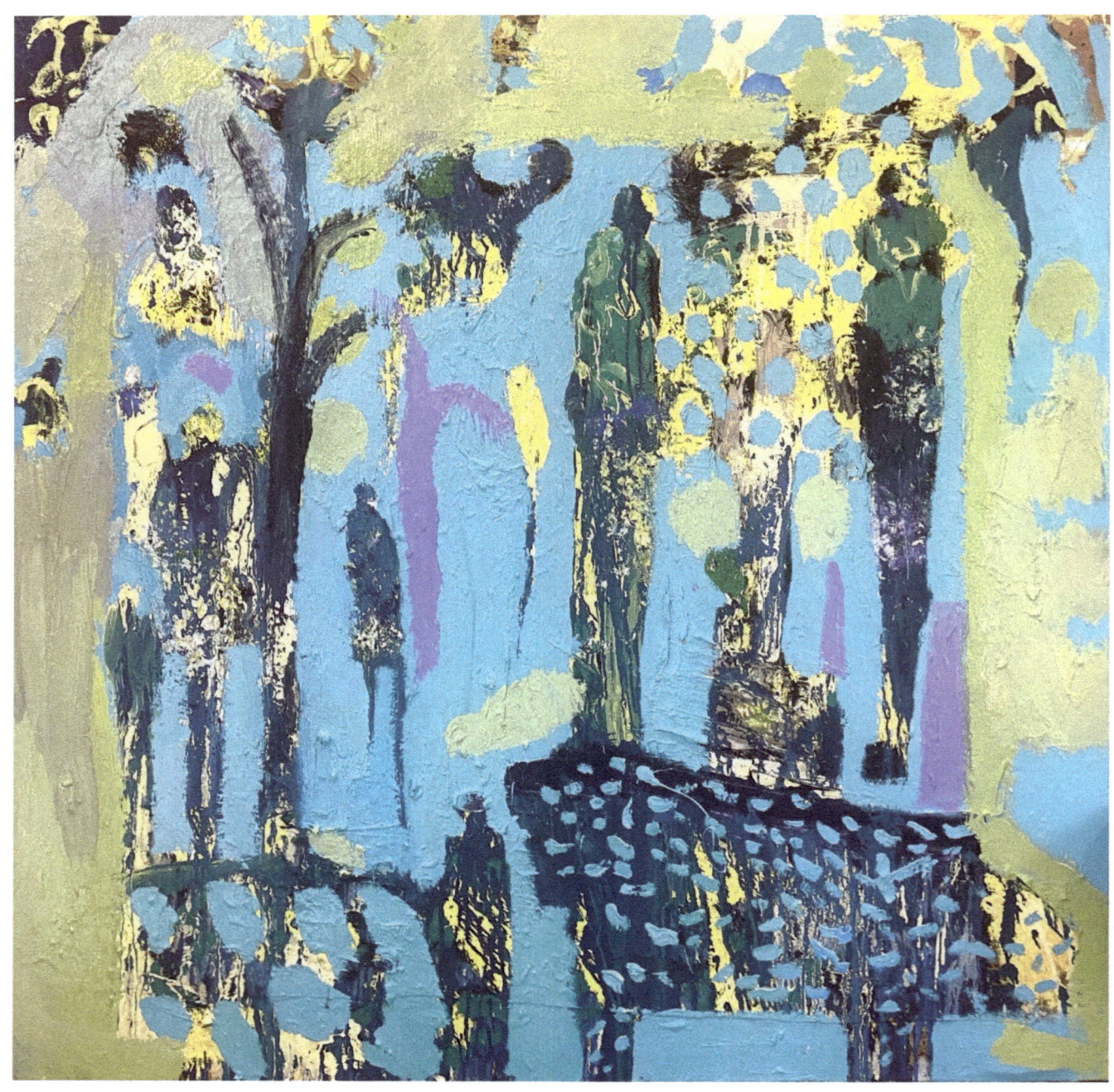

Title: Kerala life and bauty

Size: 120x120cm

Paul Wadsworth

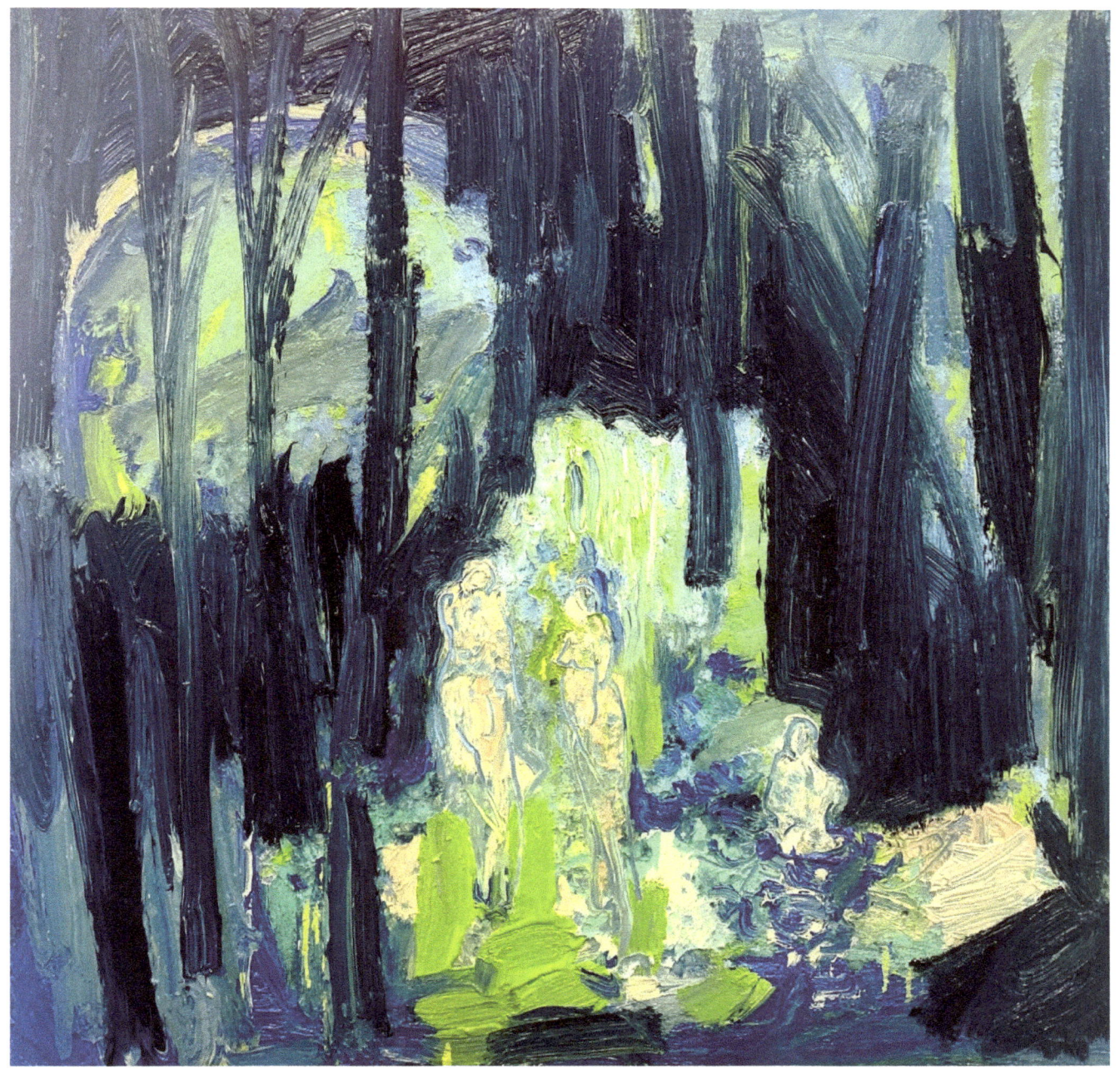

Title: Moonlit swimmer

Size: 50x50cm

Stories From The Banyan Tree

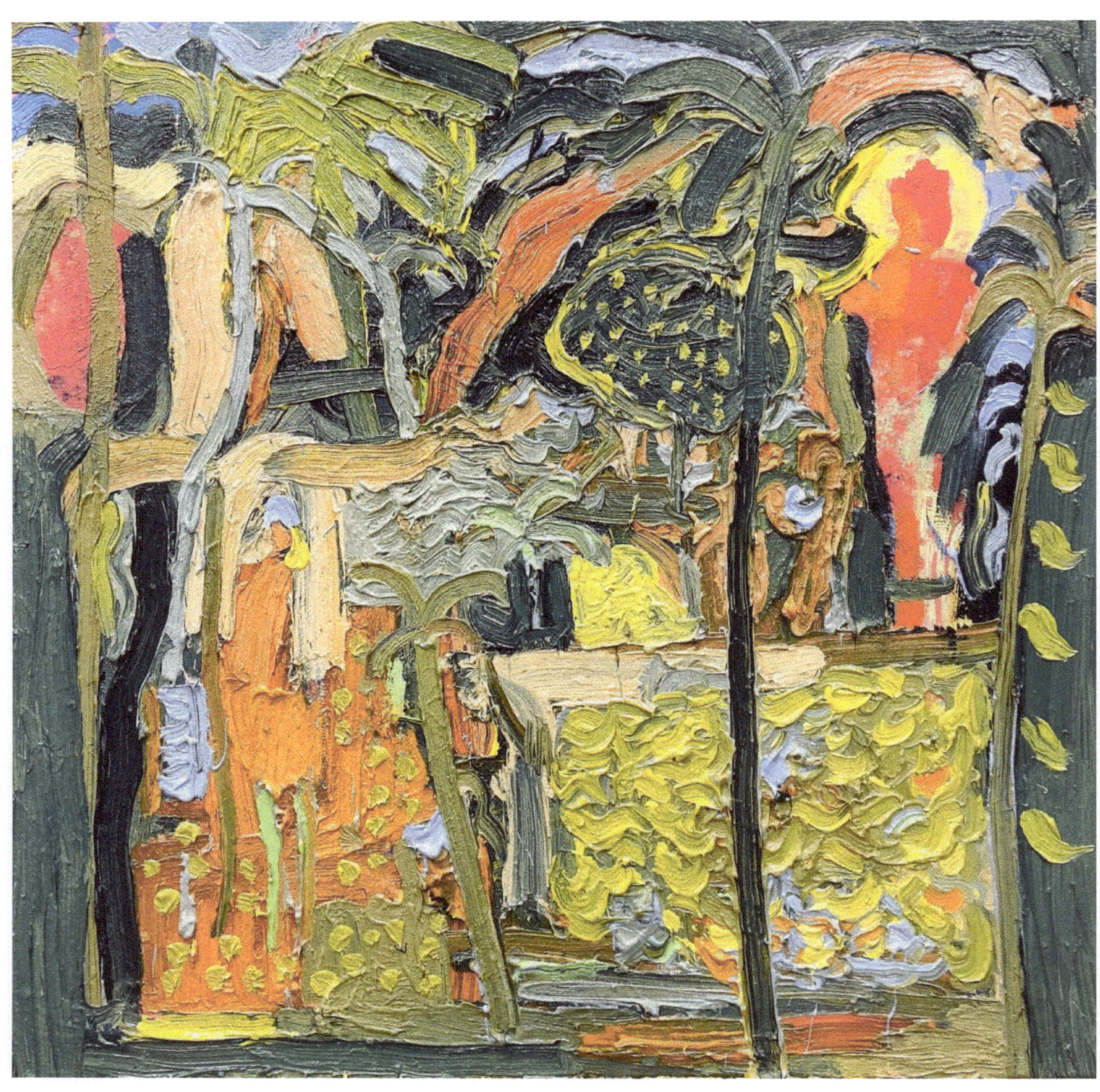

Title: Kerala's beauty

Size: 90x90cm

Paul Wadsworth

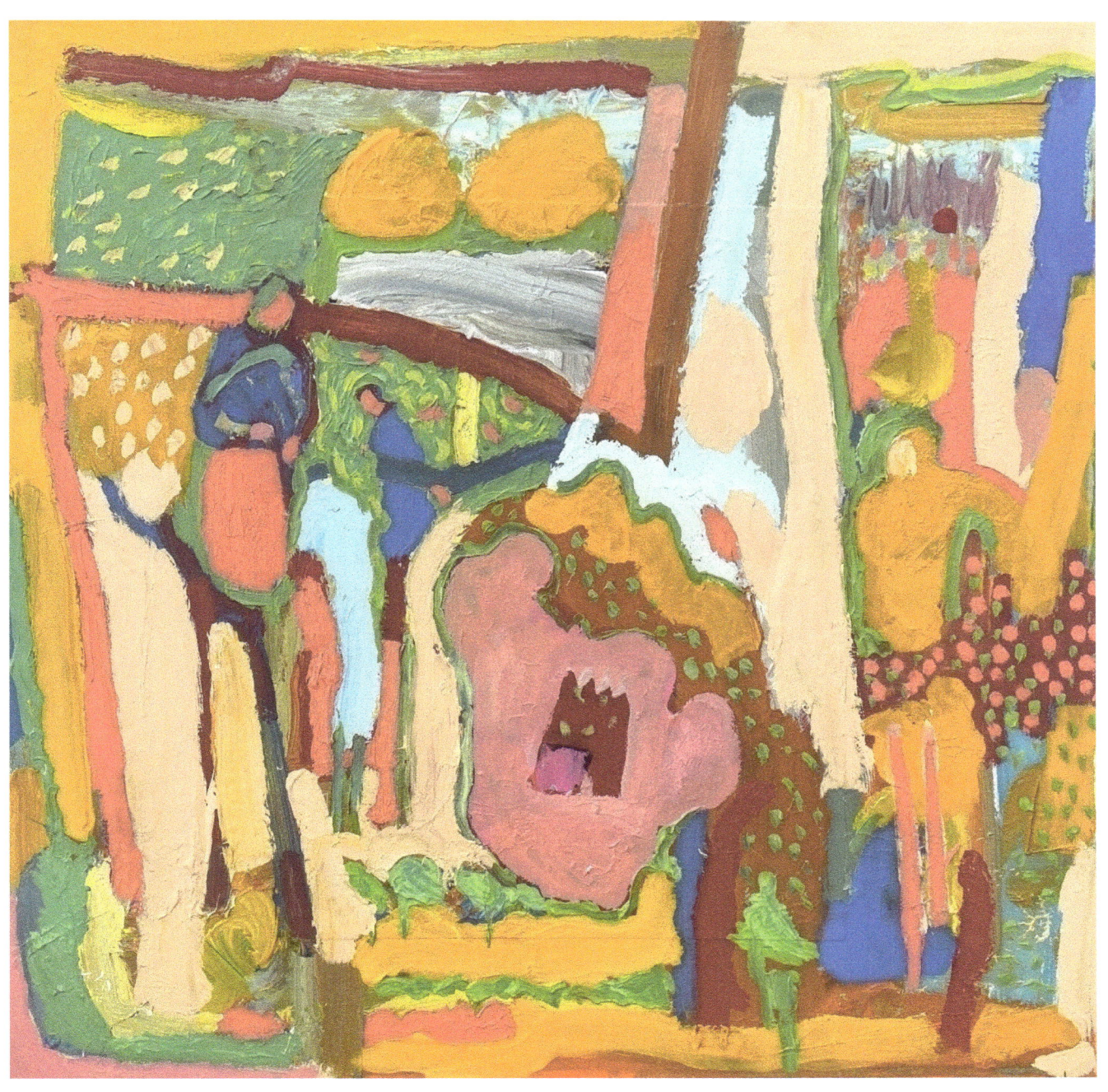

Title: Life around a small red temple

Size: 145x145cm

Stories From The Banyan Tree

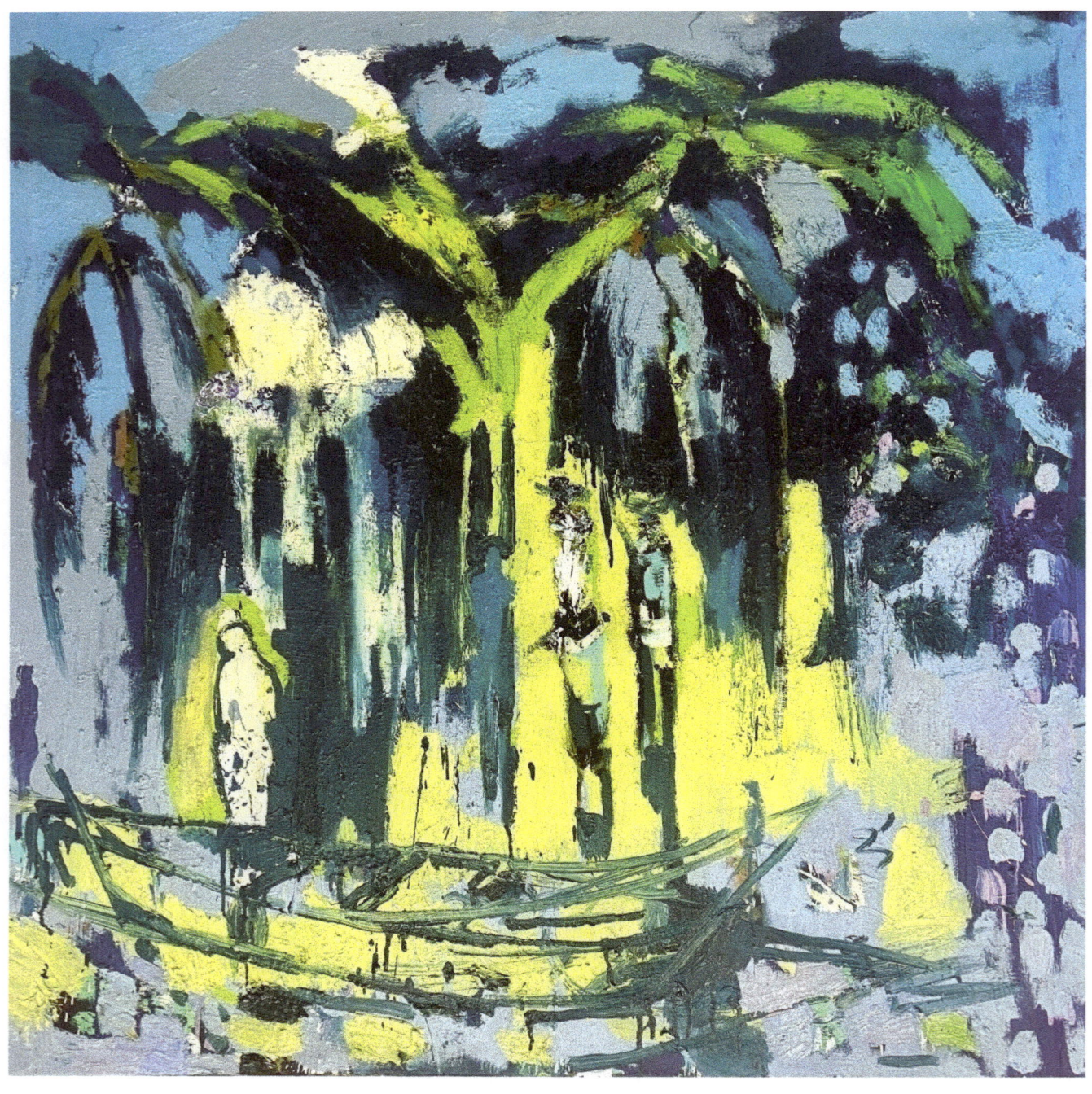

Title: Living by the sea
Size: 120x120cm

Paul Wadsworth

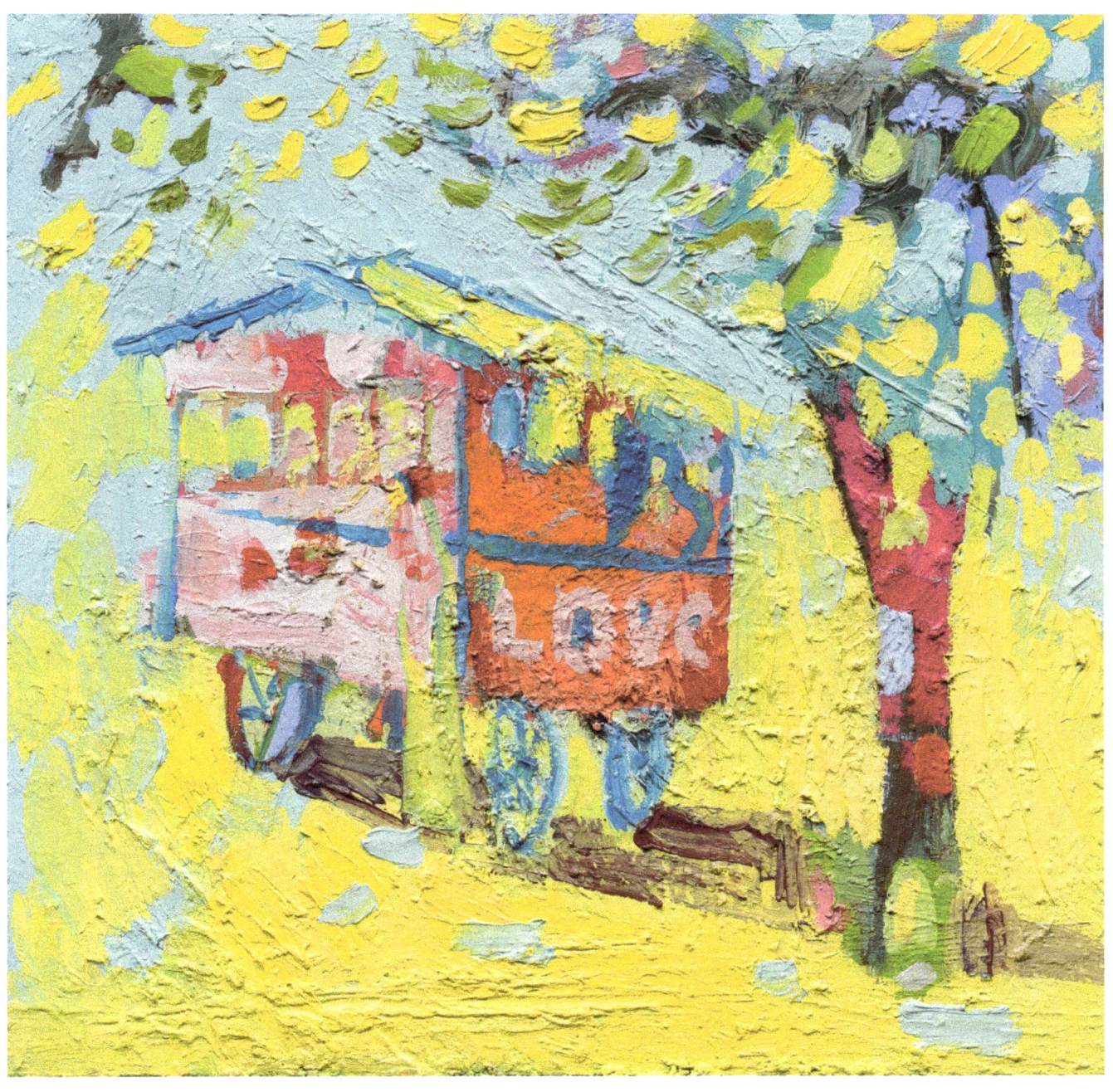

Title: Love shack

Size: 60x60cm

Stories From The Banyan Tree

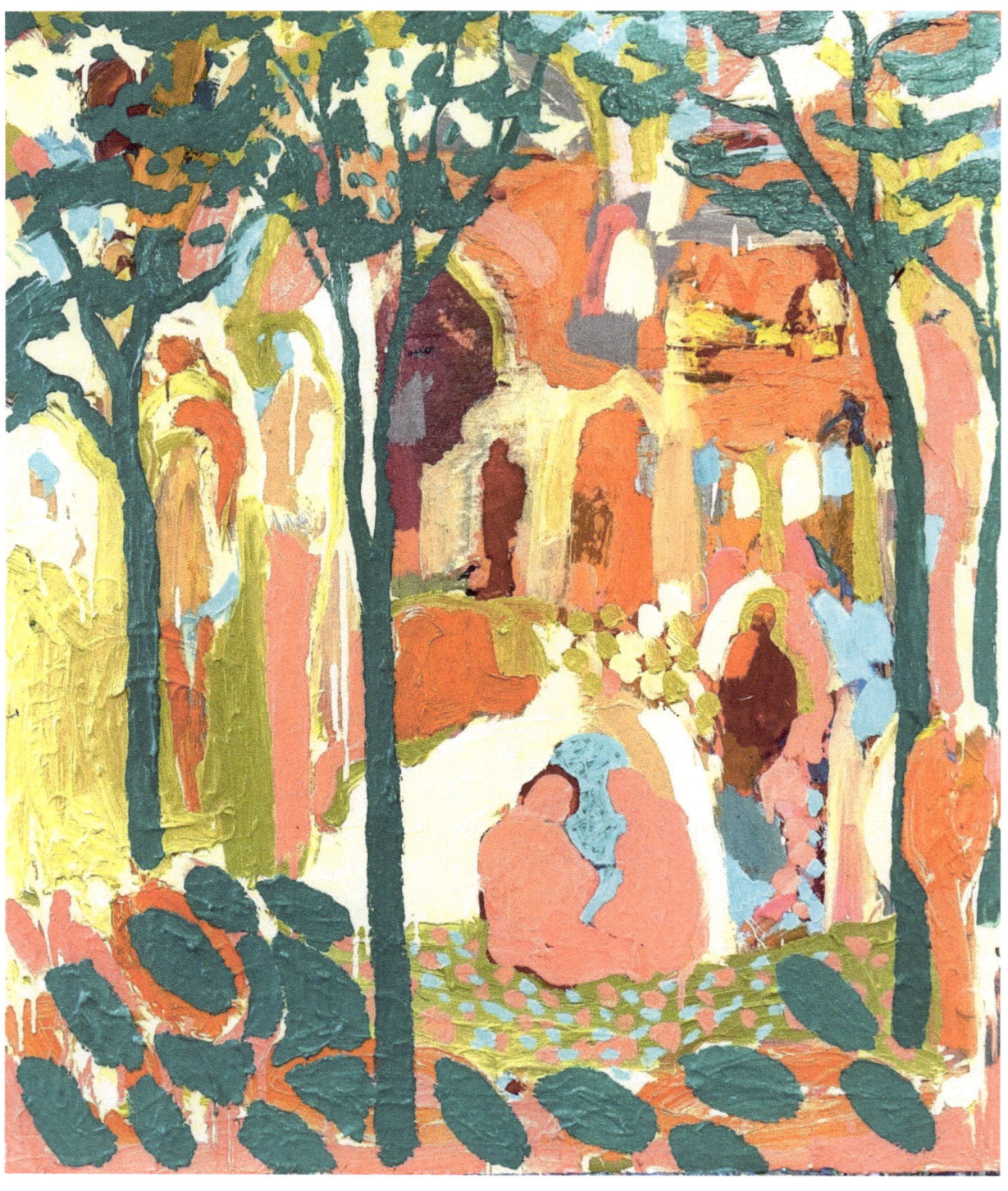

Title: Lovers
Size: 120x100cm

Paul Wadsworth

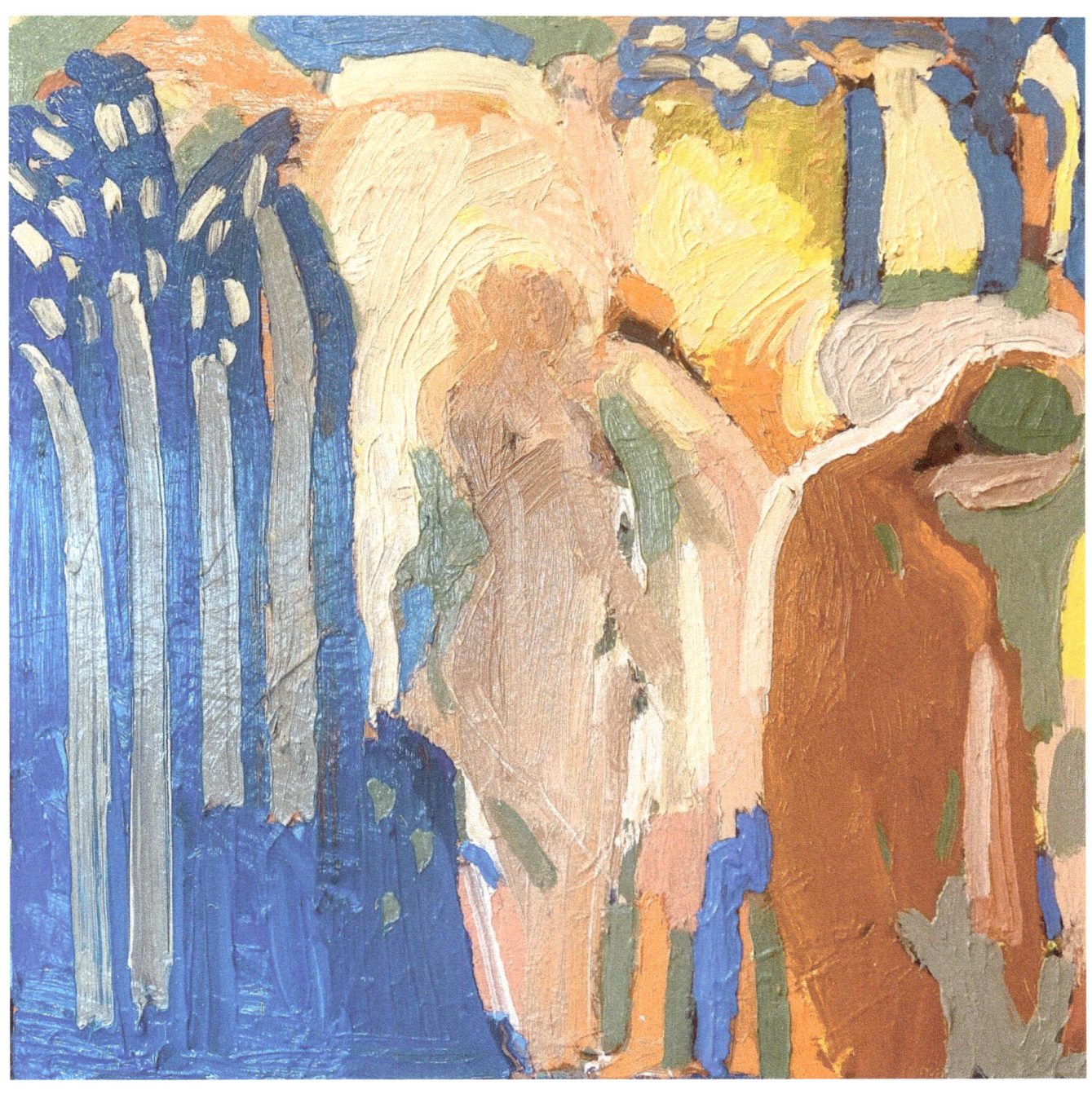

Title: Meditation

Size: 120x120cm

Stories From The Banyan Tree

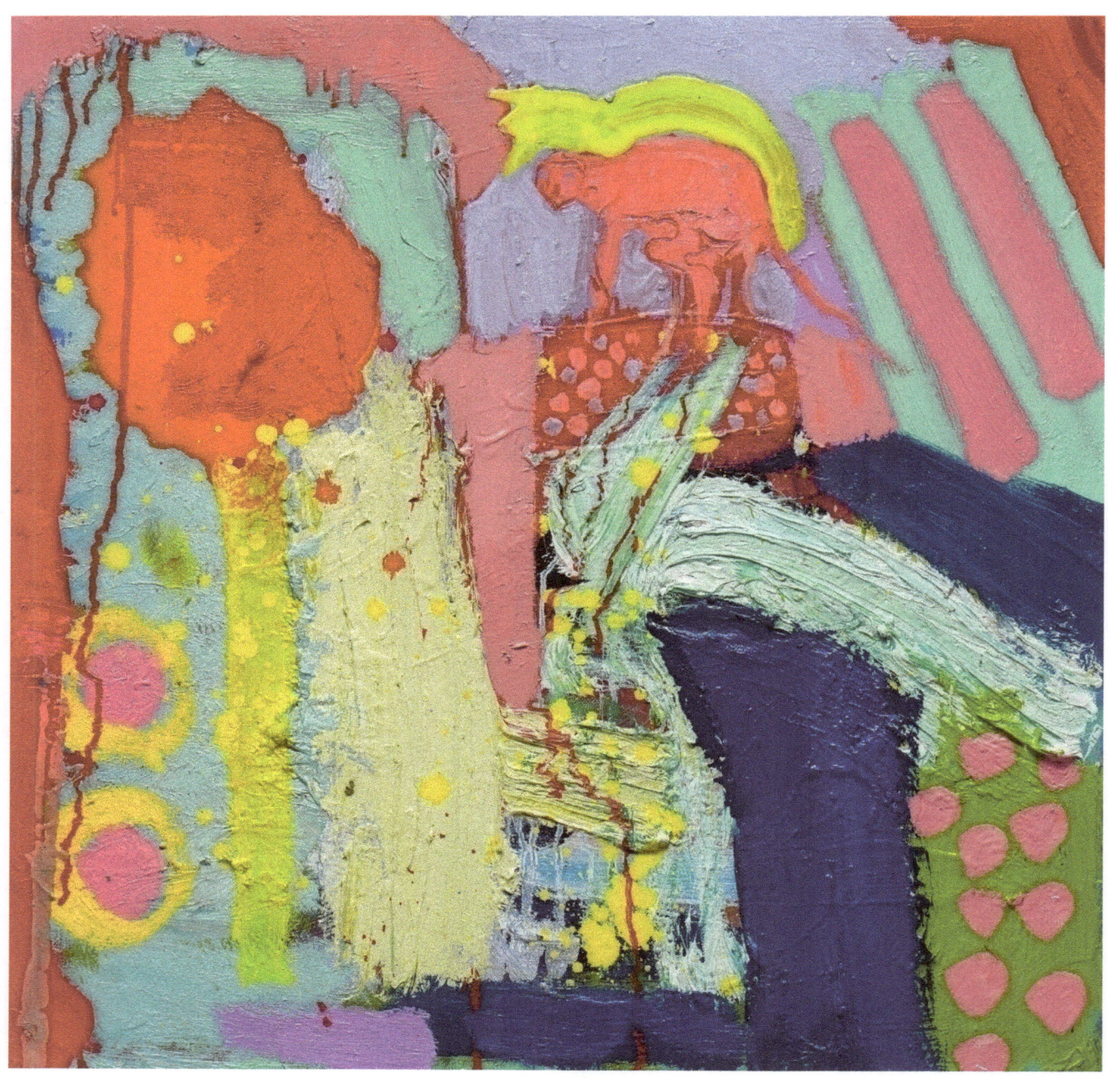

Title: Monkey temple
Size: 60x60cm

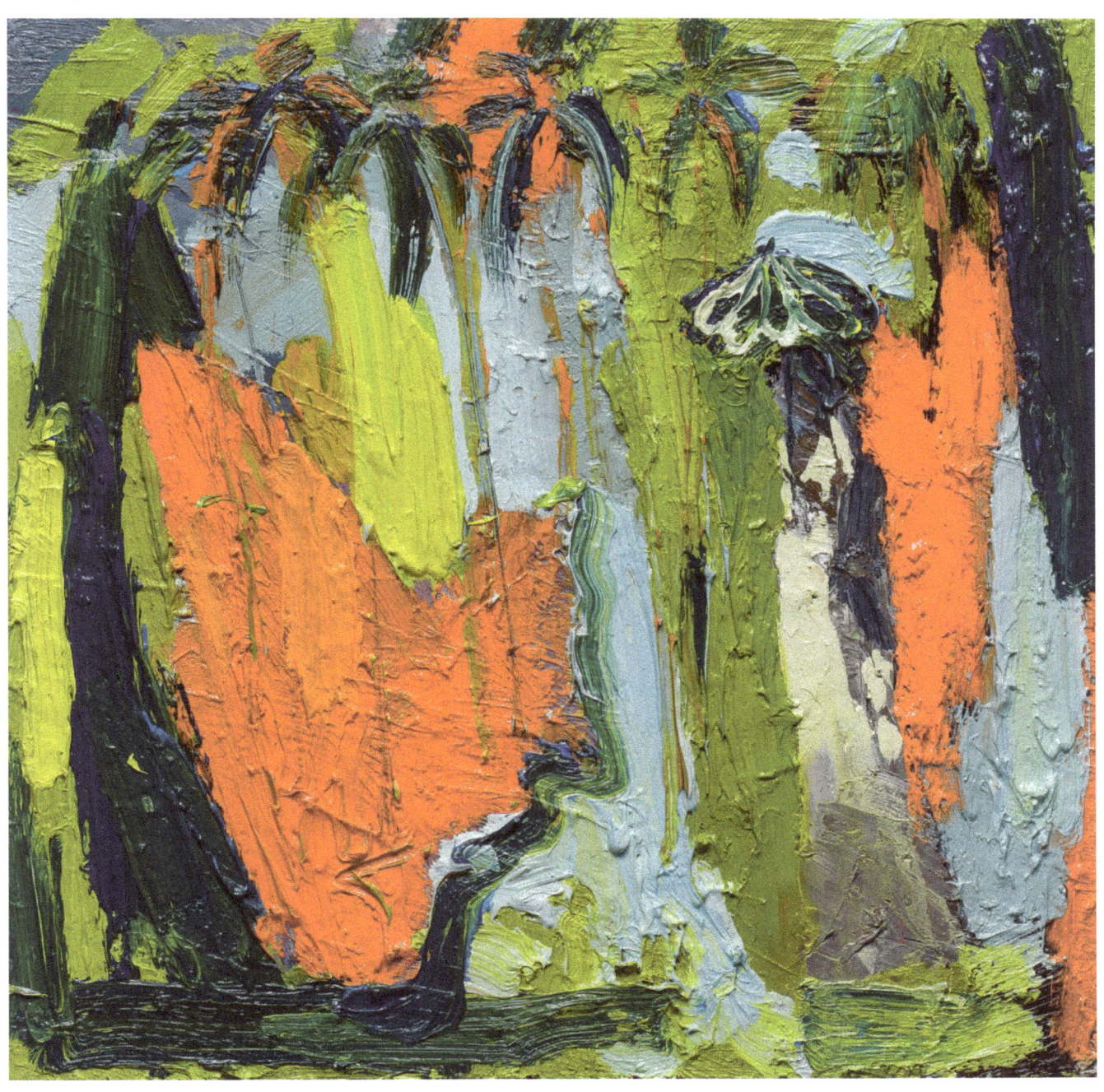

Title: Monsoon water

Size: 50x50cm

Stories From The Banyan Tree

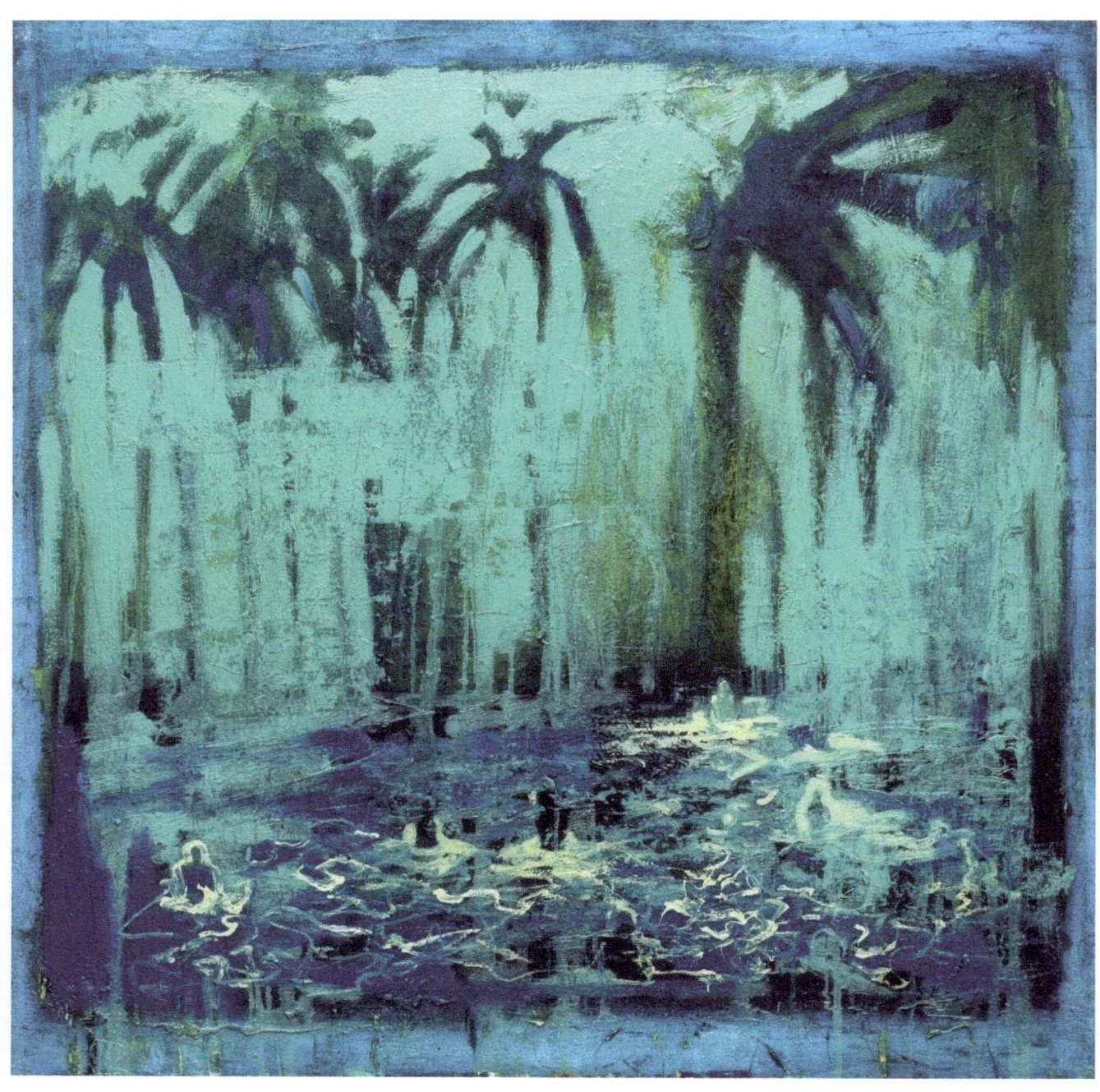

Title: Moonlight water

Size: 120x120cm

Paul Wadsworth

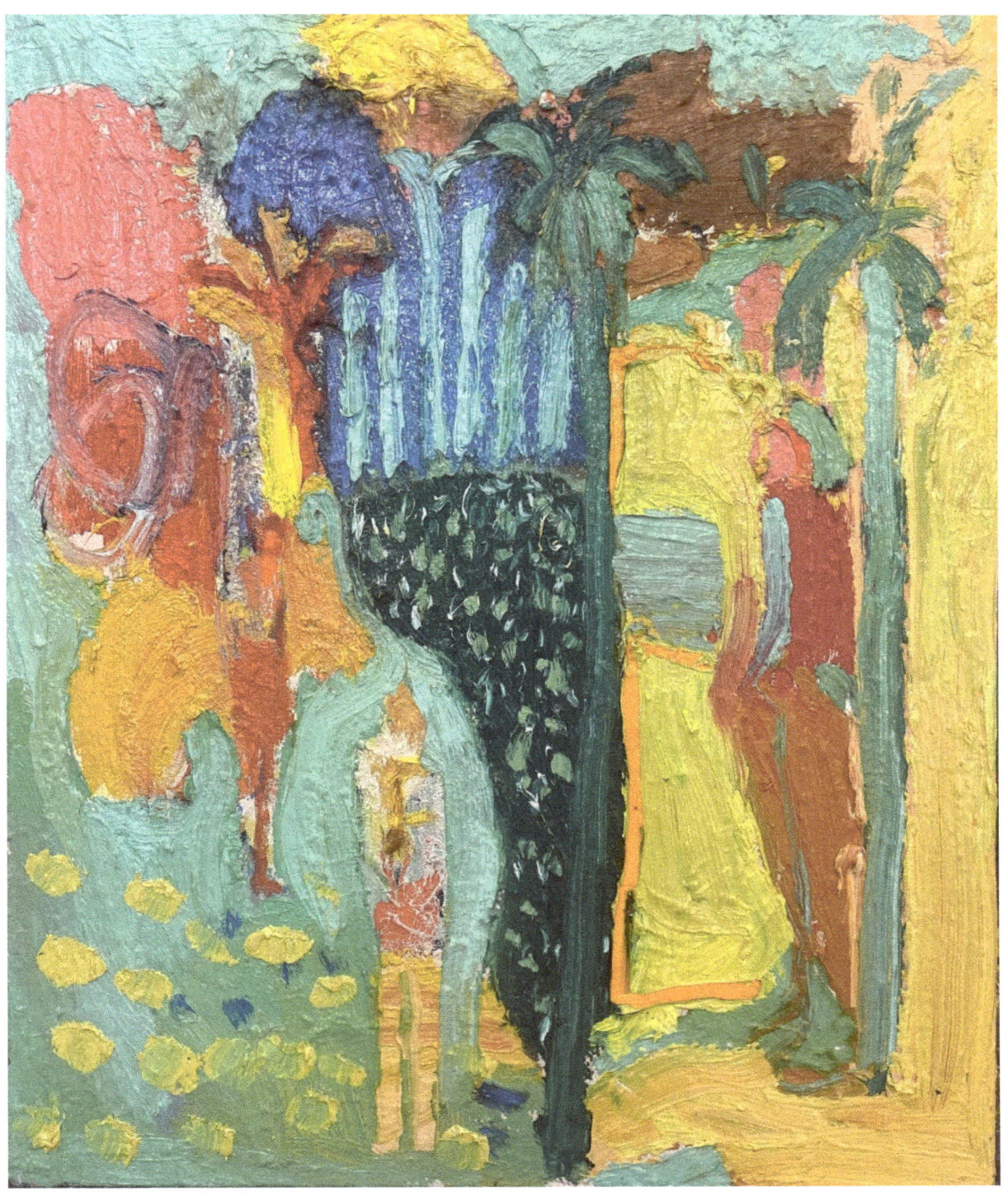

Title: Natures garden

Size: 70x60cm

Stories From The Banyan Tree

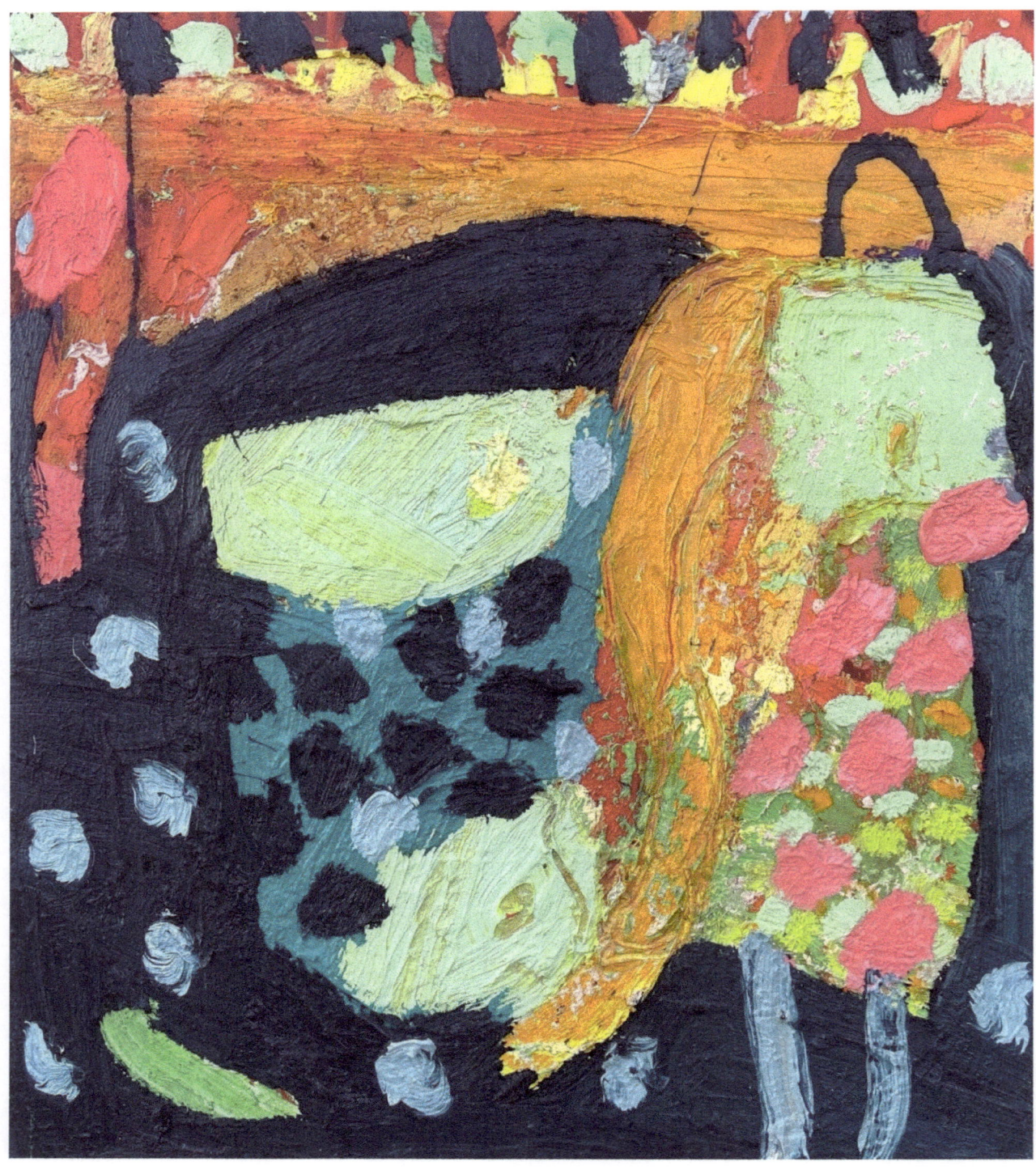

Title: Night ocean

Size: 73x67cm

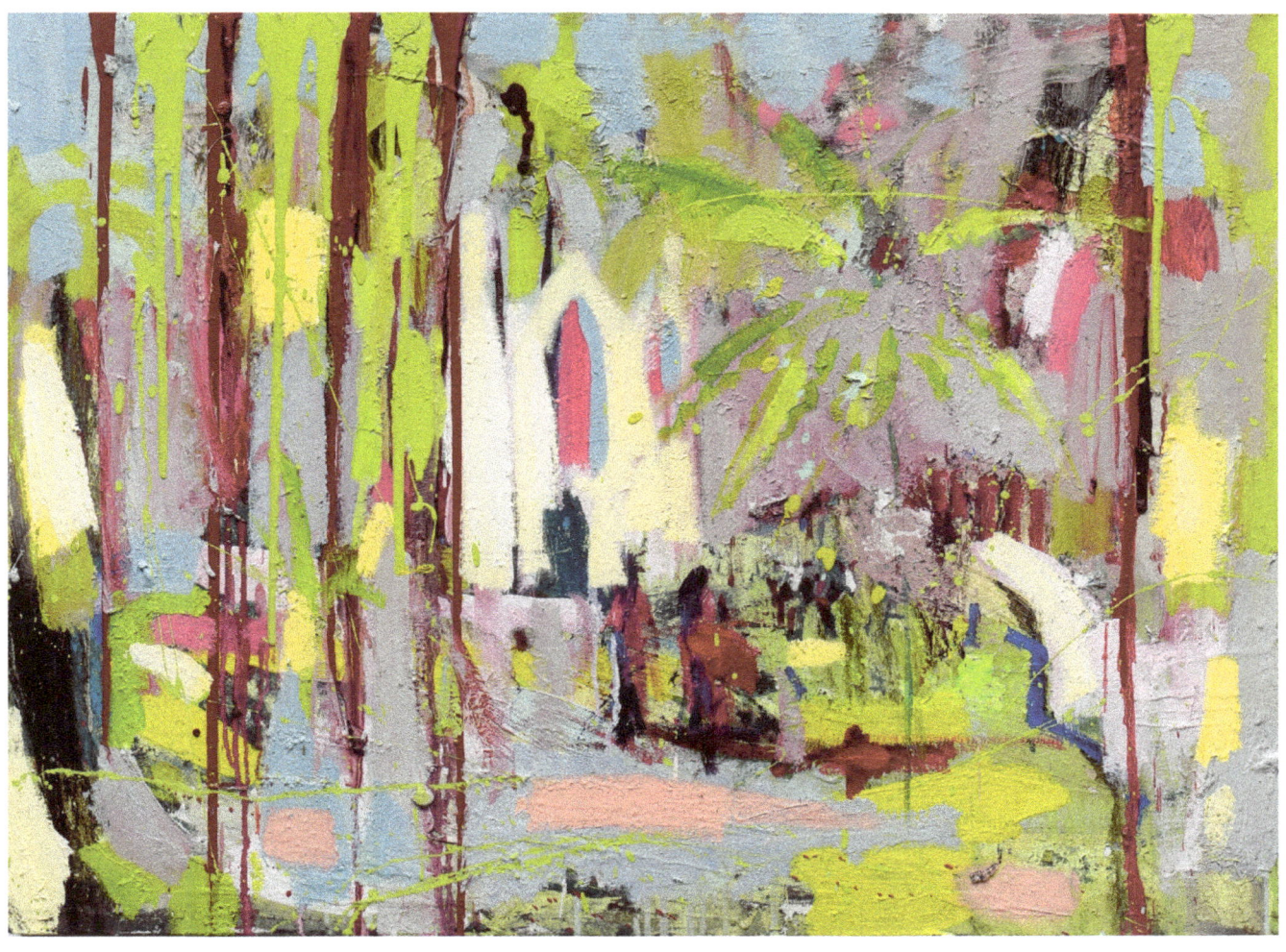

Title: Old Goa

Size: 75x90cm

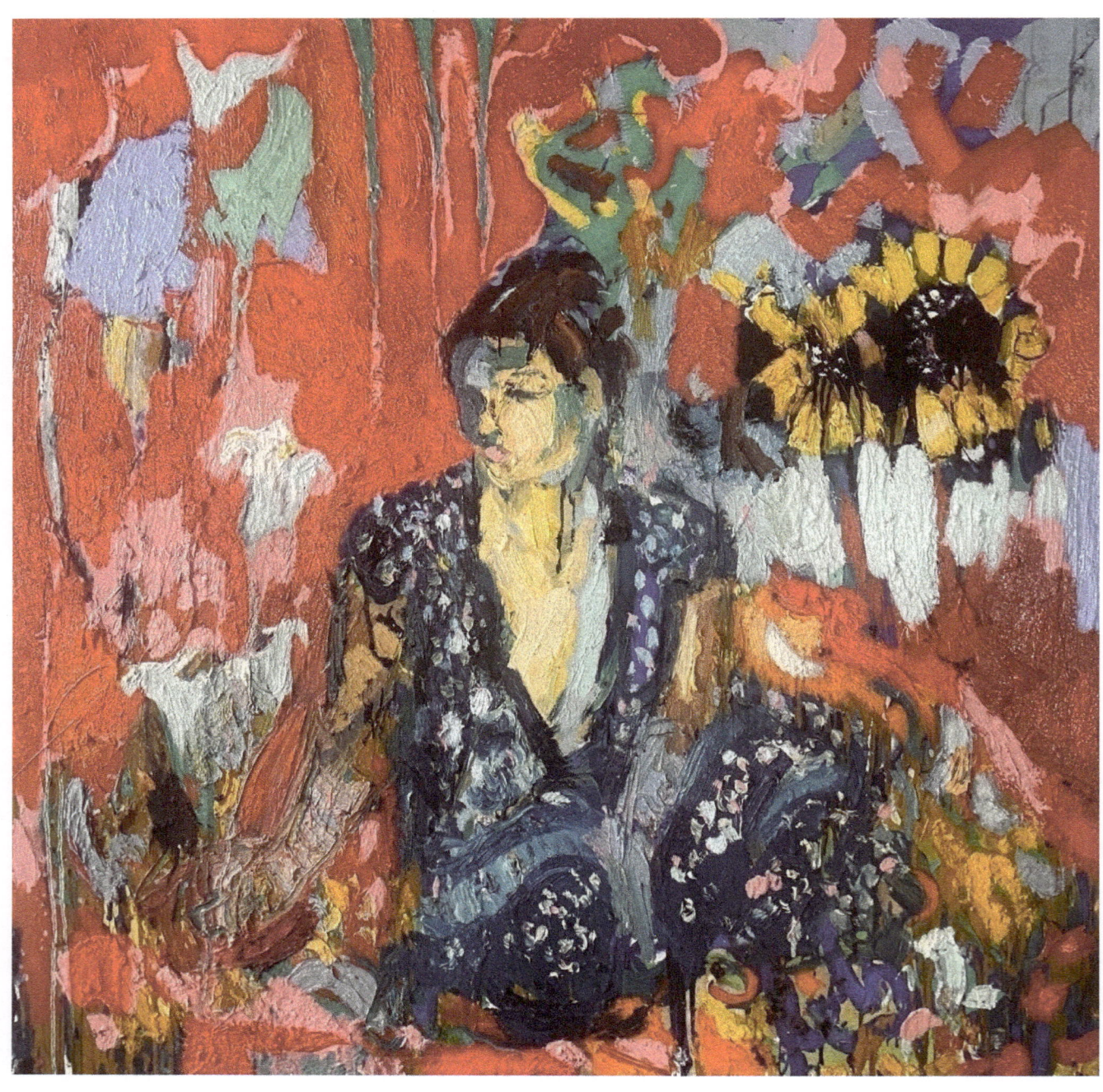

Title: Orange Garden

Size: 120x120cm

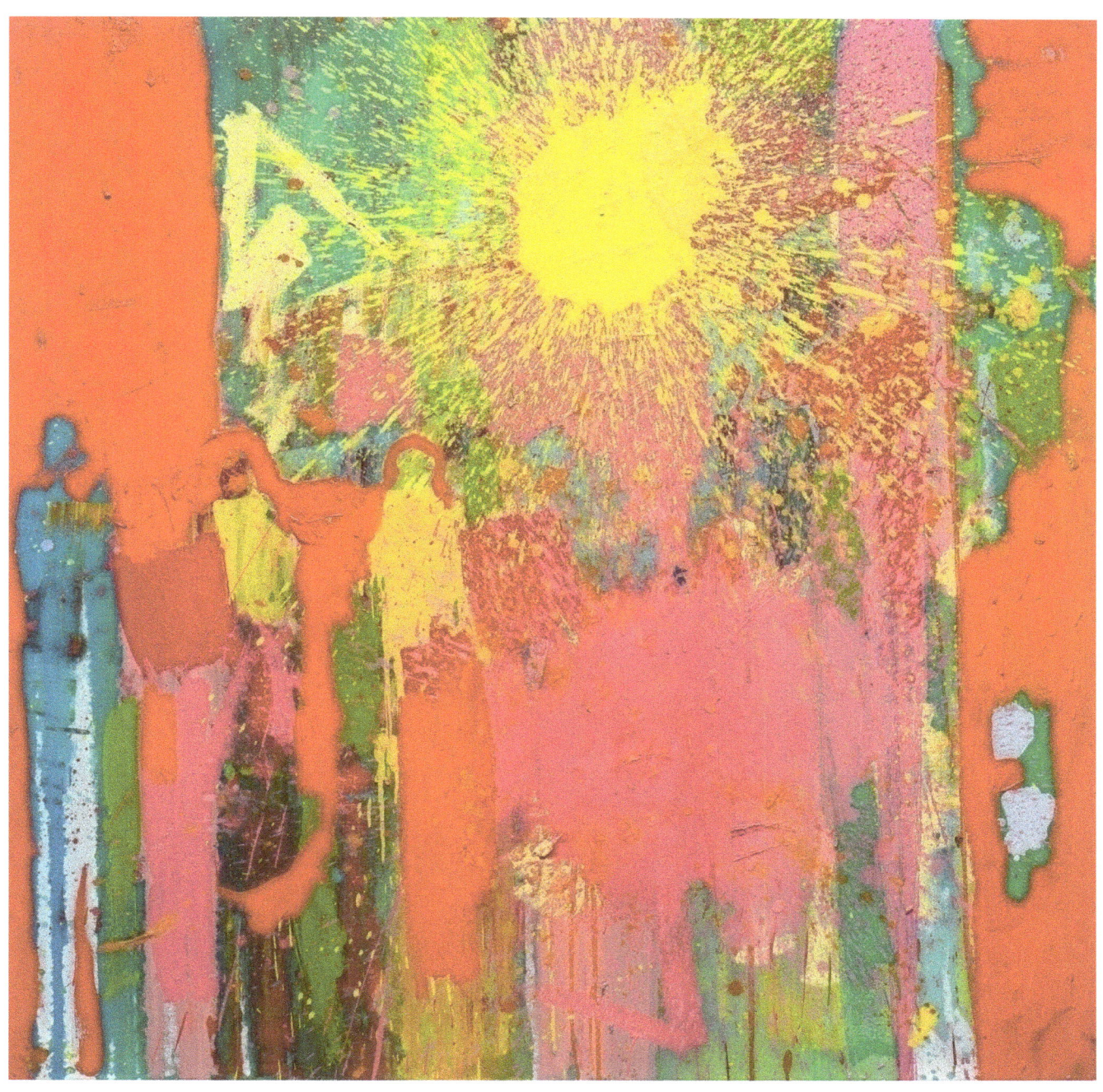

Title: Orange sunshine

Size: 126x126cm

Stories From The Banyan Tree

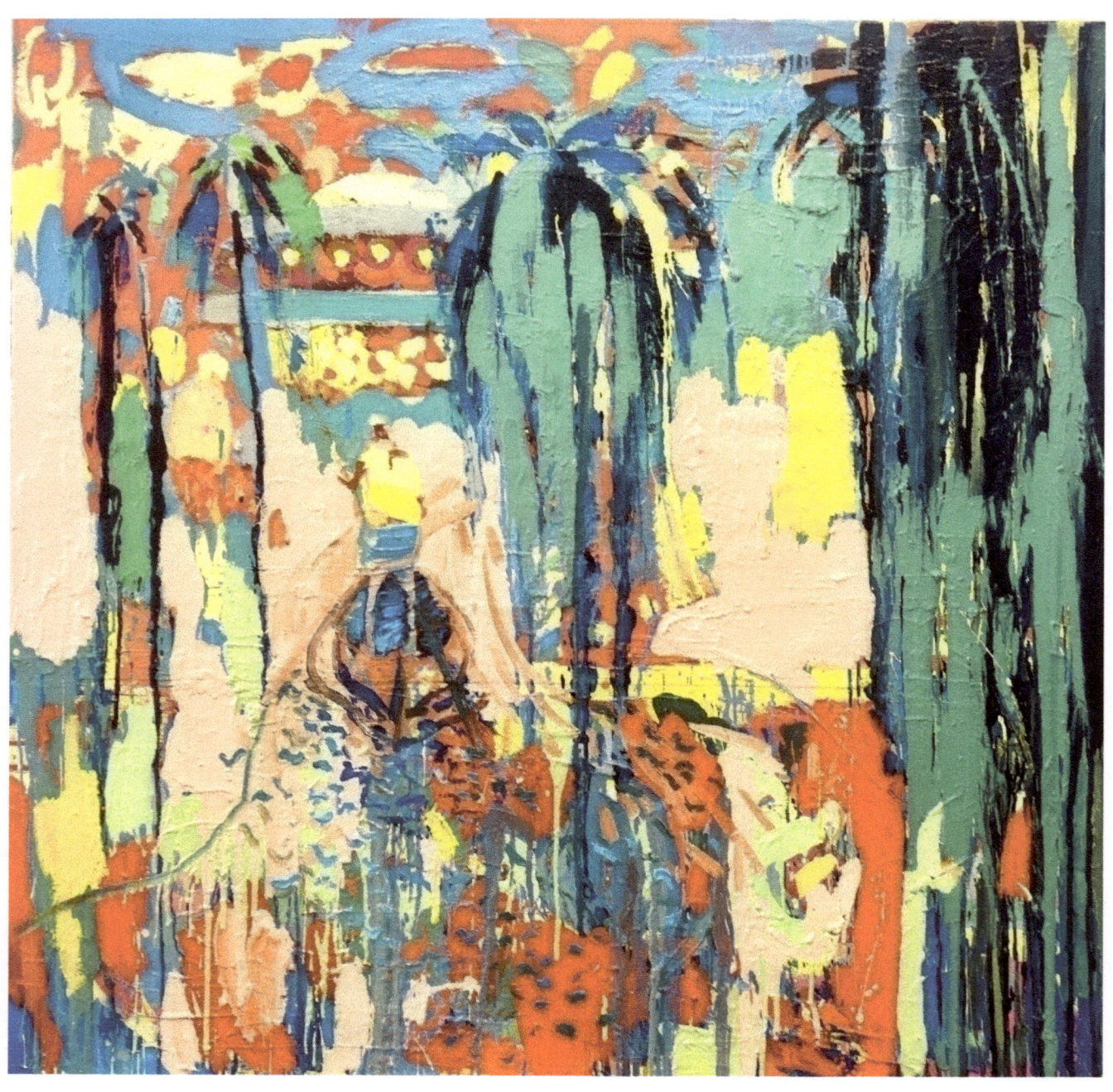

Title: Paddling through the sound of birds

Size: 140x140cm

Paul Wadsworth

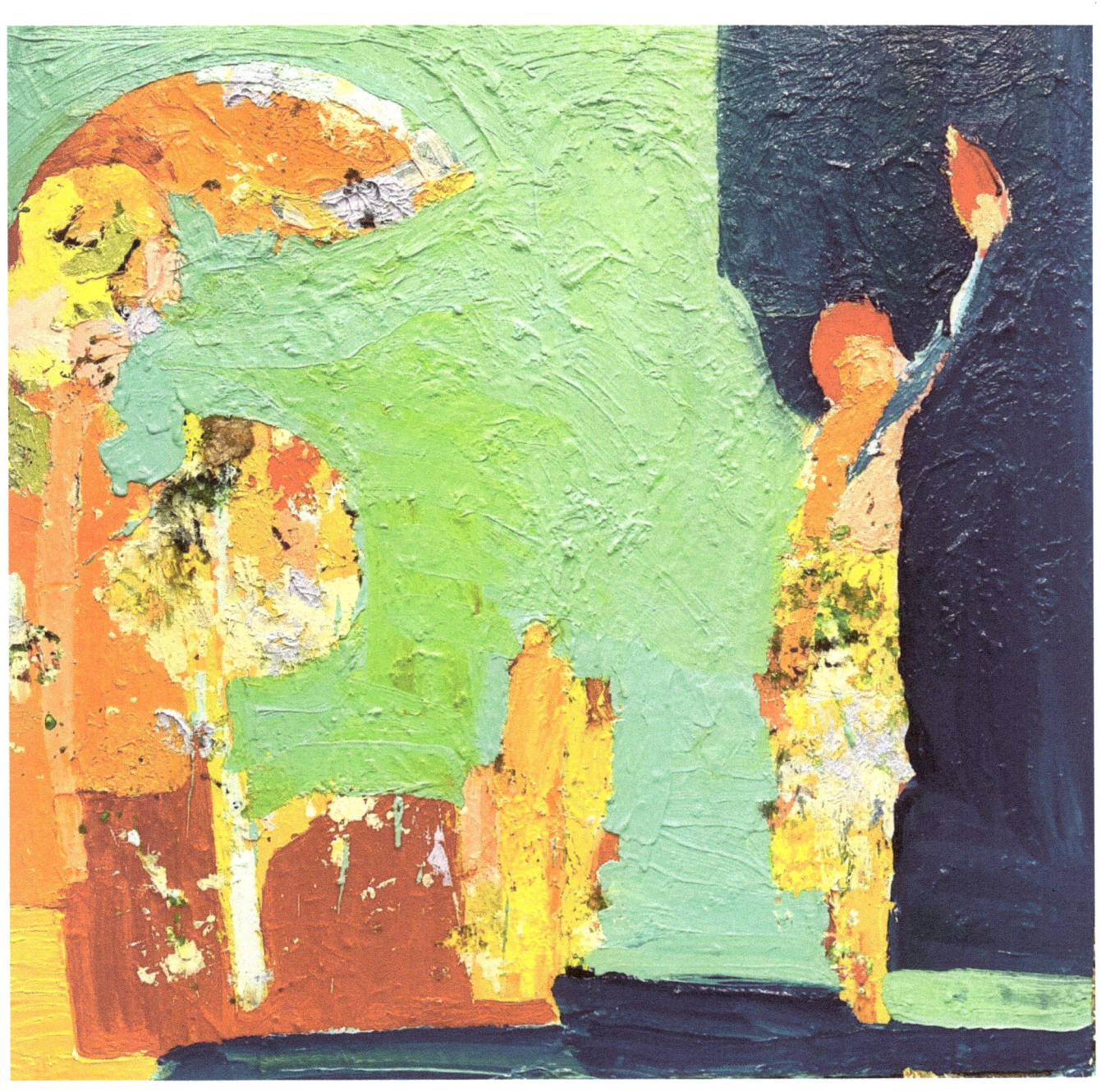

Title: Picking mangos

Size: 120x120cm

Stories From The Banyan Tree

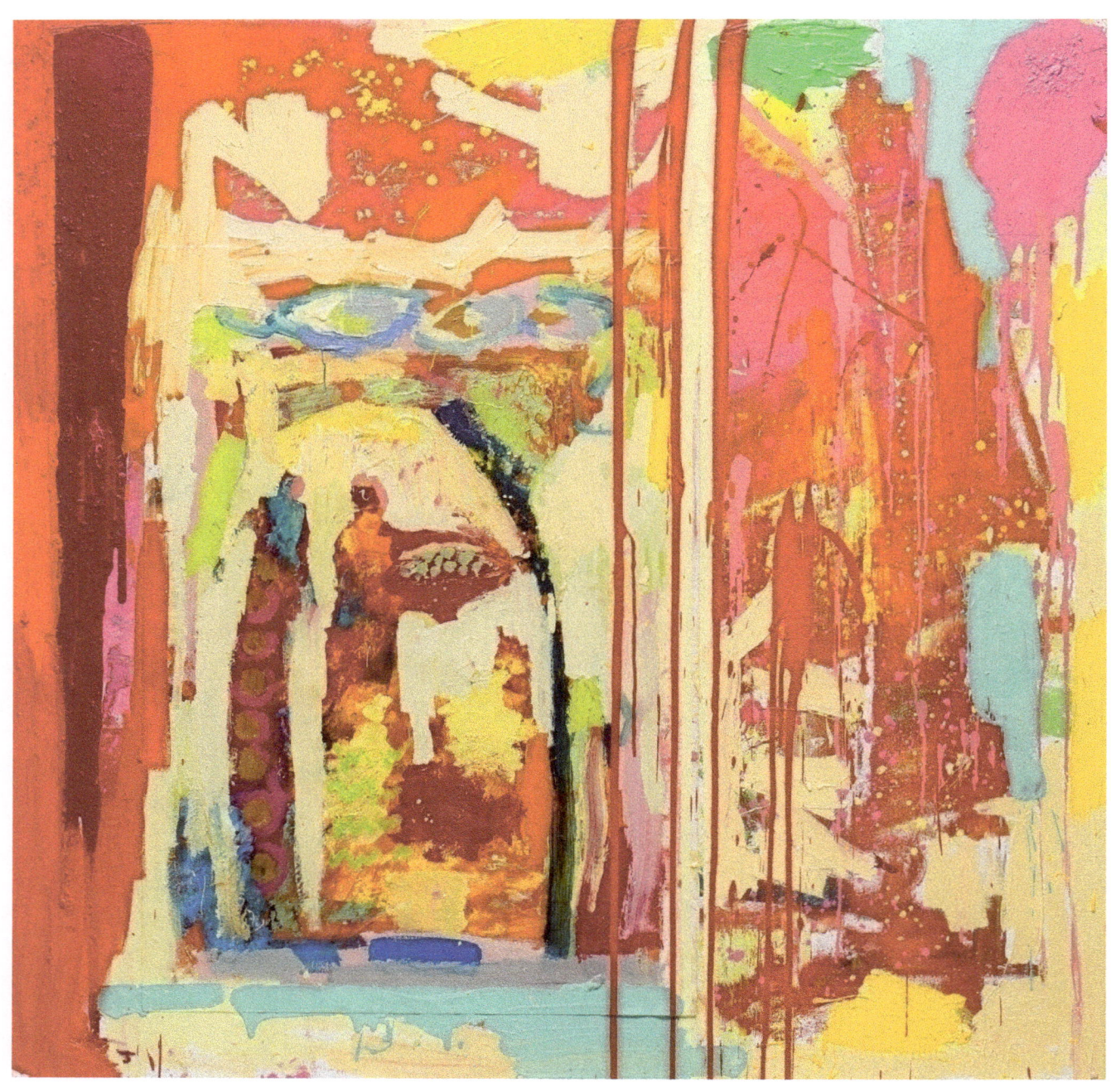

Title: Picking the fruits
Size: 140x140cm

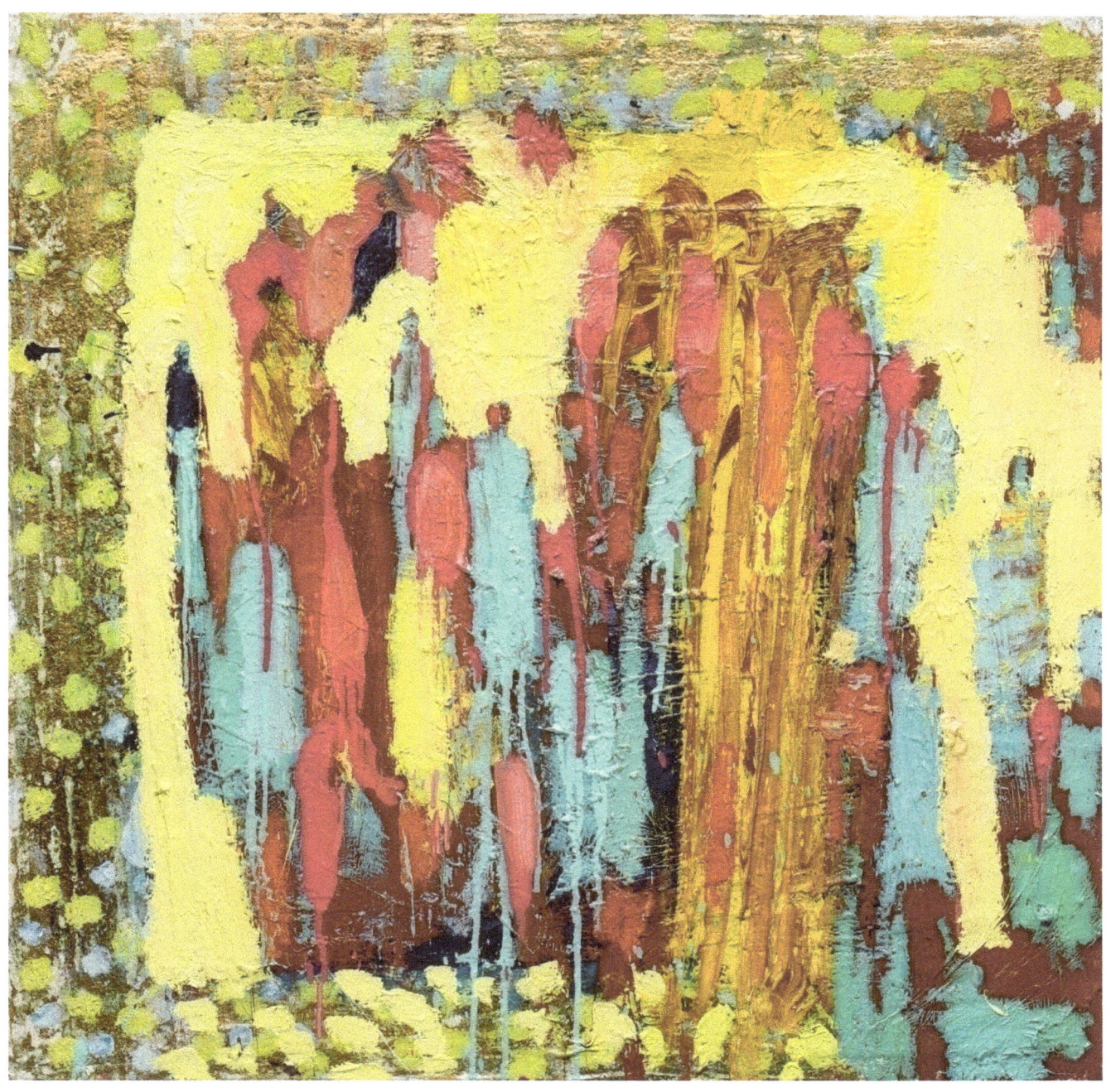

Title: Pilgrimage

Size: 84x84cm

Stories From The Banyan Tree

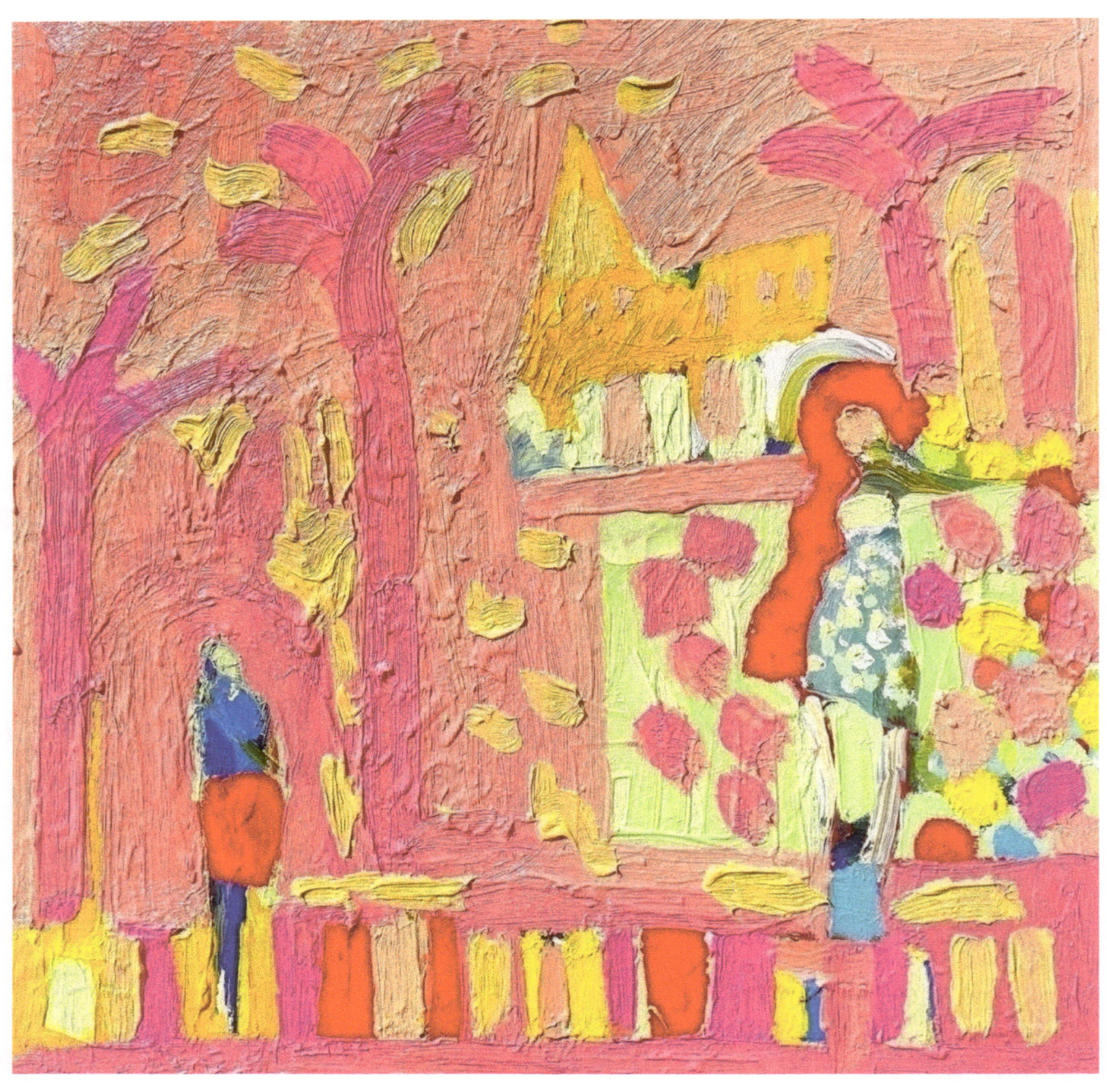

Title: Pink city
Size: 70x70cm

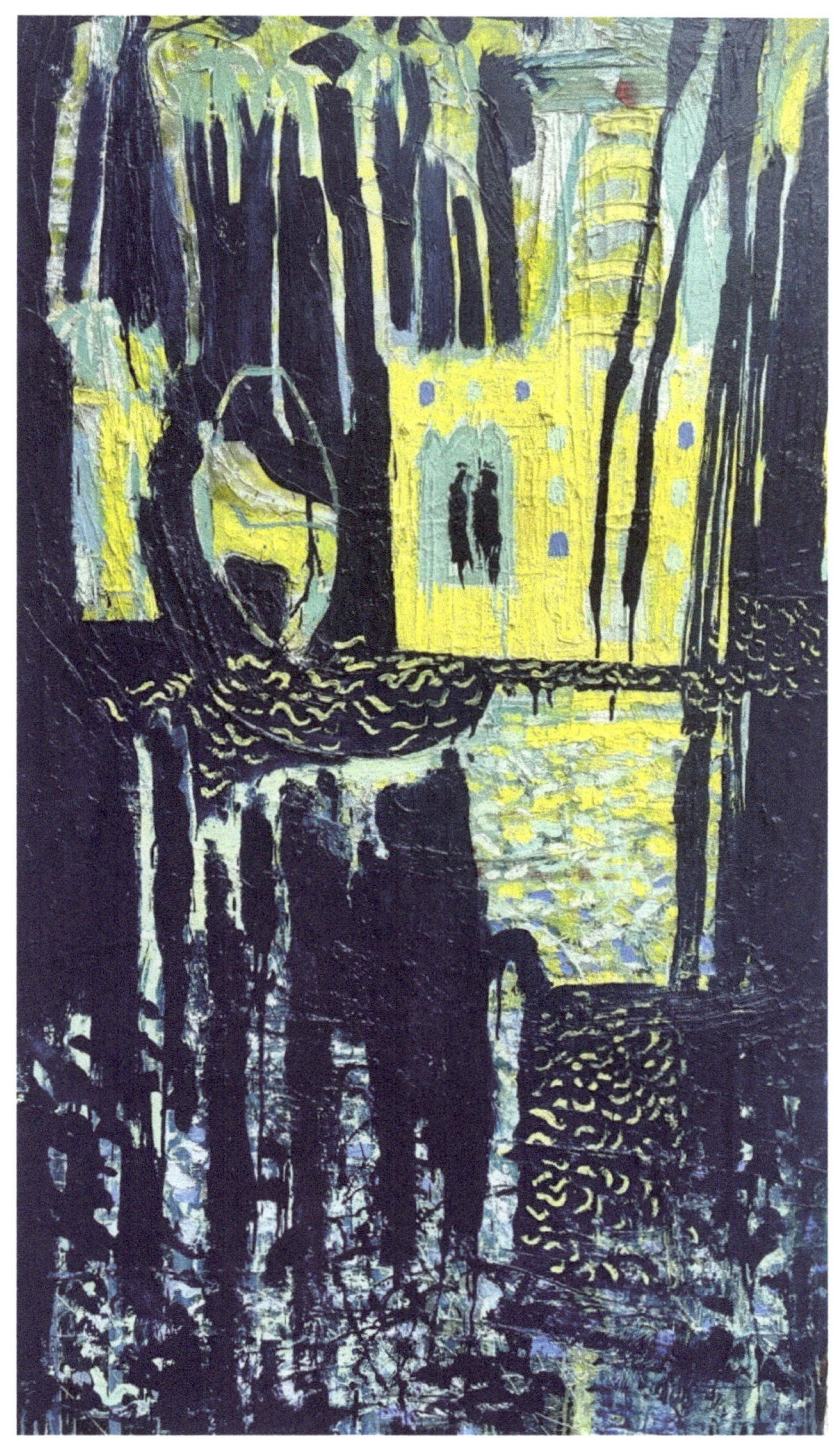

Title: Drifting in a small boat

Size: 170x116cm

Stories From The Banyan Tree

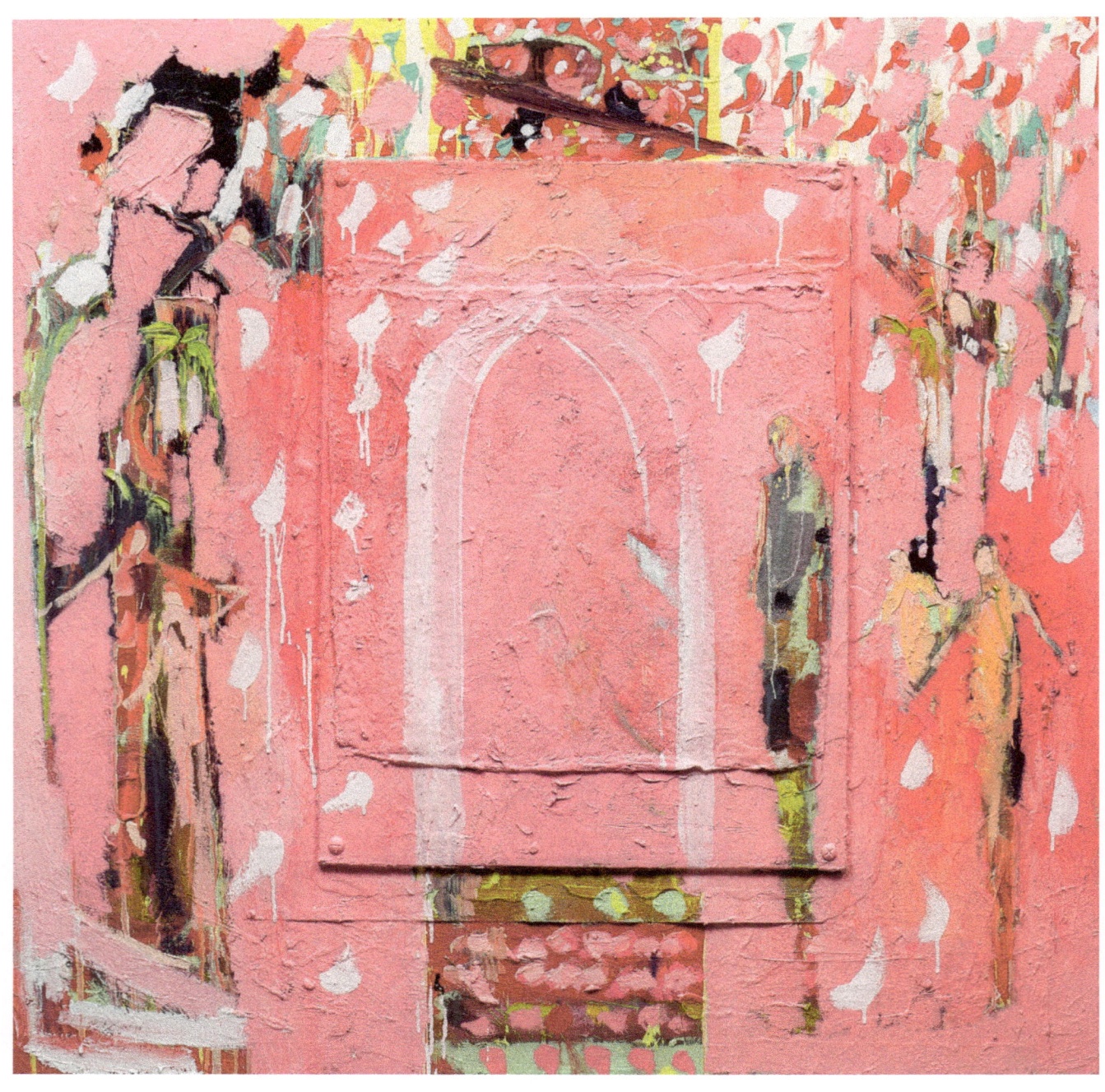

Title: Pink temple
Size: 130x130cm

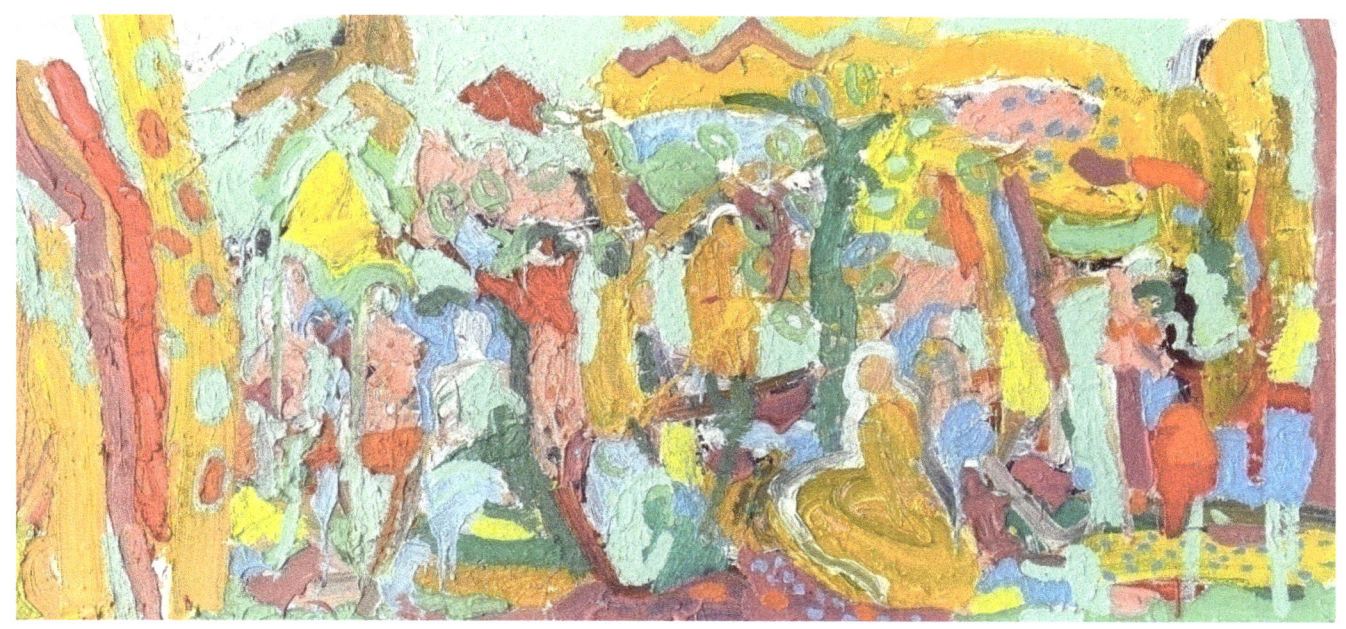

Title: Pleasure garden

Size: 78x163cm

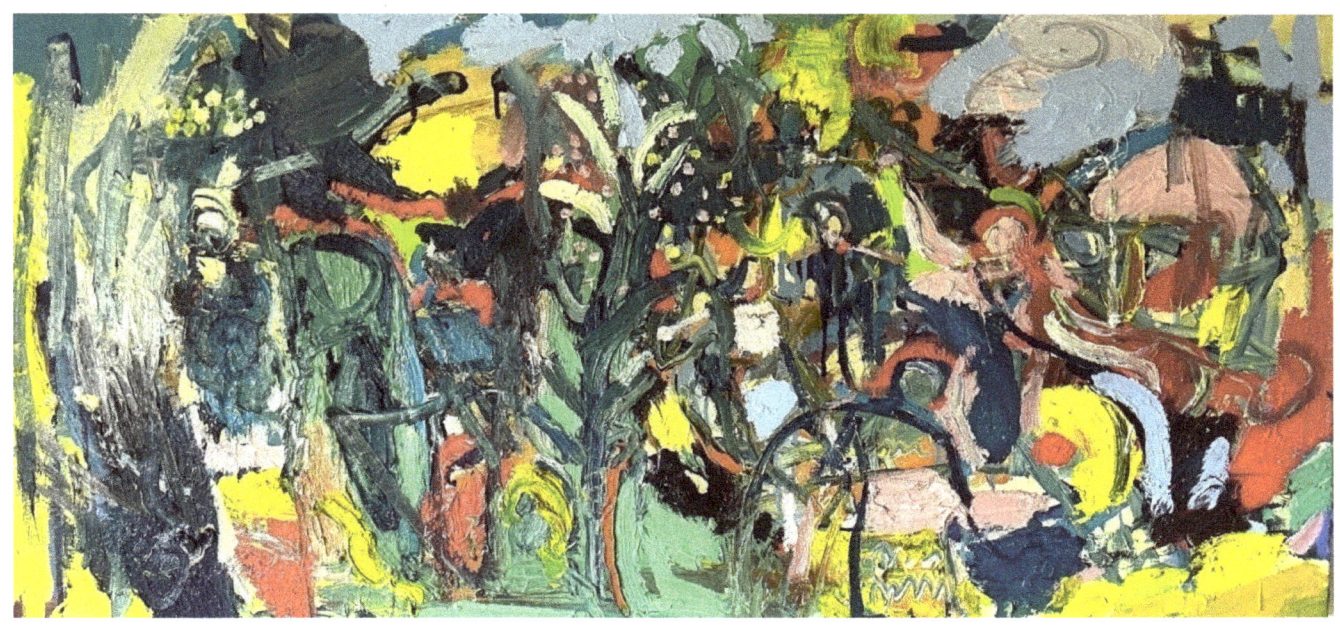

Title: Pleasure garden 2

Size: 78x163cm

Stories From The Banyan Tree

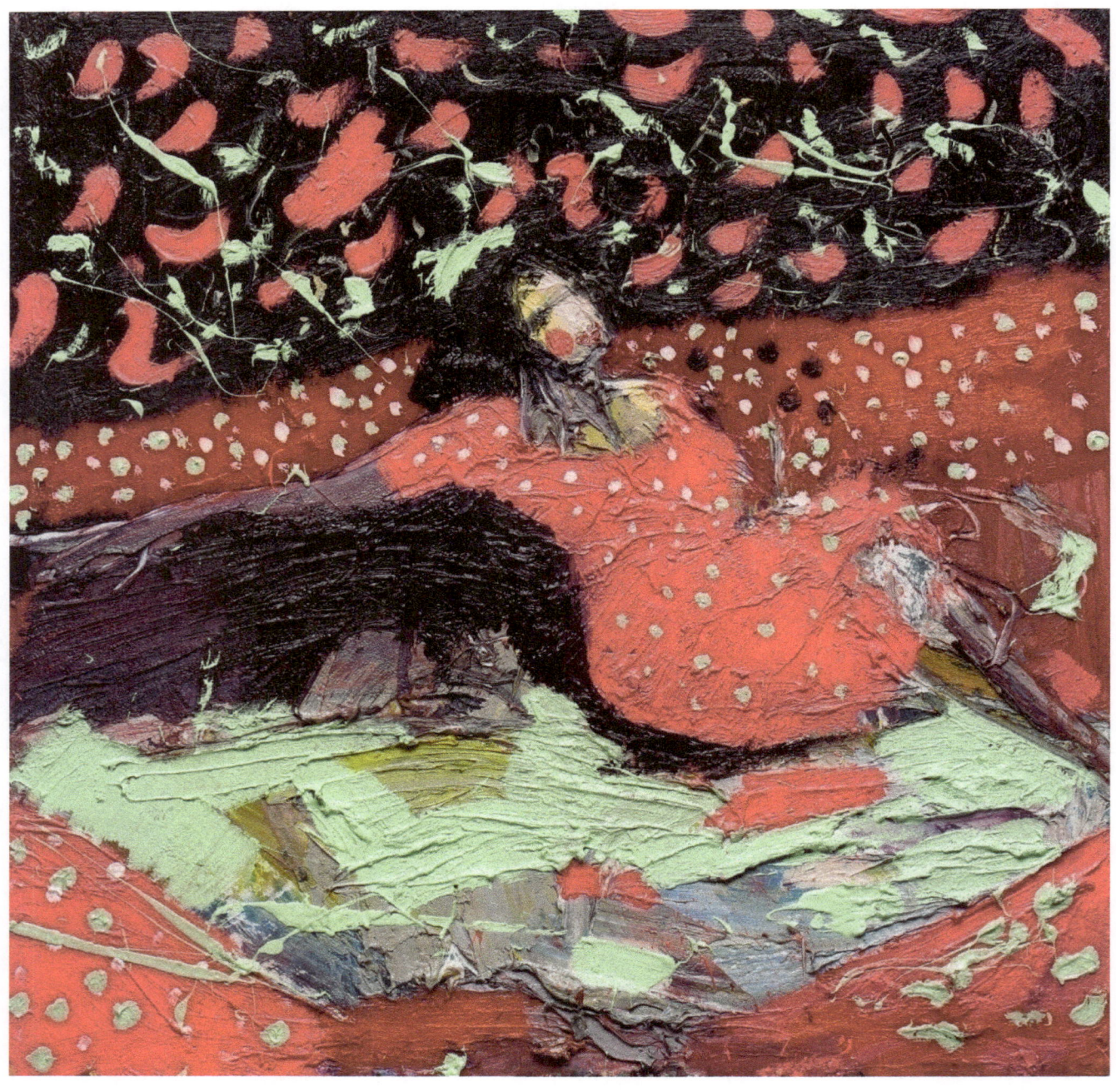

Title: Pretty in pink
Size: 73x73cm

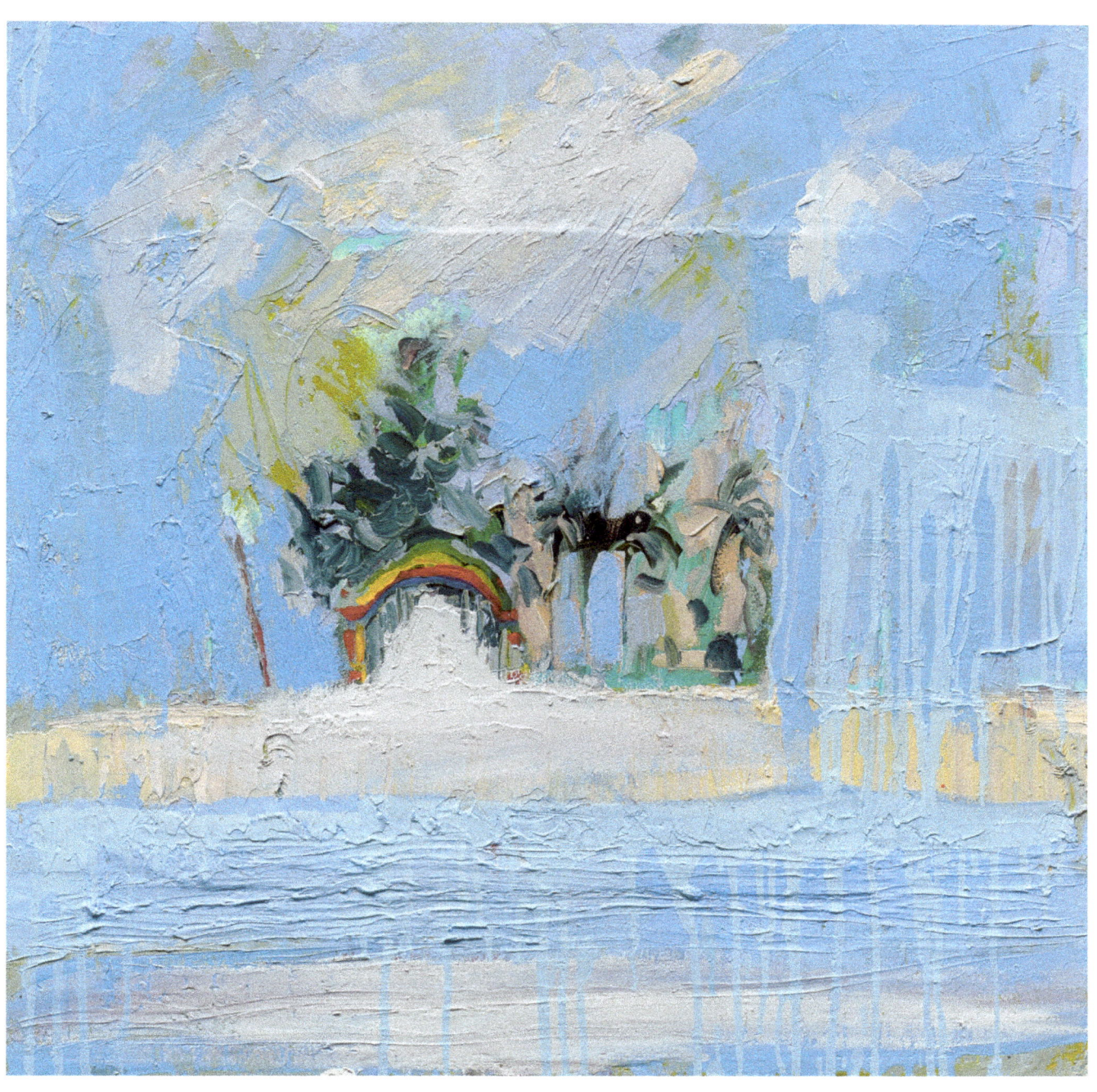

Title: Rainbow doorway

Size: 90x90cm

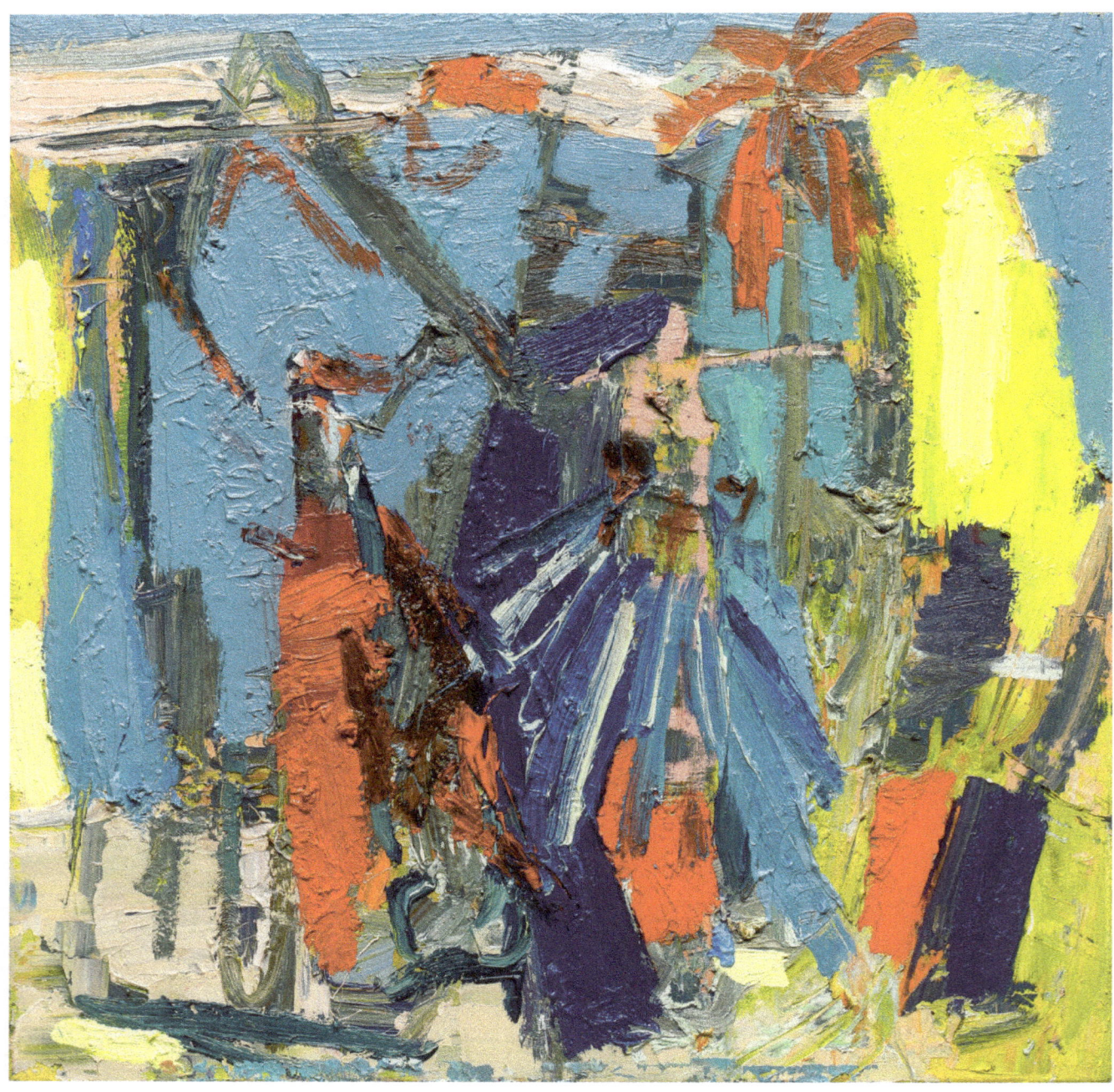

Title: Rajasthan gypsy dancer

Size: 90x90cm

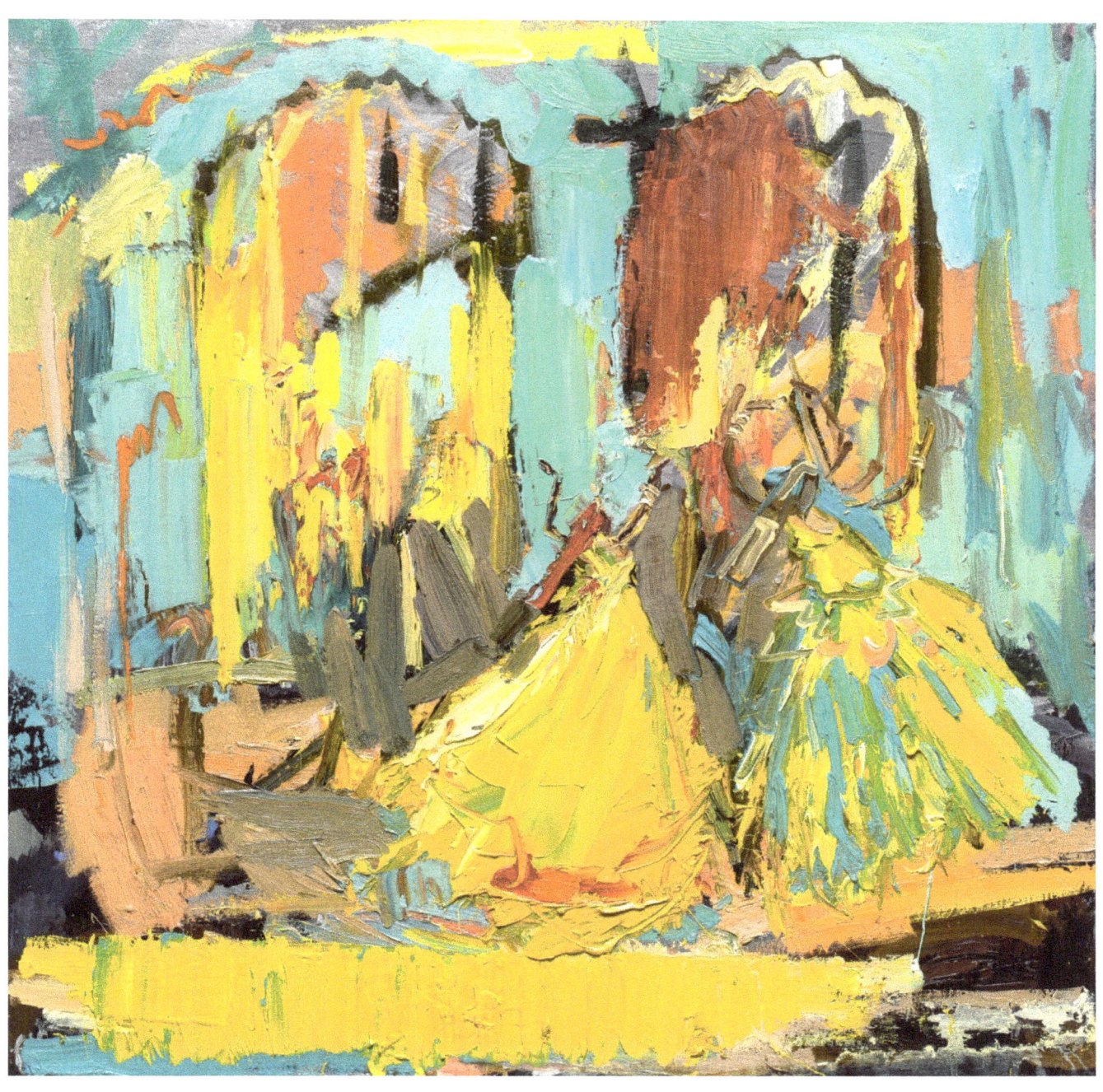

Title: Rajasthan gypsy dancer 2

Size: 100x100cm

Stories From The Banyan Tree

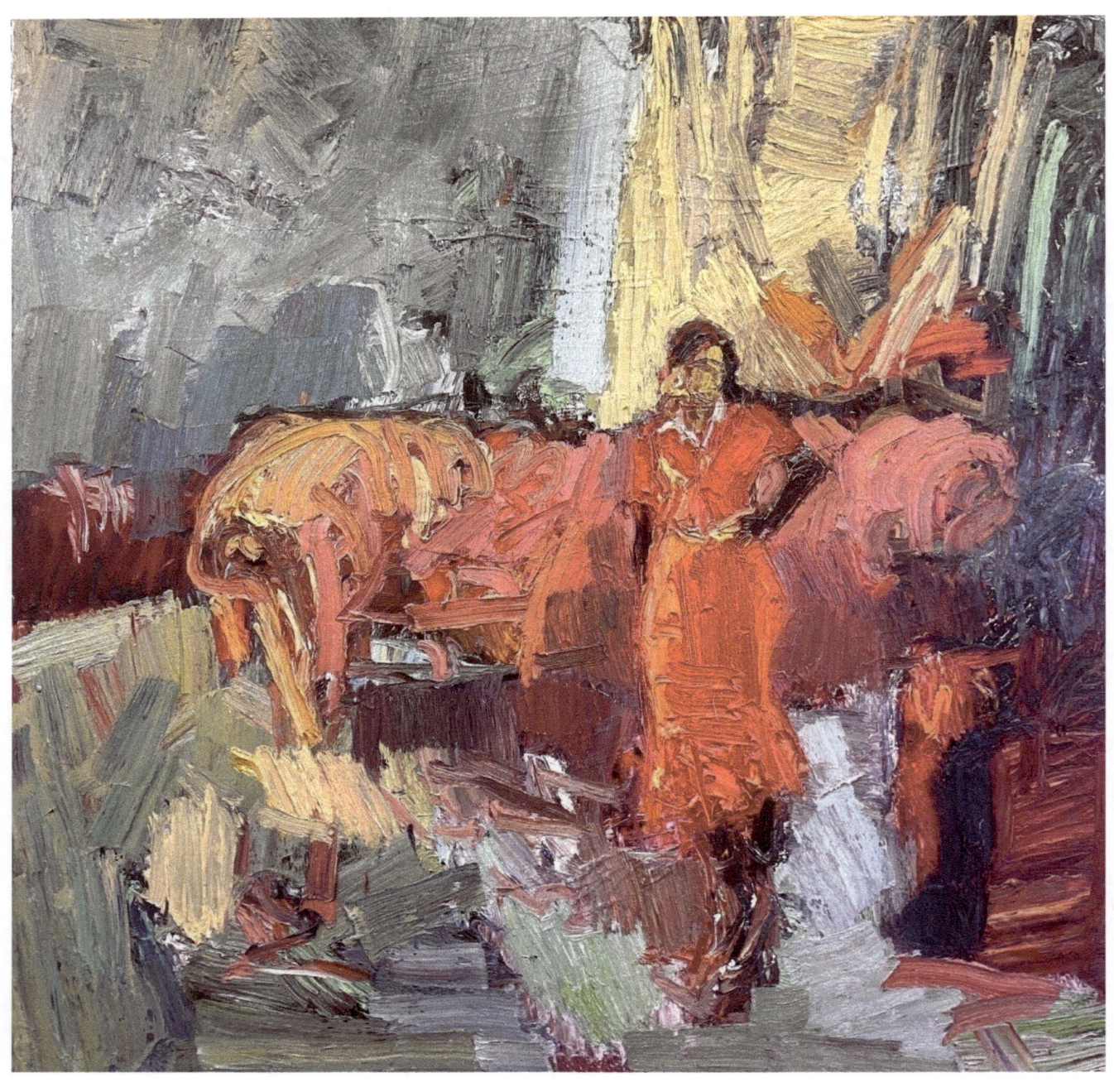

Title: Red dress
Size: 140x140cm

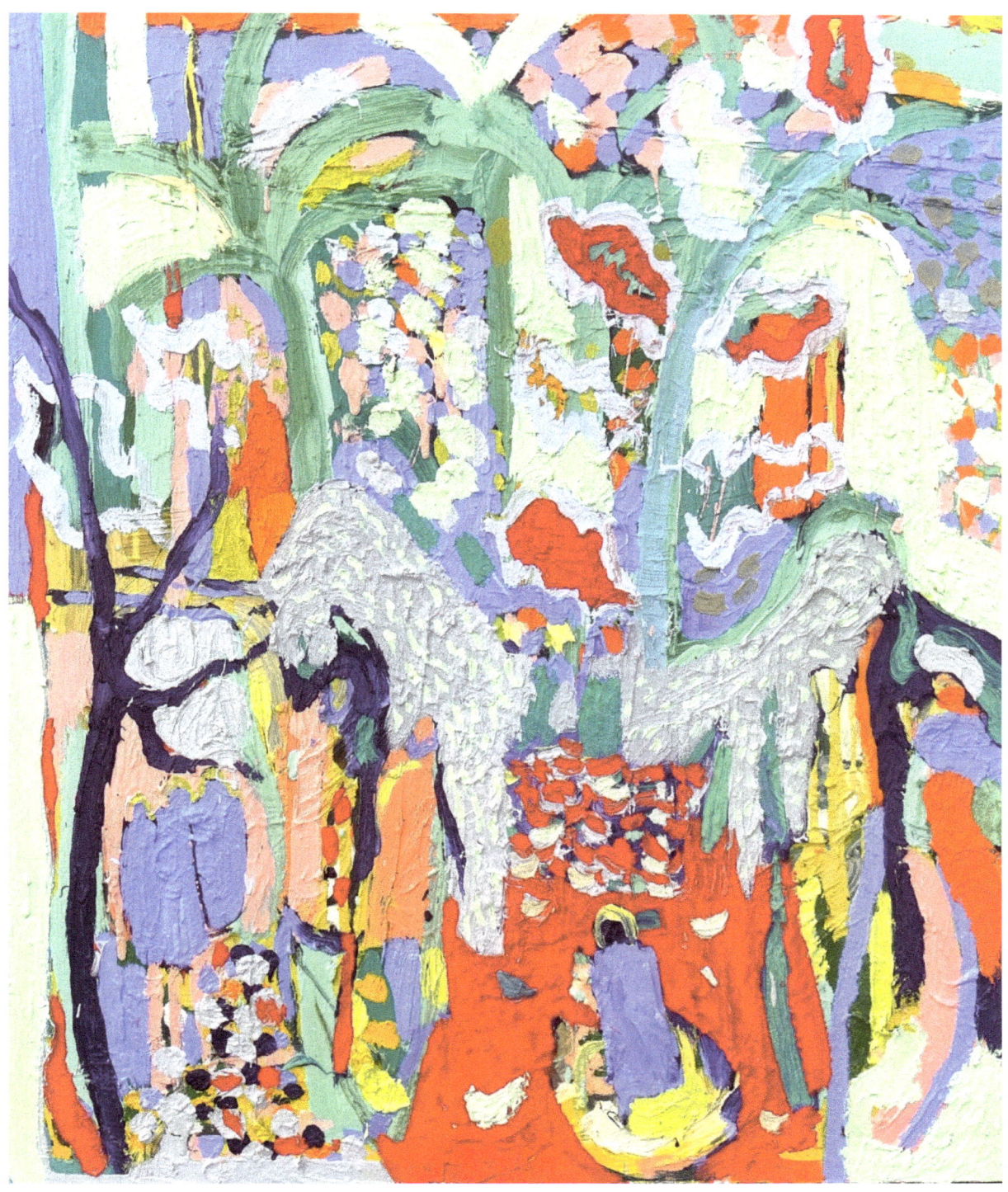

Title: Red river shore

Size: 120x100cm

Stories From The Banyan Tree

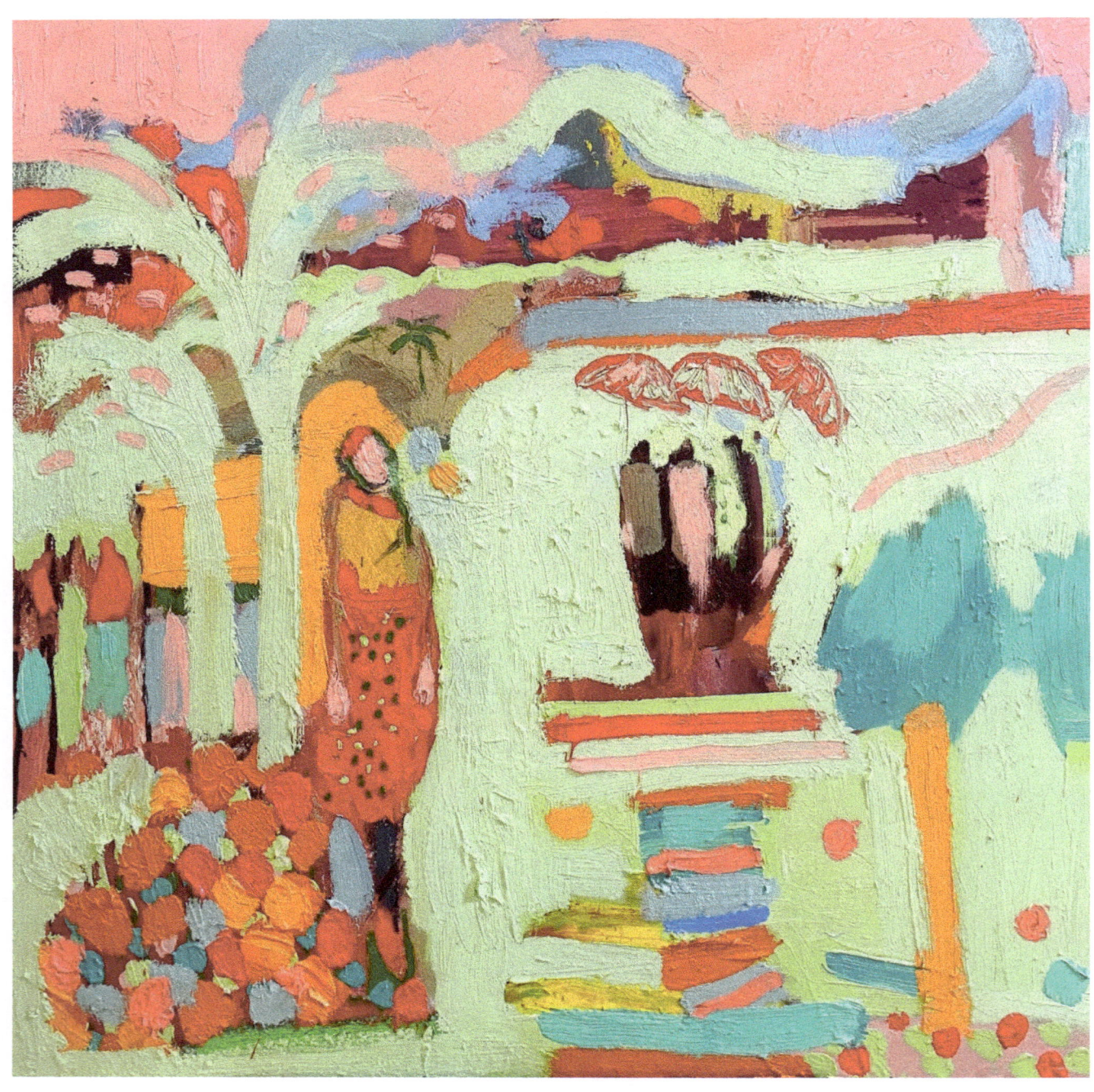

Title: Red umbrellas
Size: 90x90cm

Paul Wadsworth

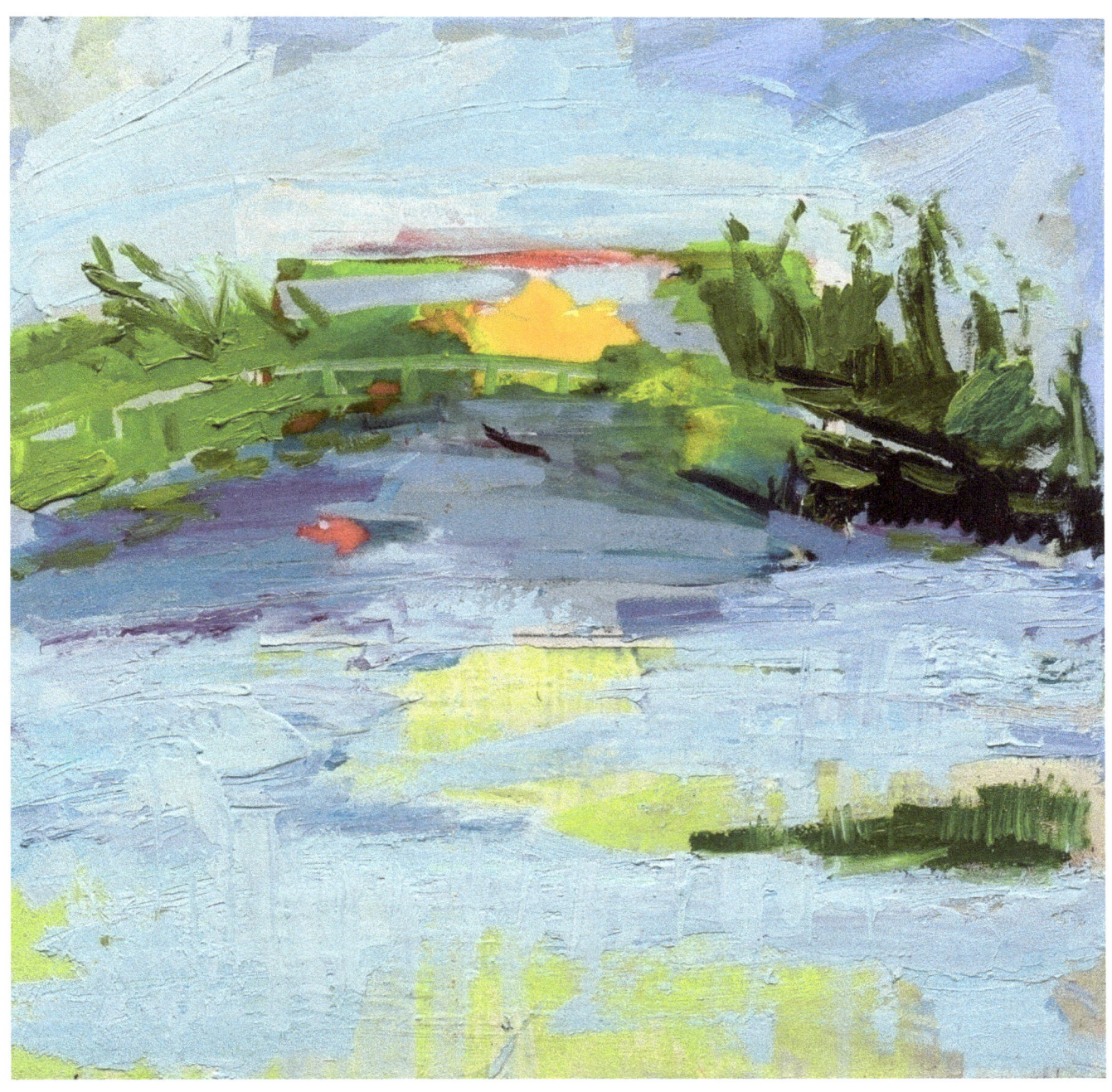

Title: River journey

Size: 90x90cm

Stories From The Banyan Tree

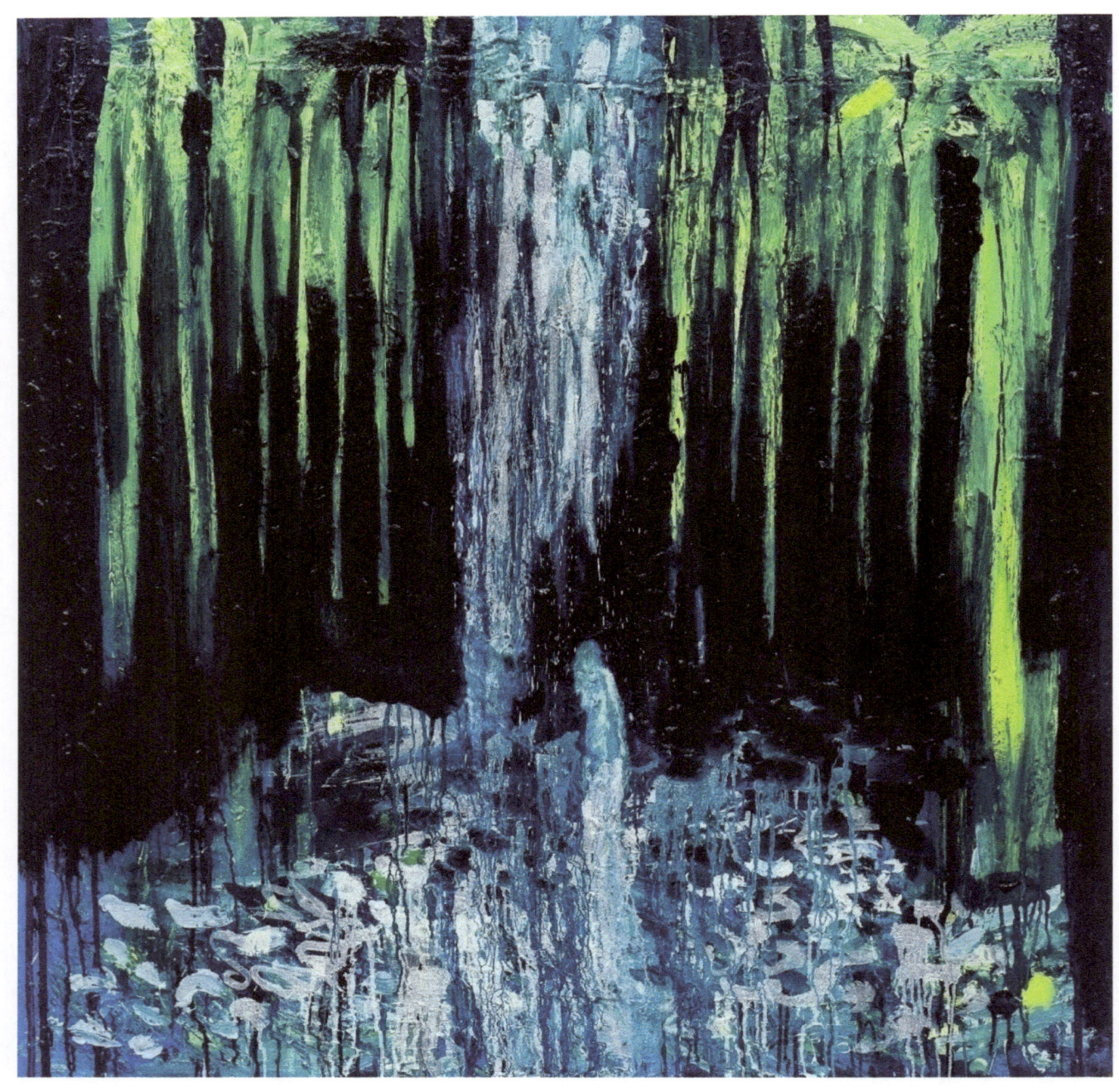

Title: Sweet isolation
Size: 120x120cm

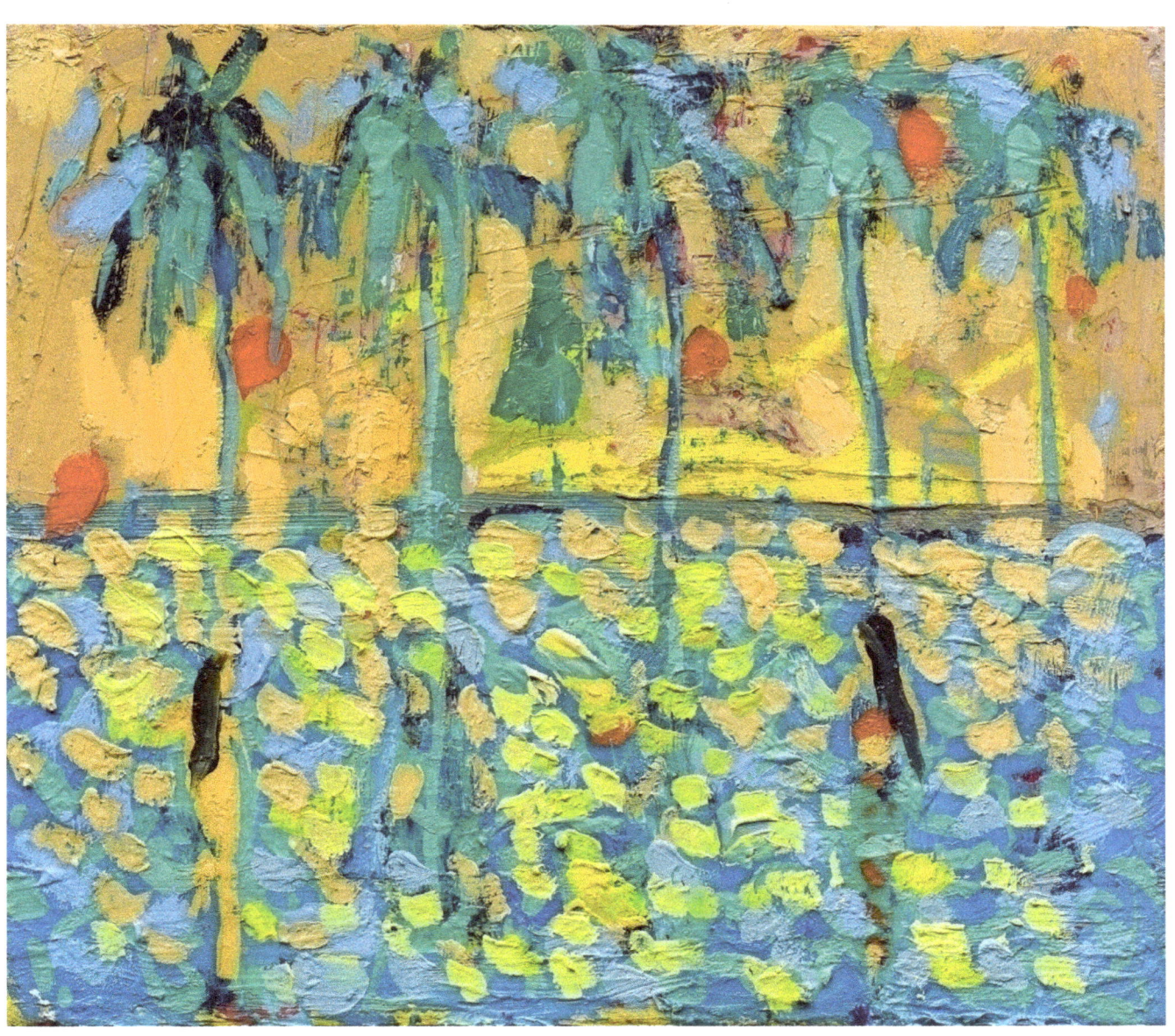

Title: River swimmer

Size: 63x77cm

Stories From The Banyan Tree

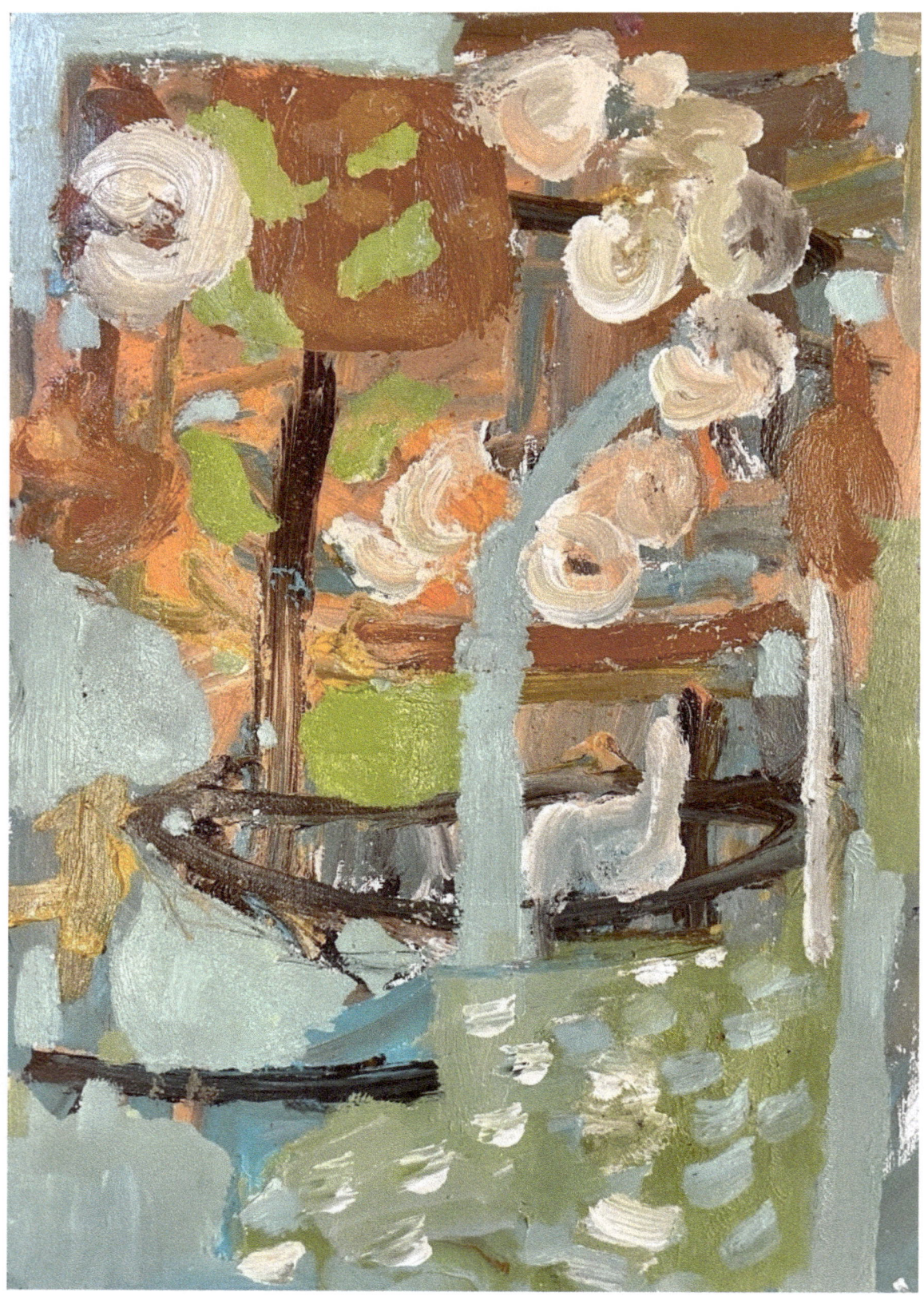

Title: River takes you

Size: 100x100cm

Paul Wadsworth

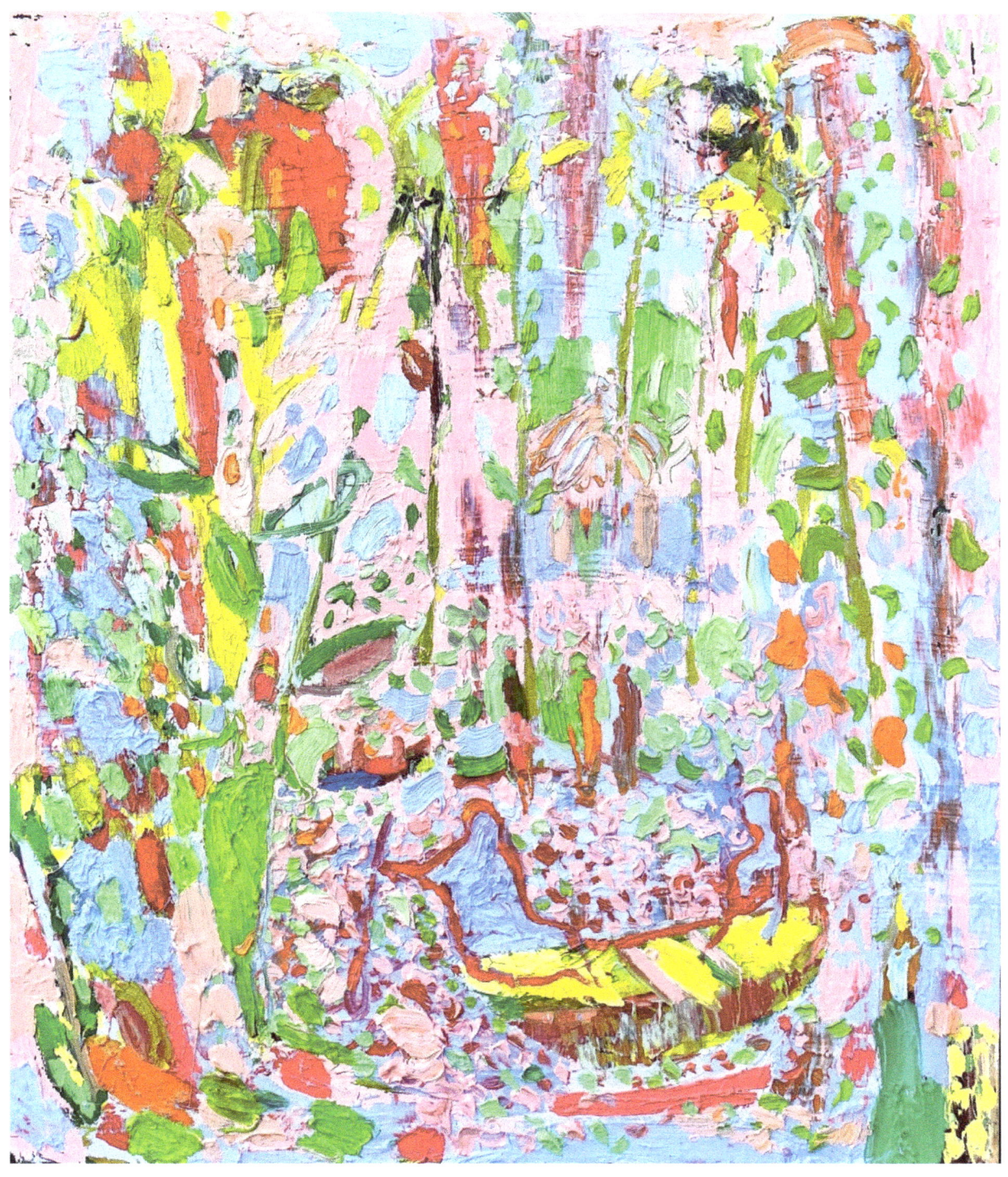

Title: Round boat river
Size: 120x100cm

Stories From The Banyan Tree

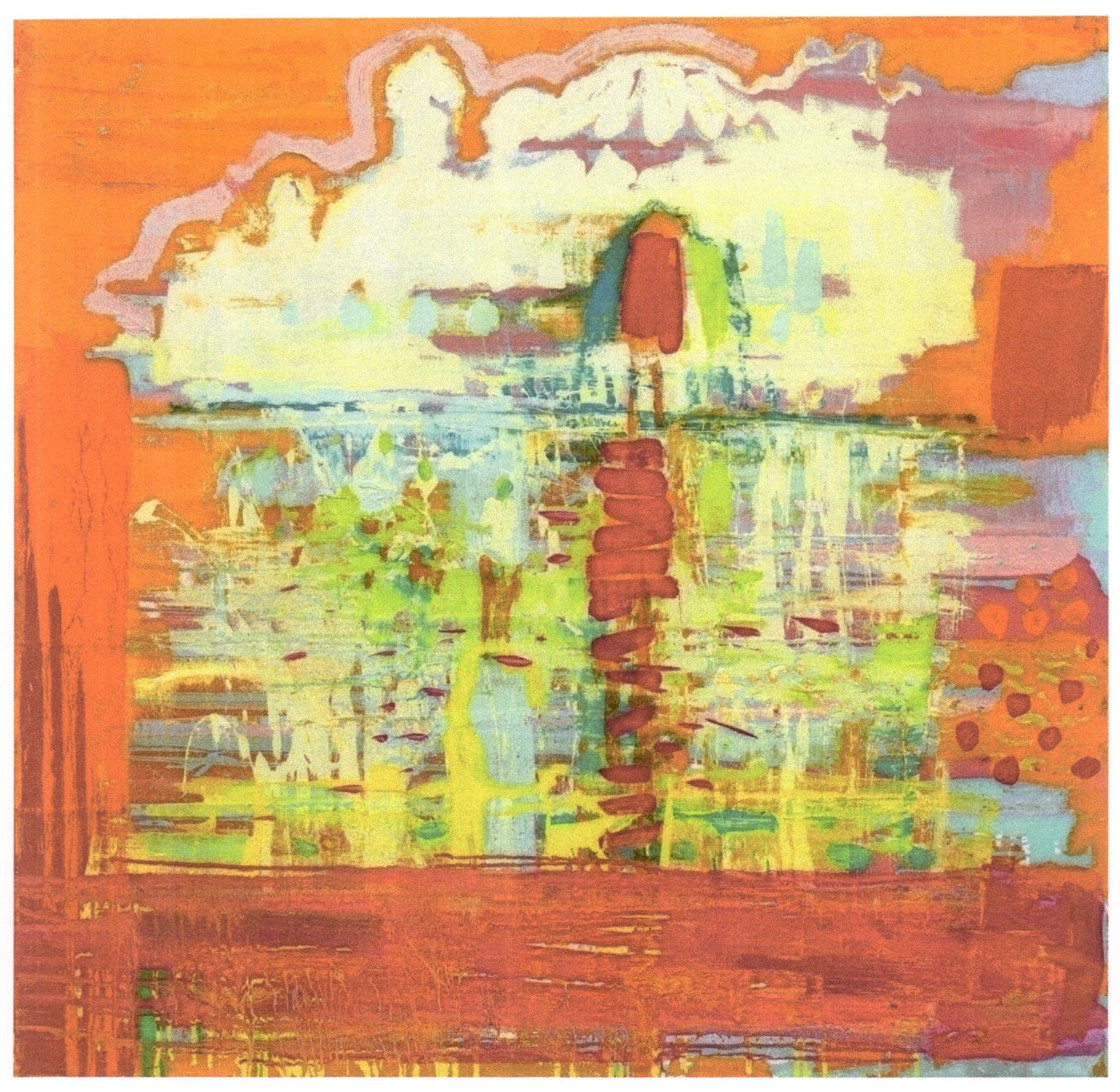

Title: Sacred water
Size: 126x126cm

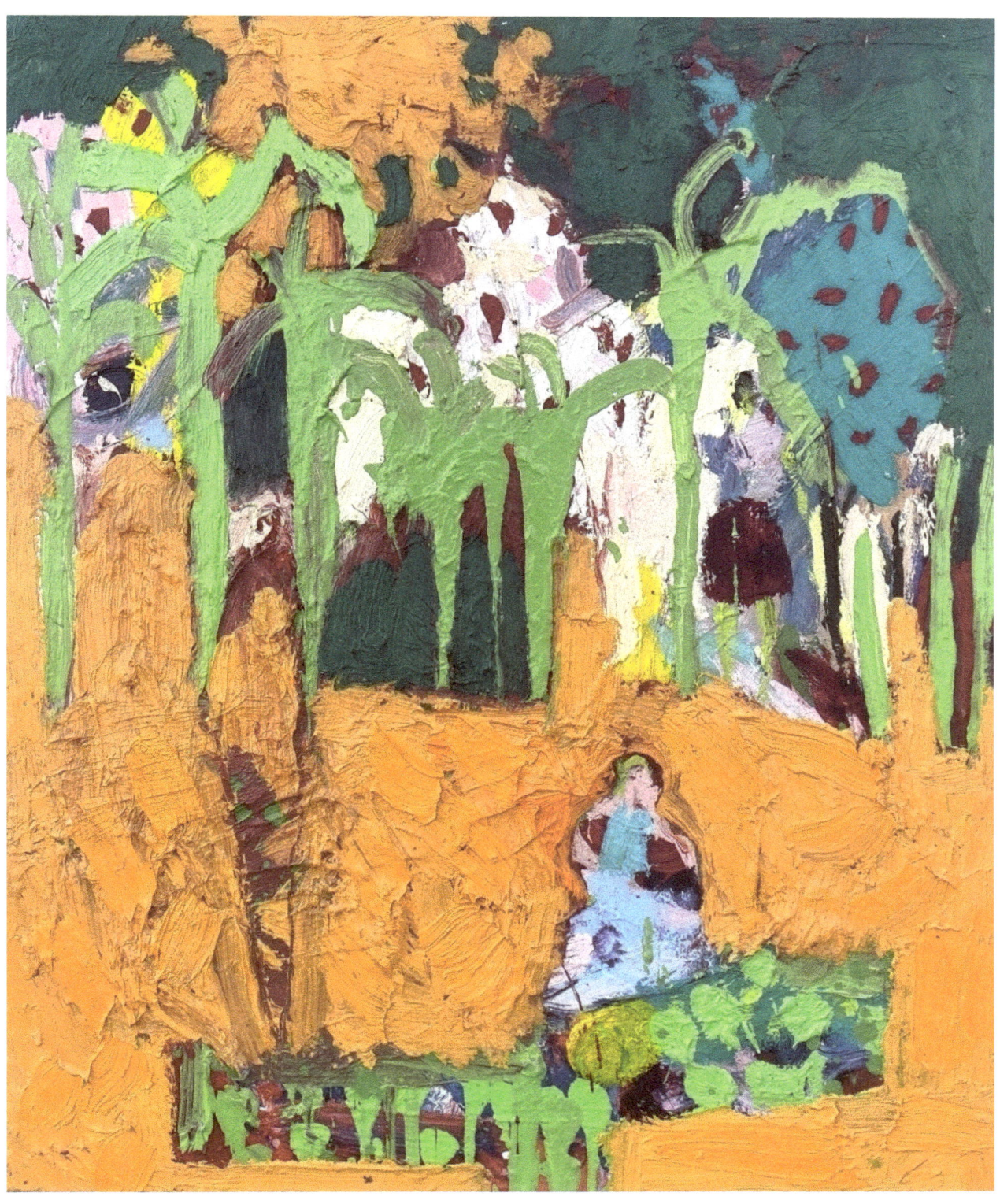

Title: She lives by the beach

Size: 130x130cm

Stories From The Banyan Tree

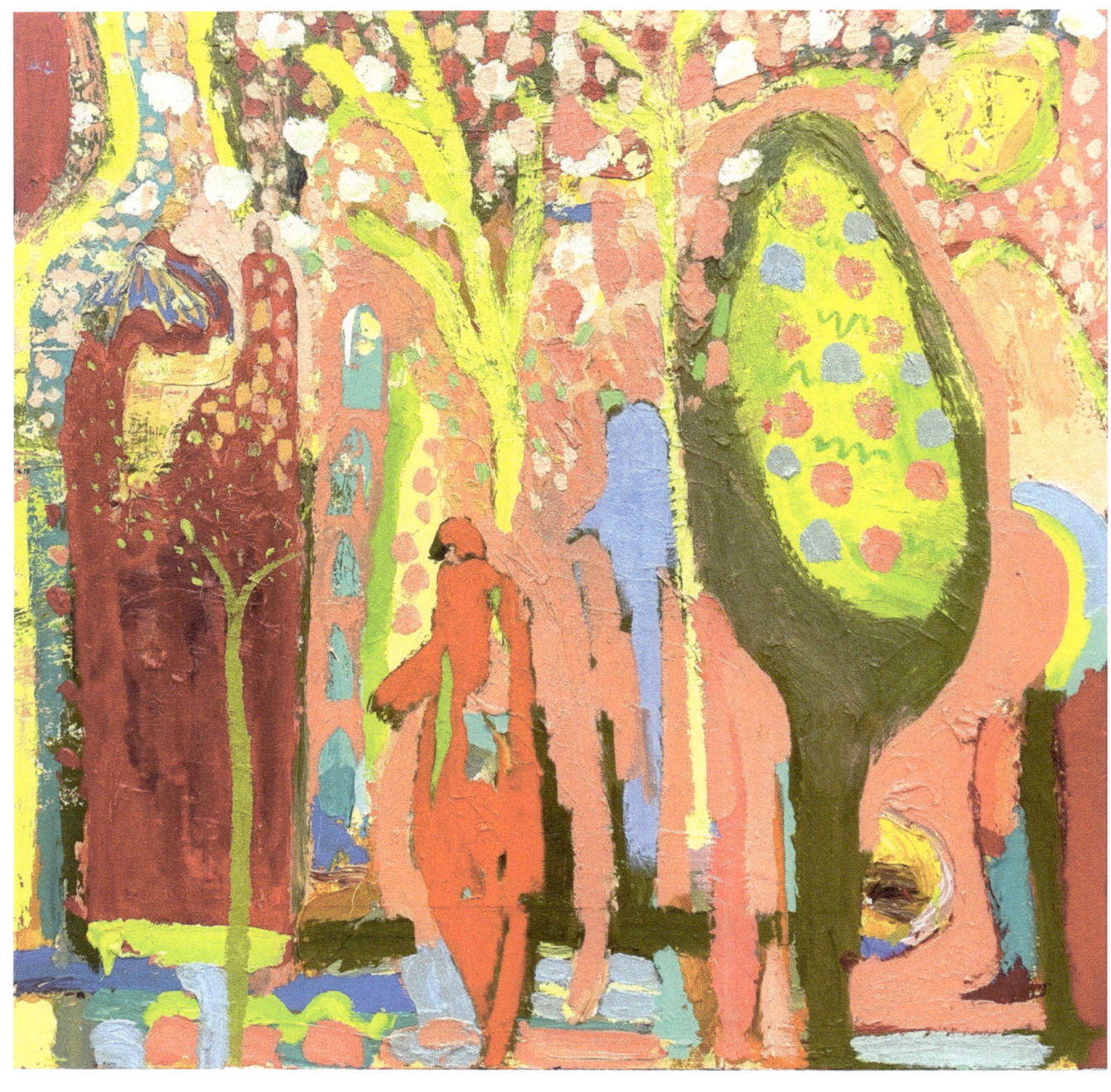

Title: Silent air

Size: 145x145cm

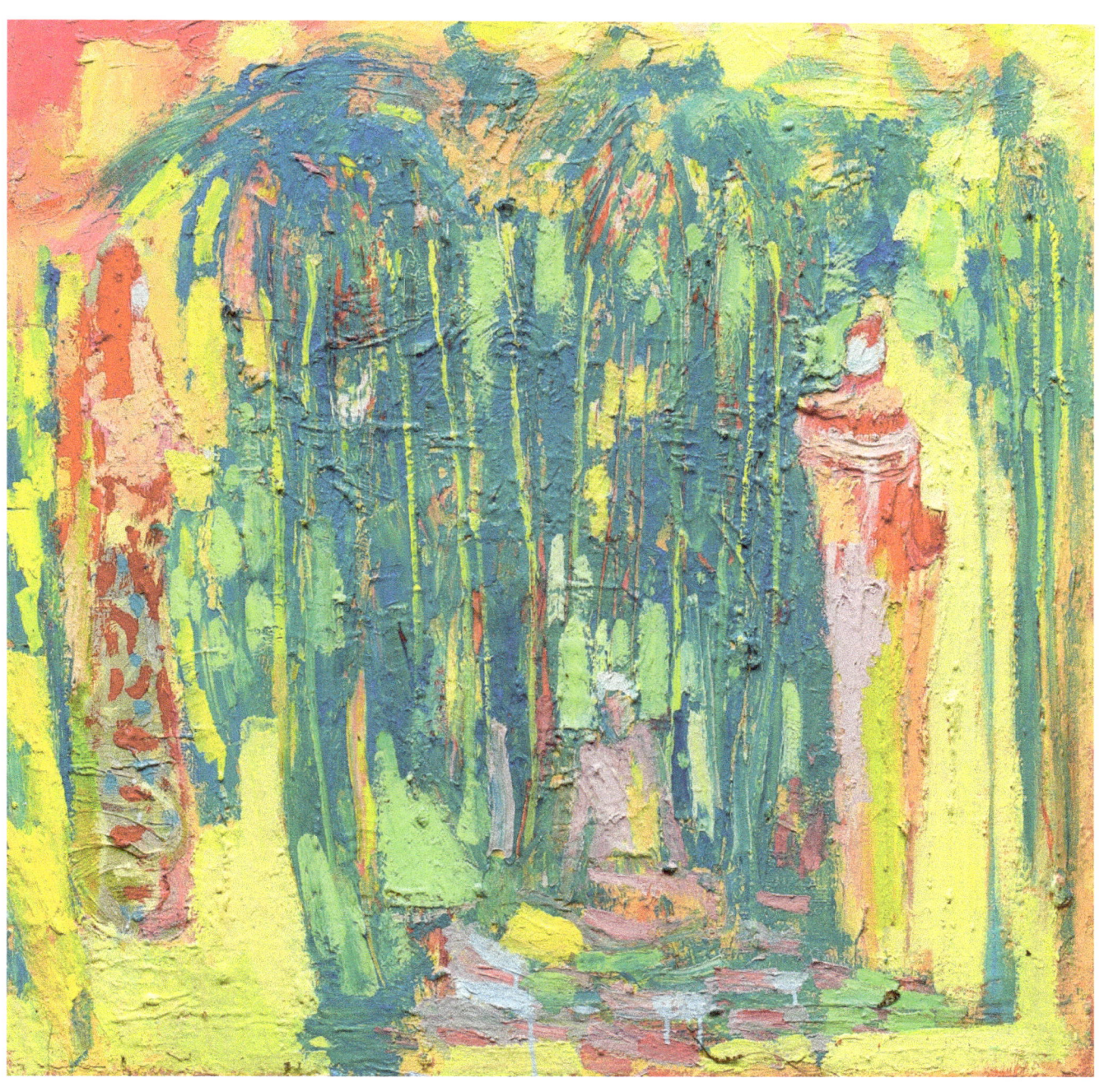

Title: Silent colour

Size: 120x120cm

Stories From The Banyan Tree

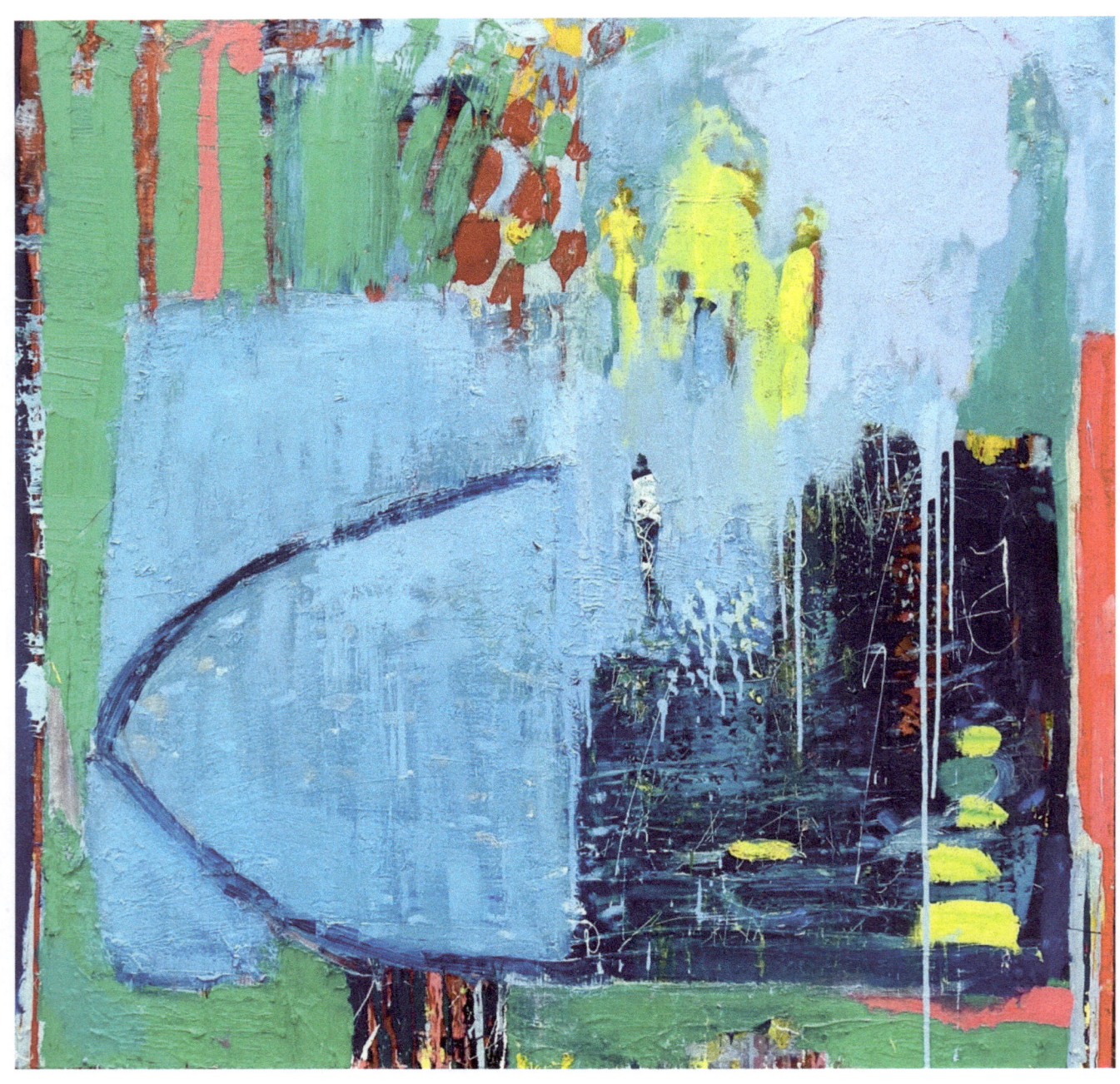

Title: Silent lake
Size: 140x140cm

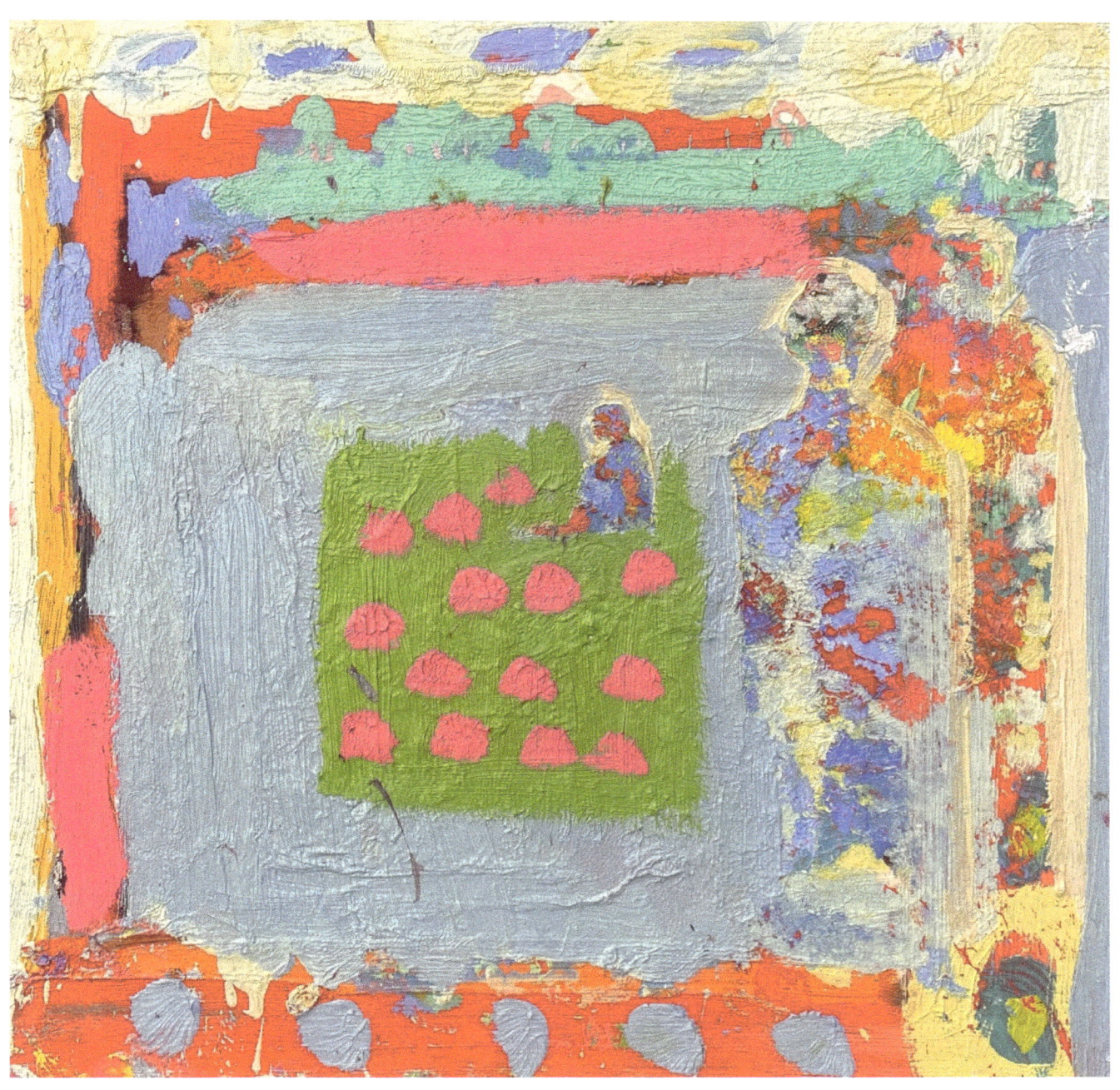

Title: Sitting in the rose garden
Size: 60x60cm

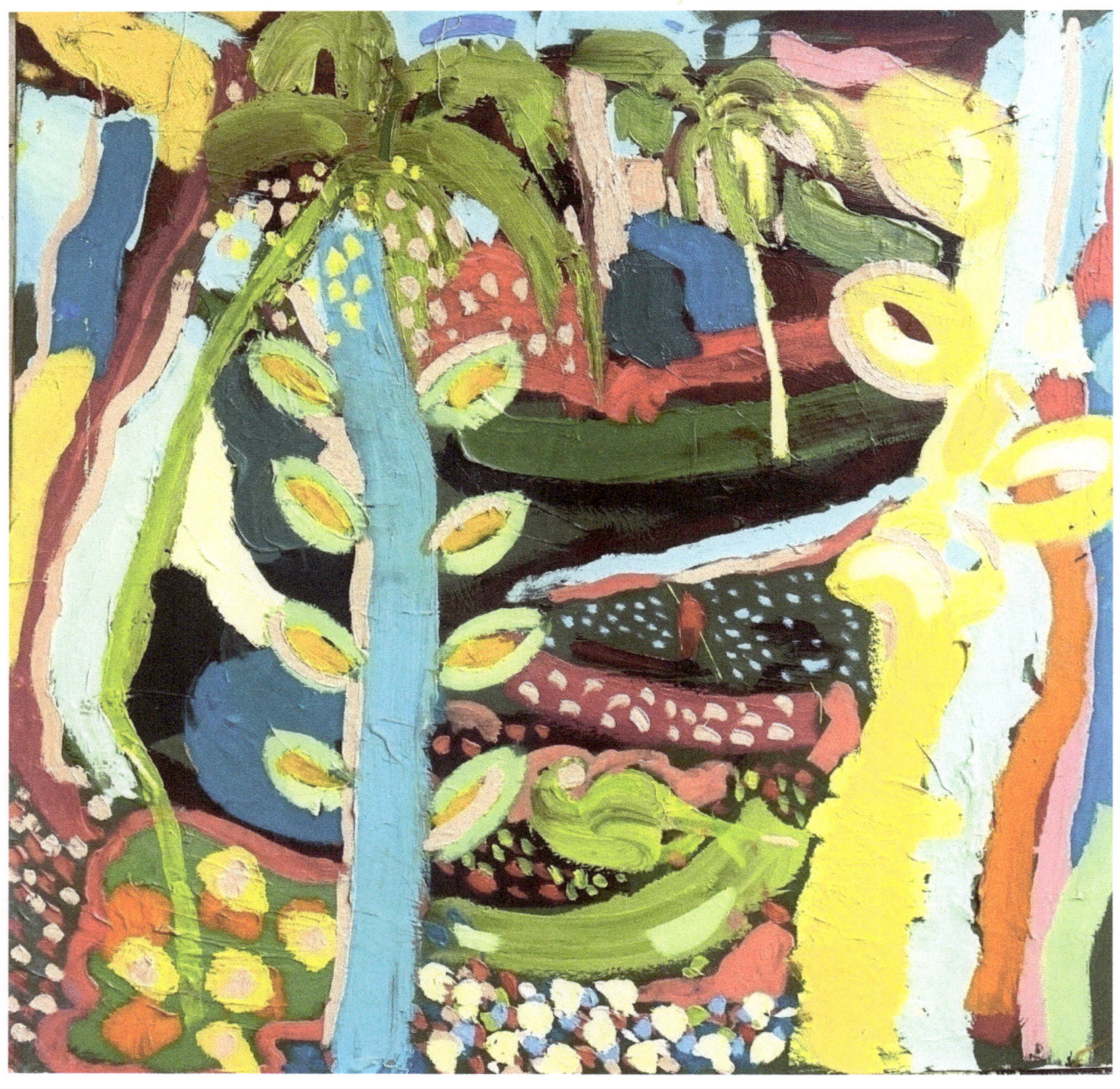

Title: Sleeping by the lake
Size: 120x120cm

Paul Wadsworth

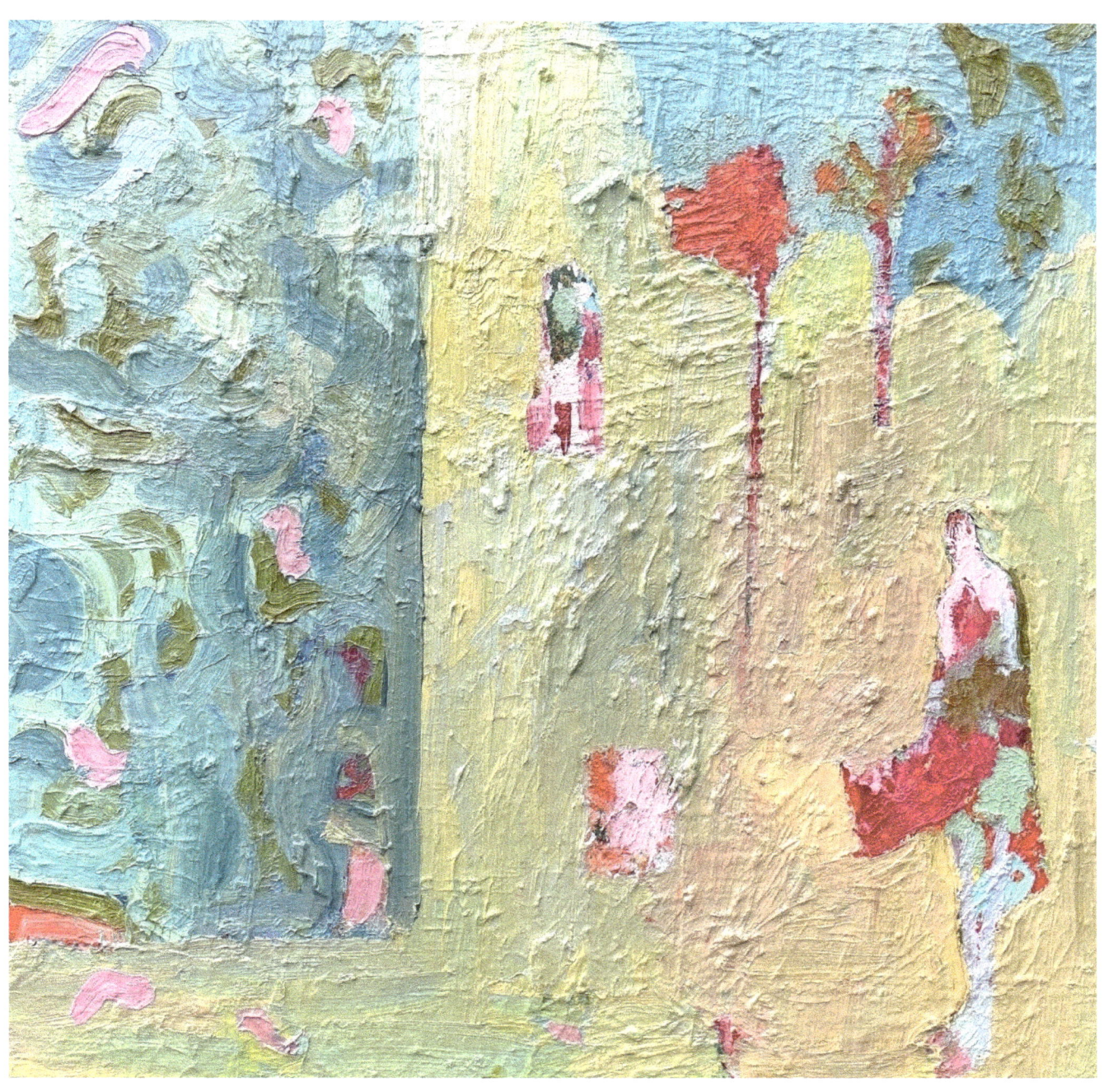

Title: Small pink temple

Size: 120x120cm

Stories From The Banyan Tree

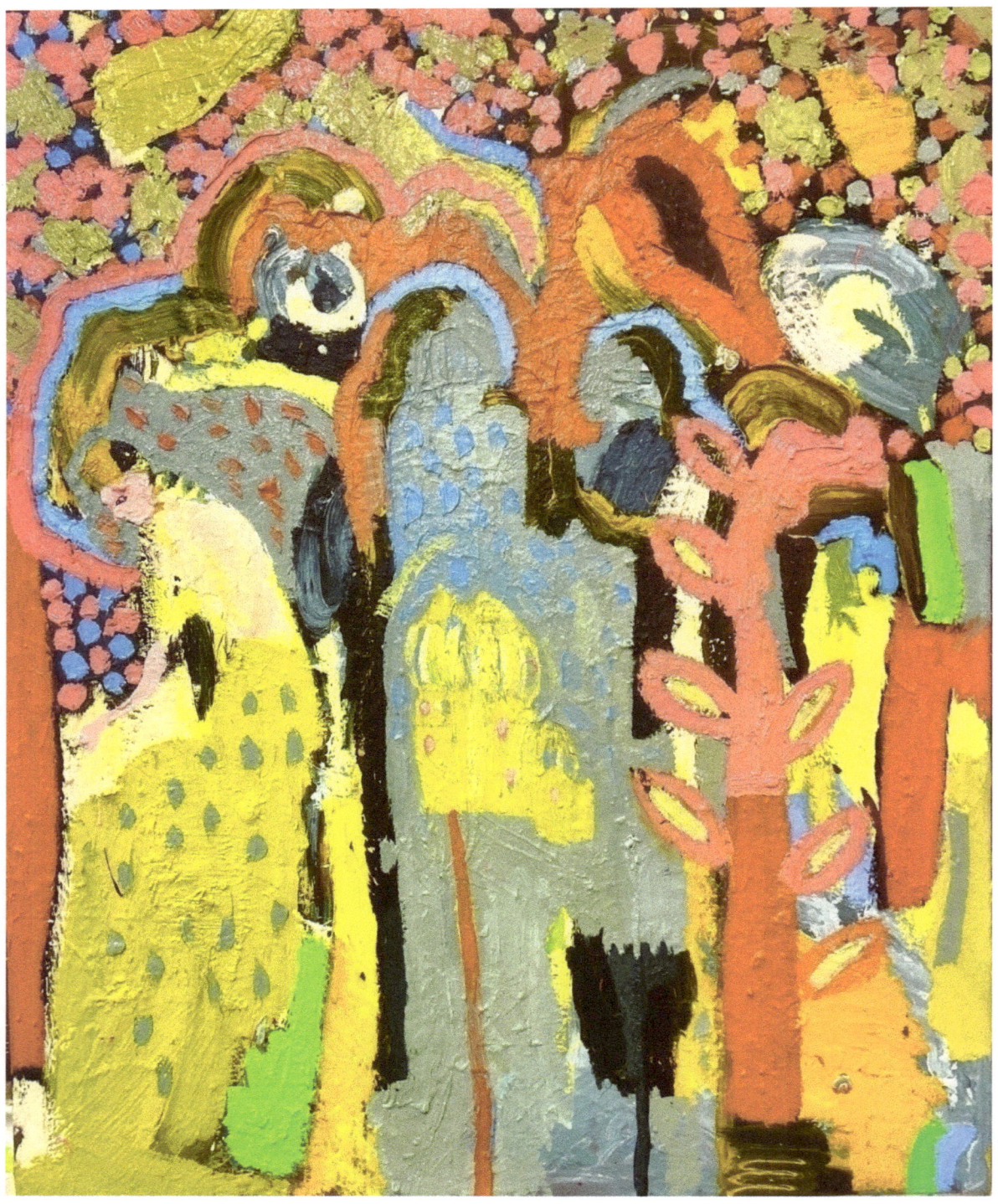

Title: Small yellow temple
Size: 120x100cm

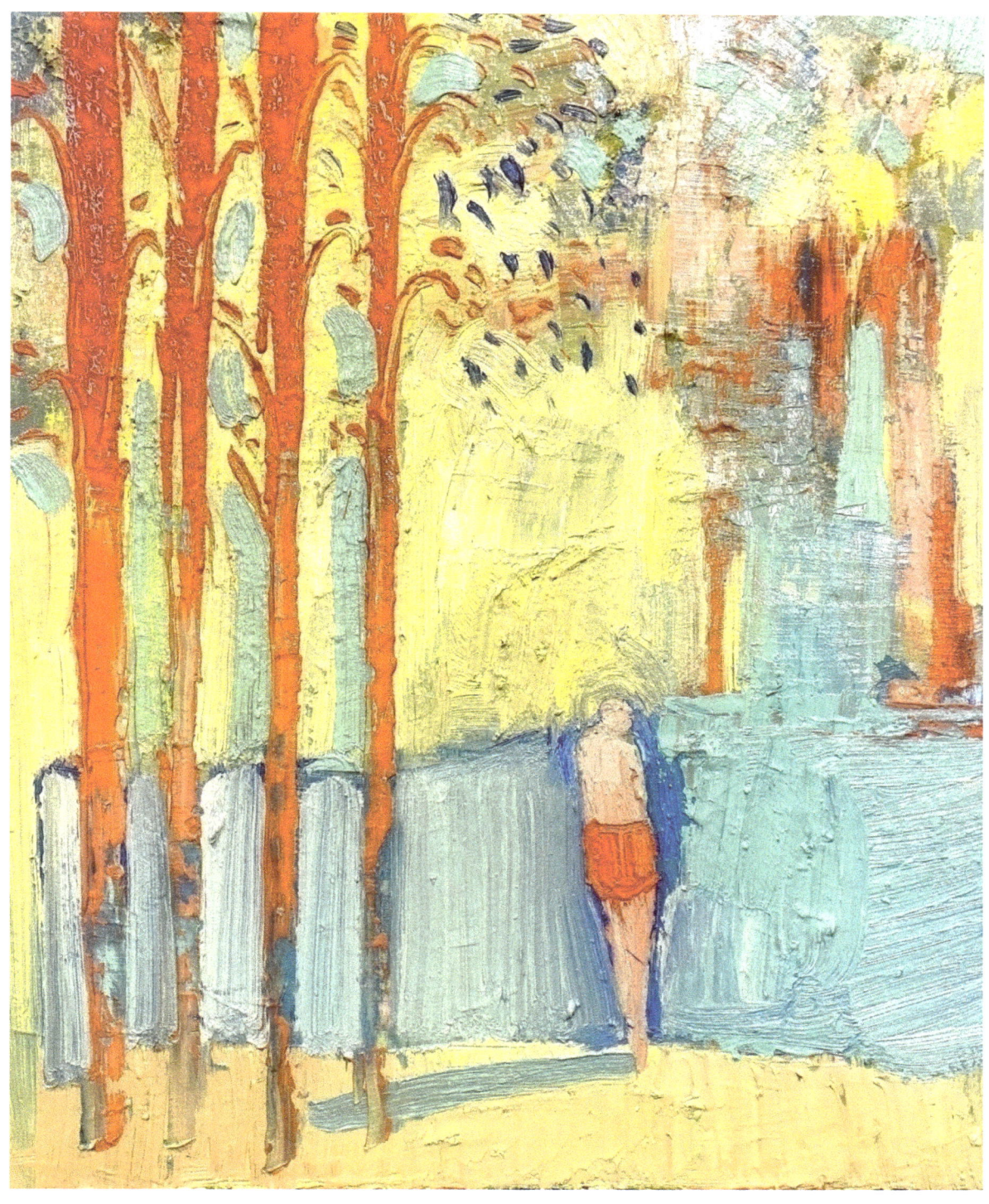

Title: Standing by the sacred river
Size: 76x63cm

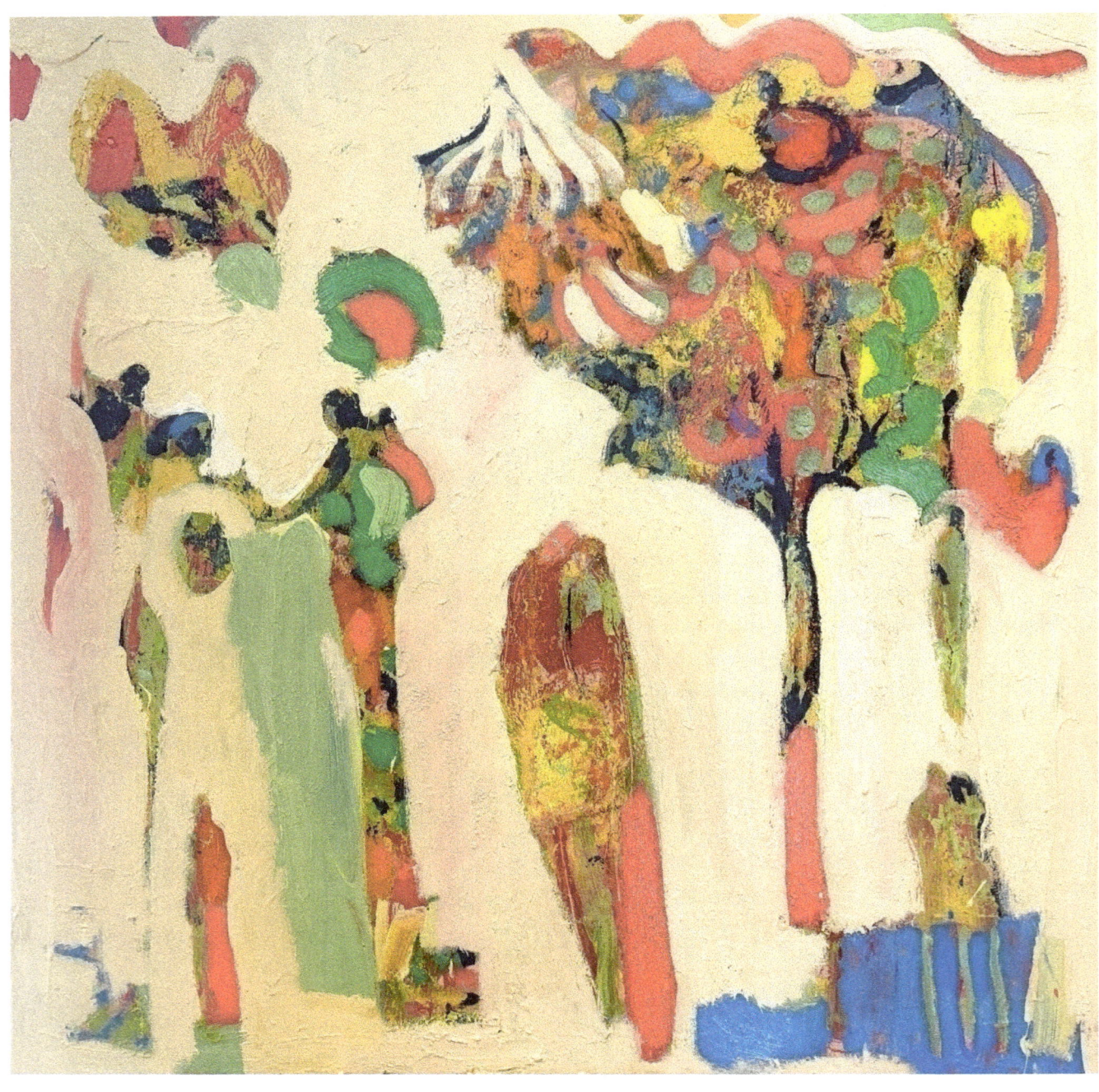

Title: Stories from the banyan tree

Size: 100x100cm

Paul Wadsworth

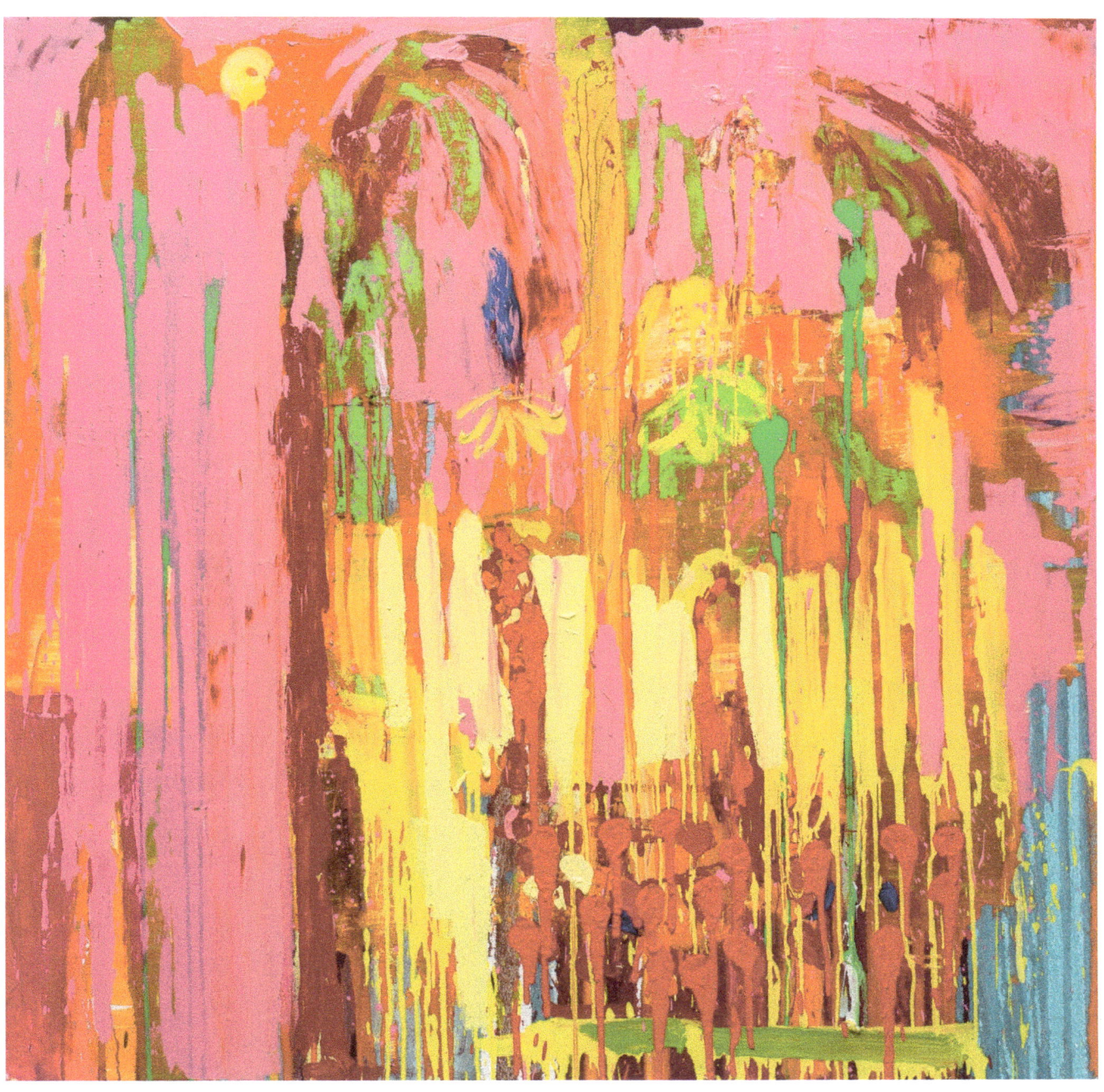

Title: Sun umbrellas

Size: 140x140cm

Stories From The Banyan Tree

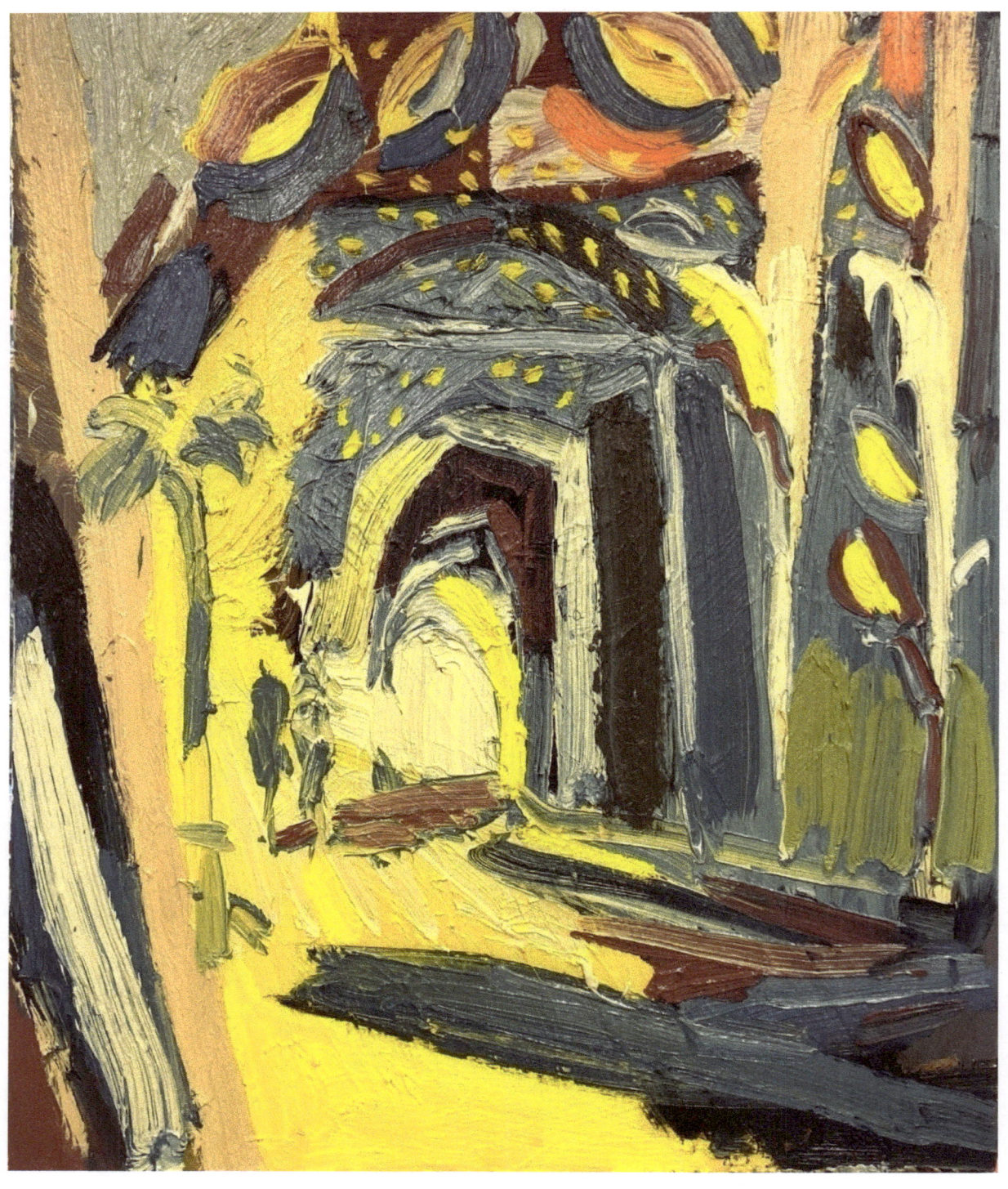

Title: Sunlit path
Size: 77x63cm

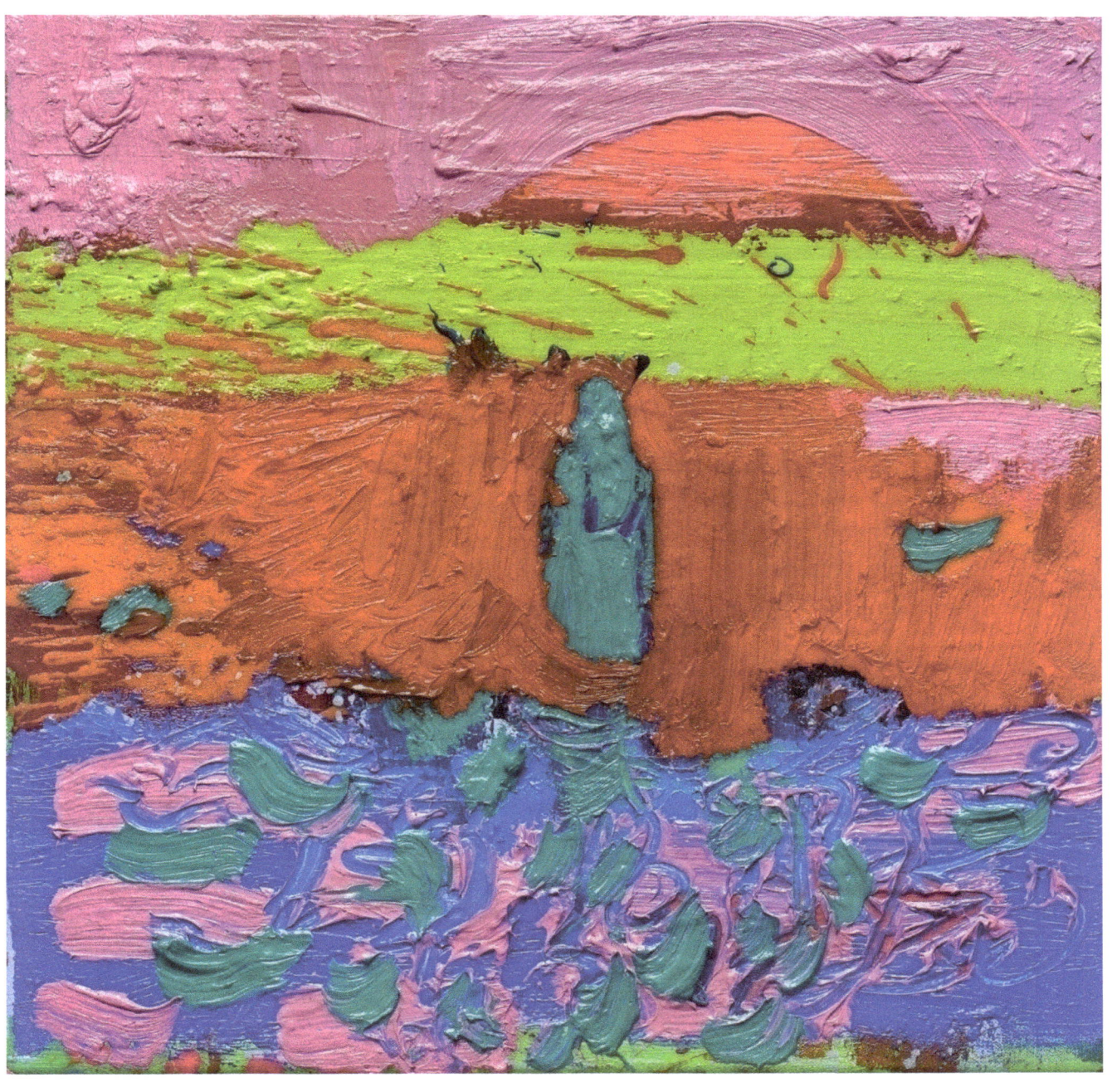

Title: Sunset

Size: 40x40cm

Stories From The Banyan Tree

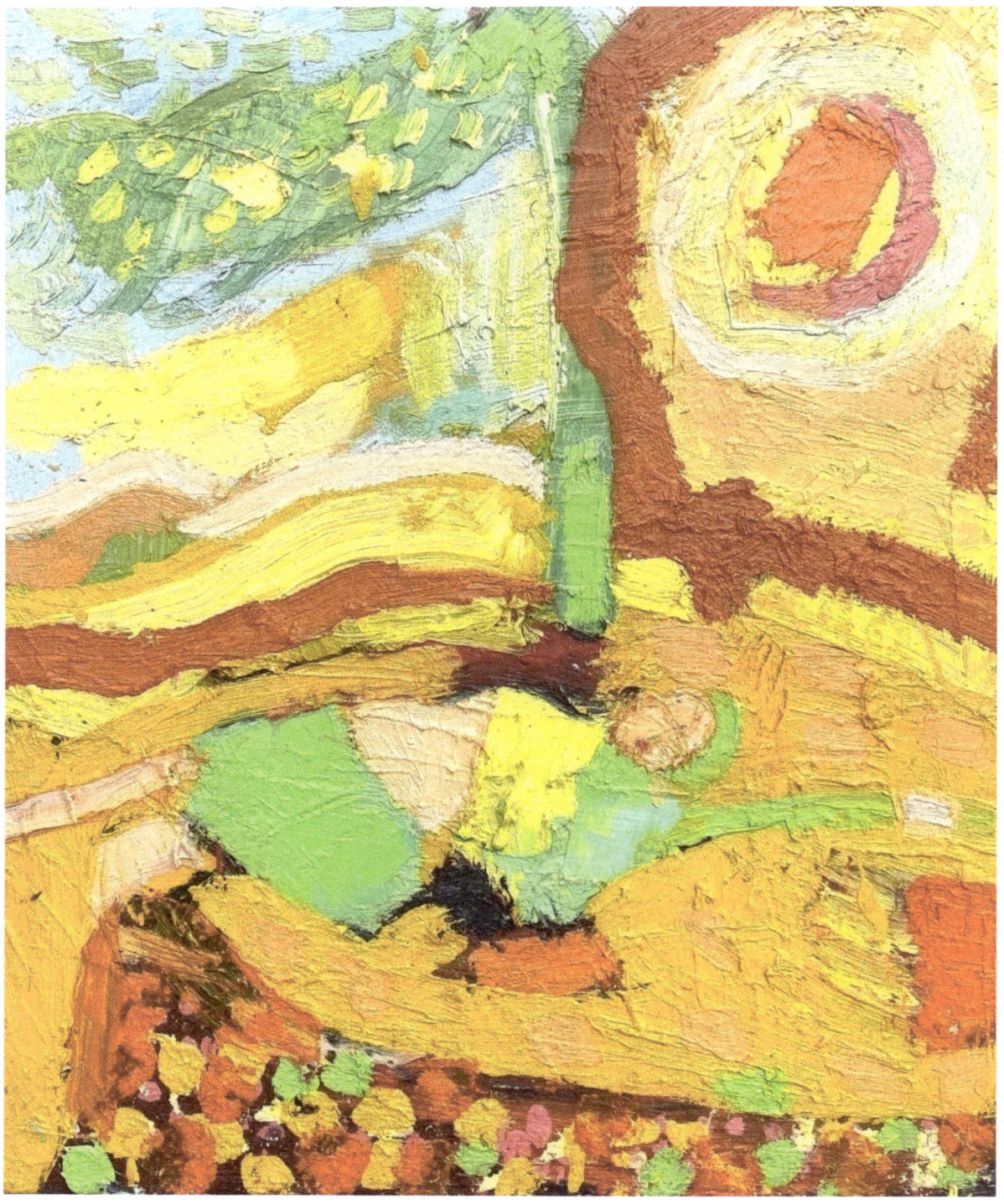

Title: Sunshine
Size: 78x63cm

Paul Wadsworth

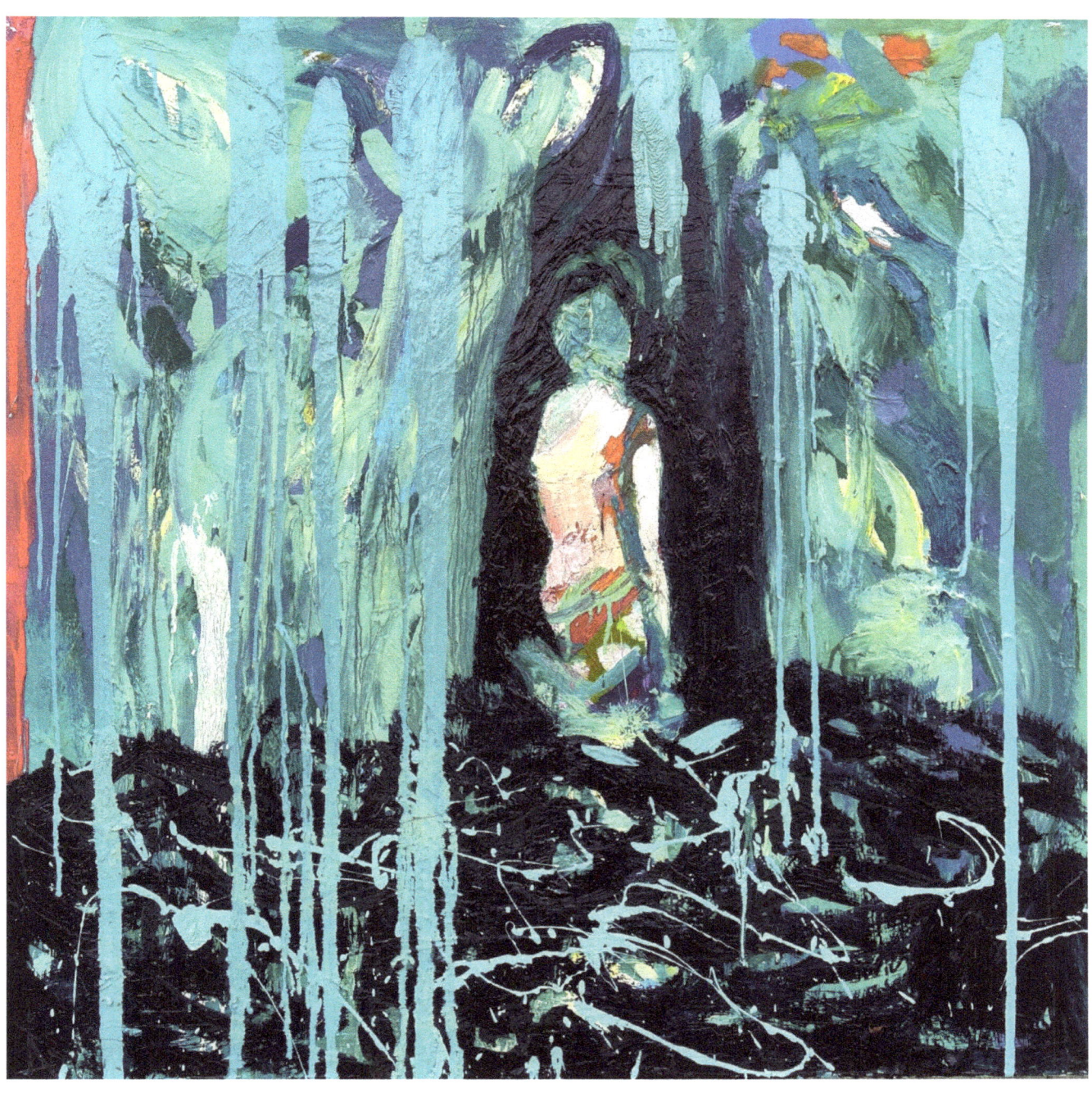

Title: Swimmer and blue bird

Size: 120x120cm

Stories From The Banyan Tree

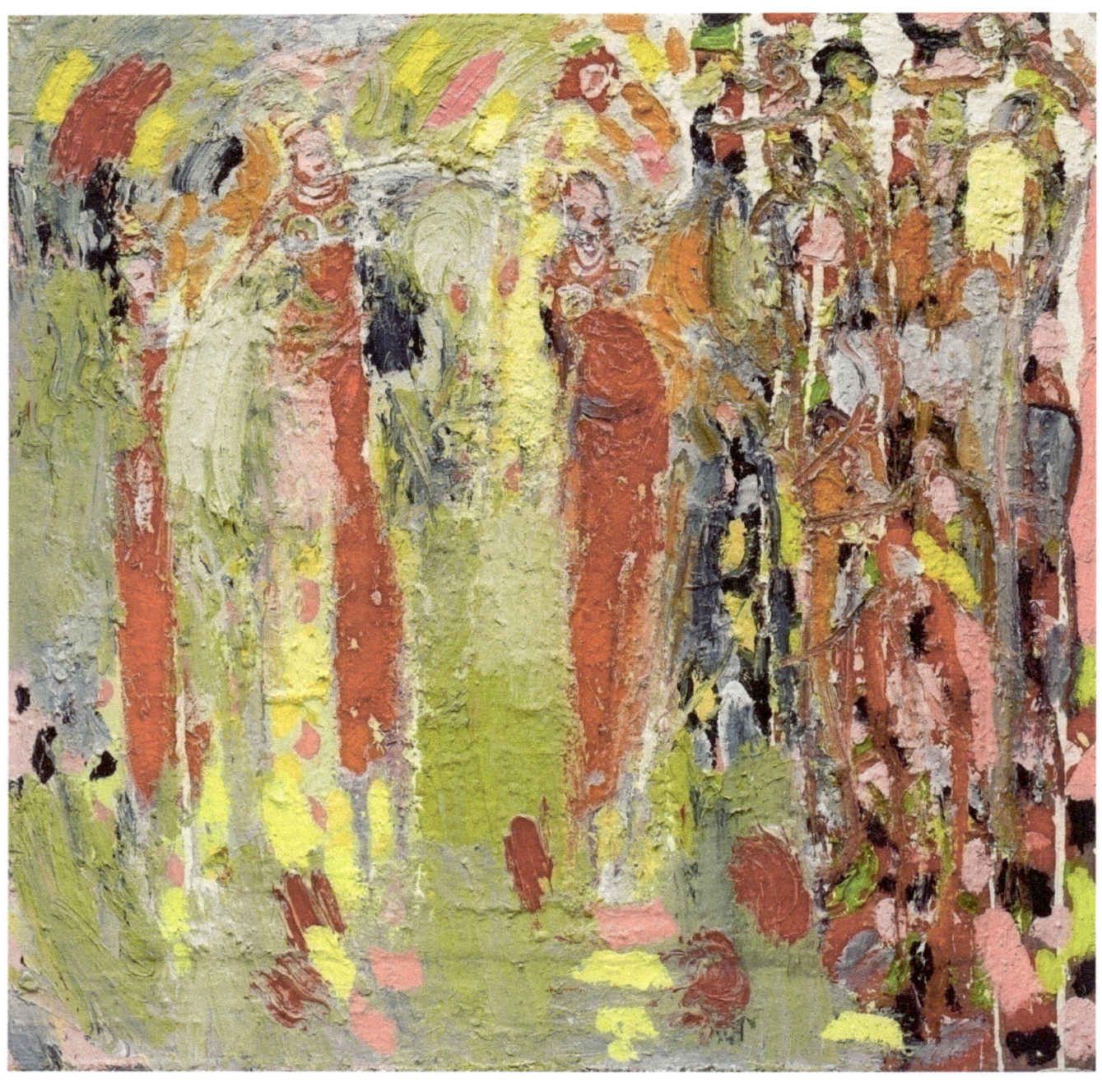

Title: Tantric dancers
Size: 126x126cm

Paul Wadsworth

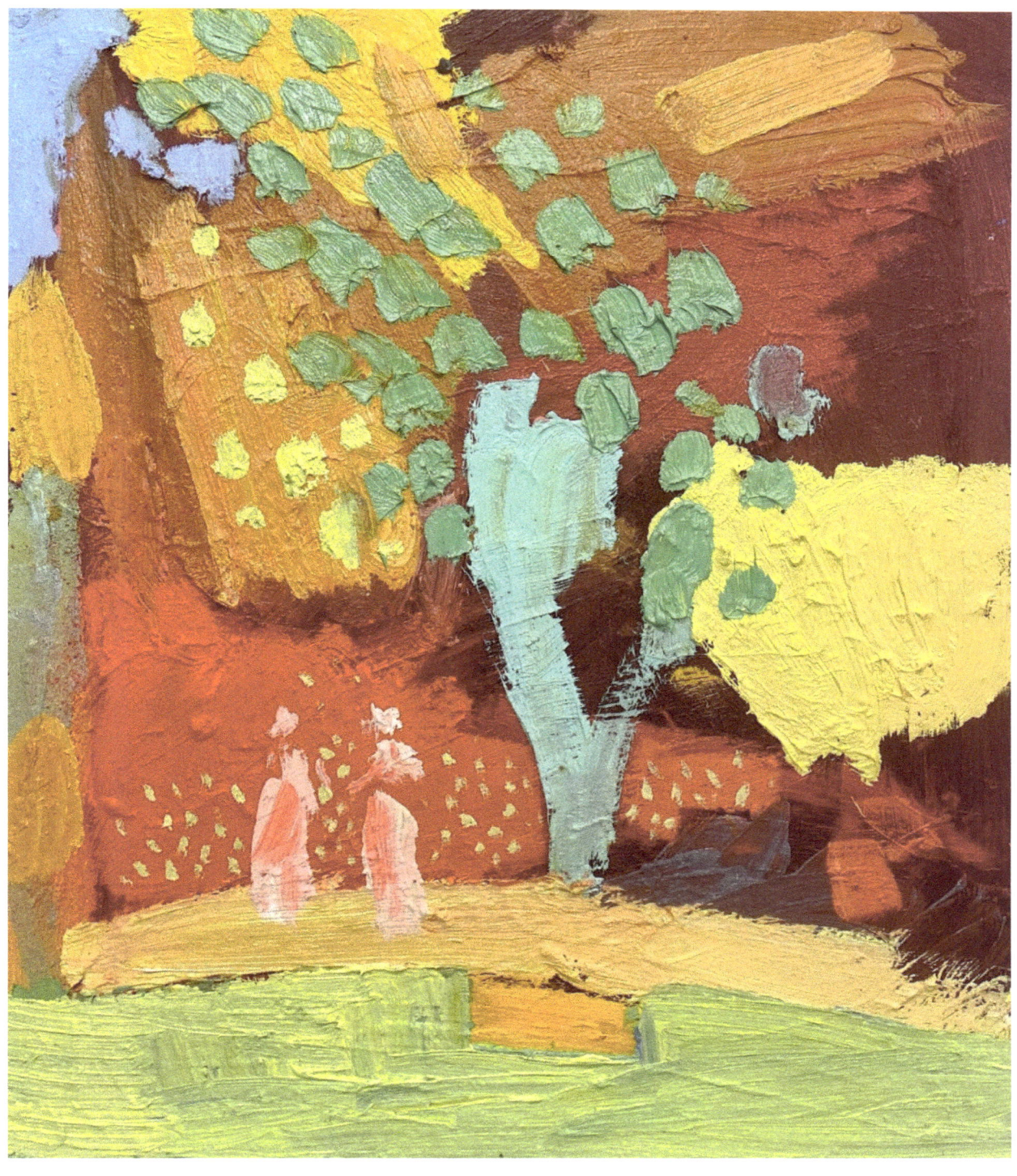

Title: Tea pickers
Size:70x60cm

Stories From The Banyan Tree

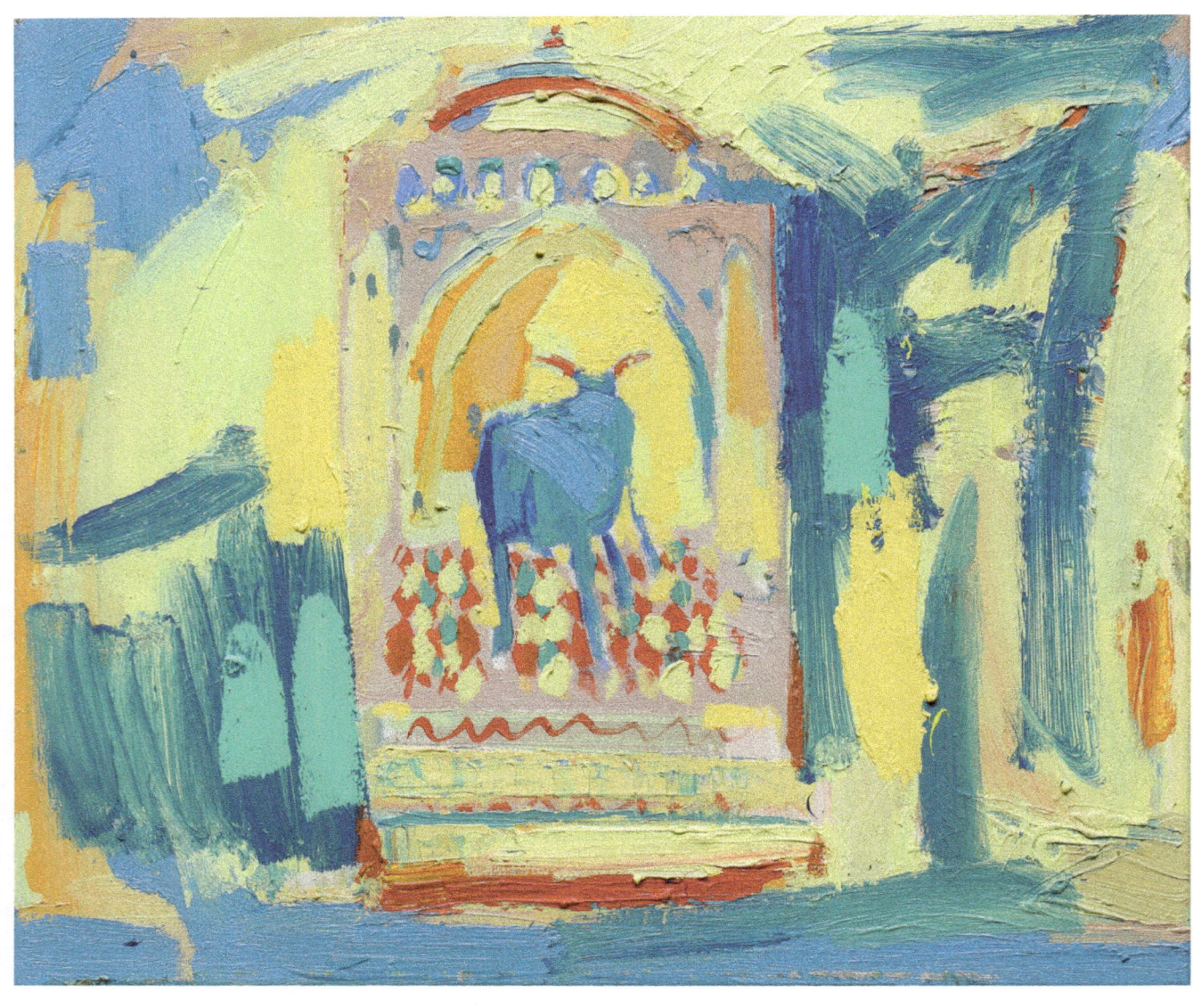

Title: Temple cow
Size: 60x70cm

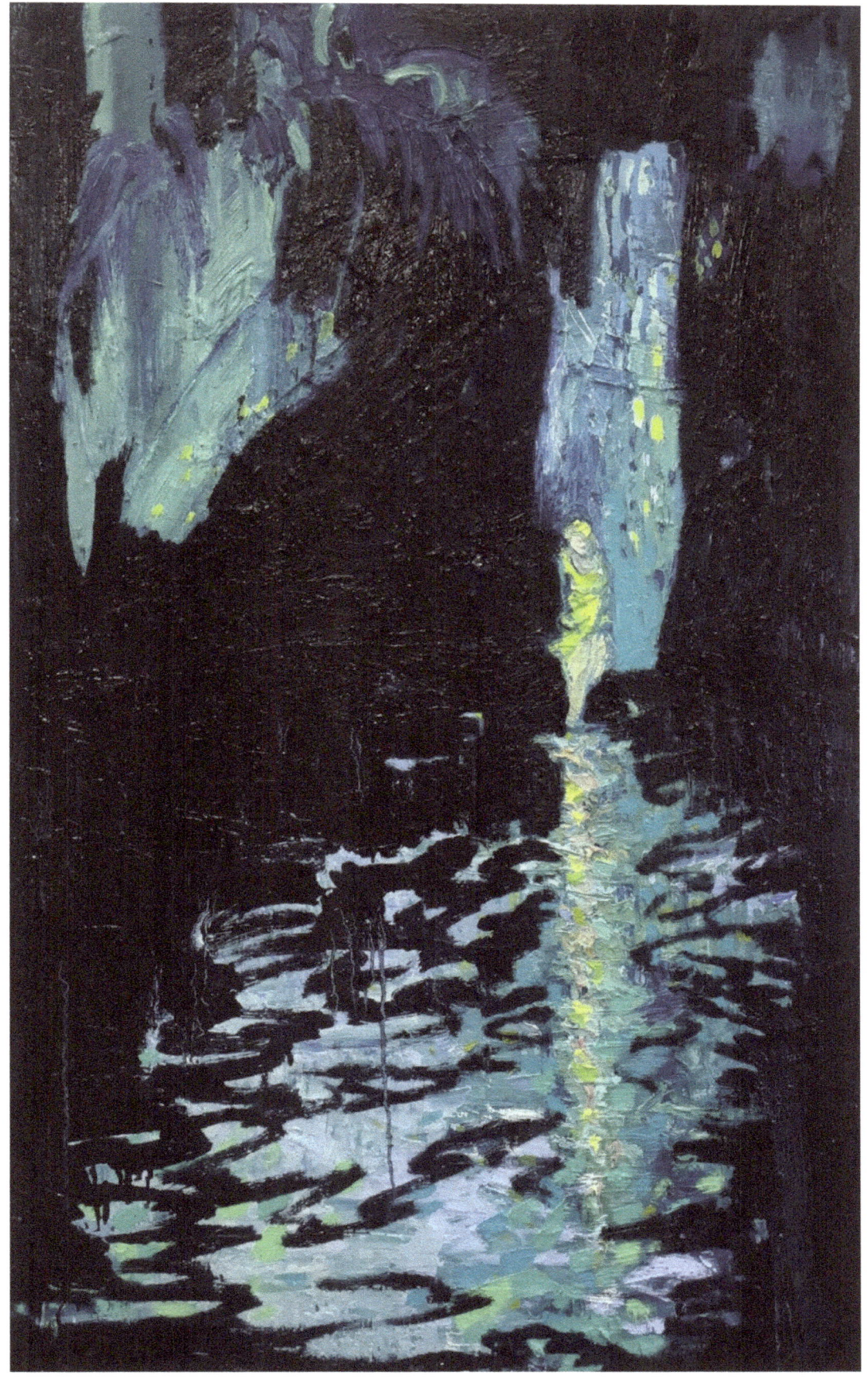

Title: Stream reflection

Size: 160x110cm

Stories From The Banyan Tree

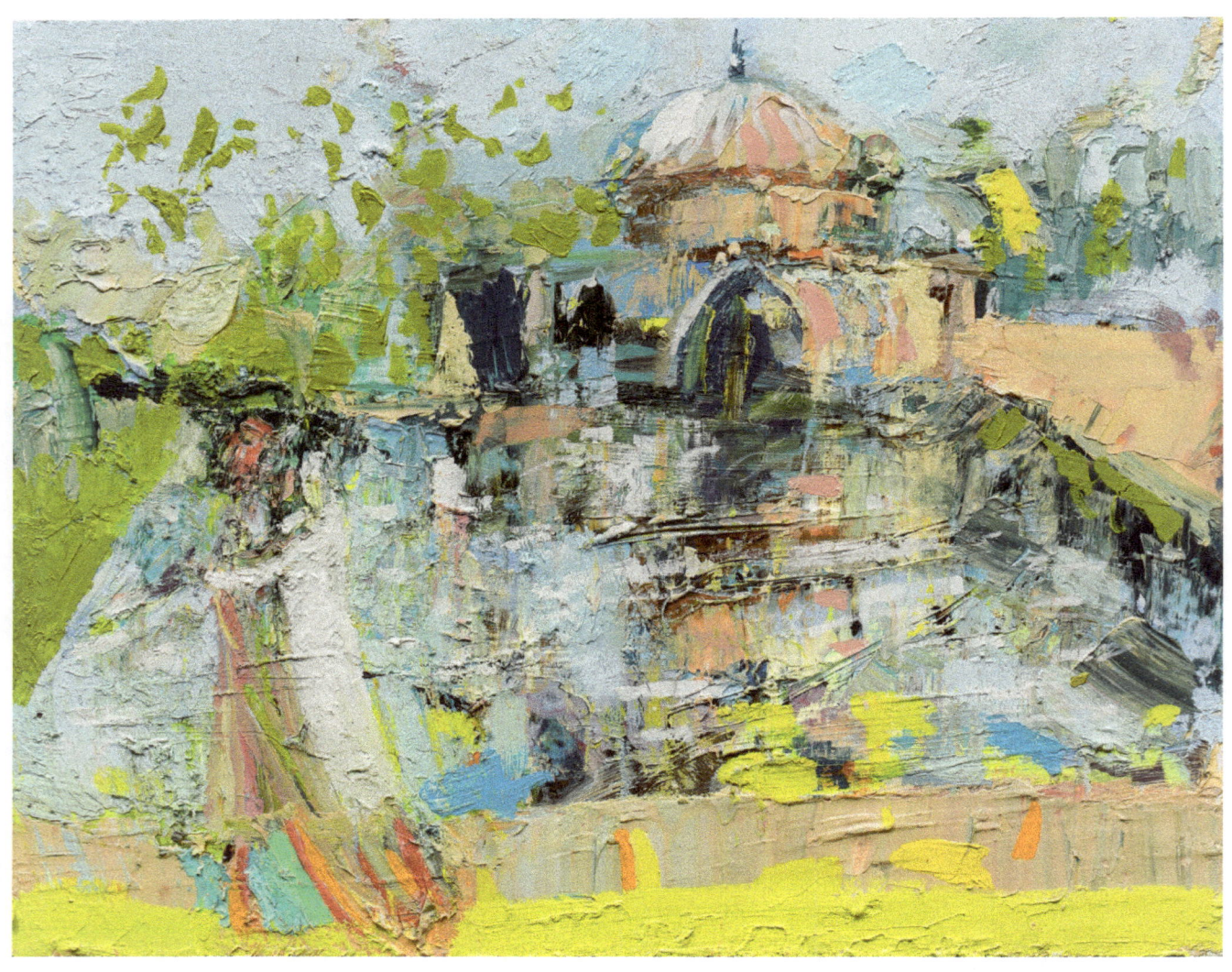

Title: Temple lake dancers
Size: 60x70cm

Paul Wadsworth

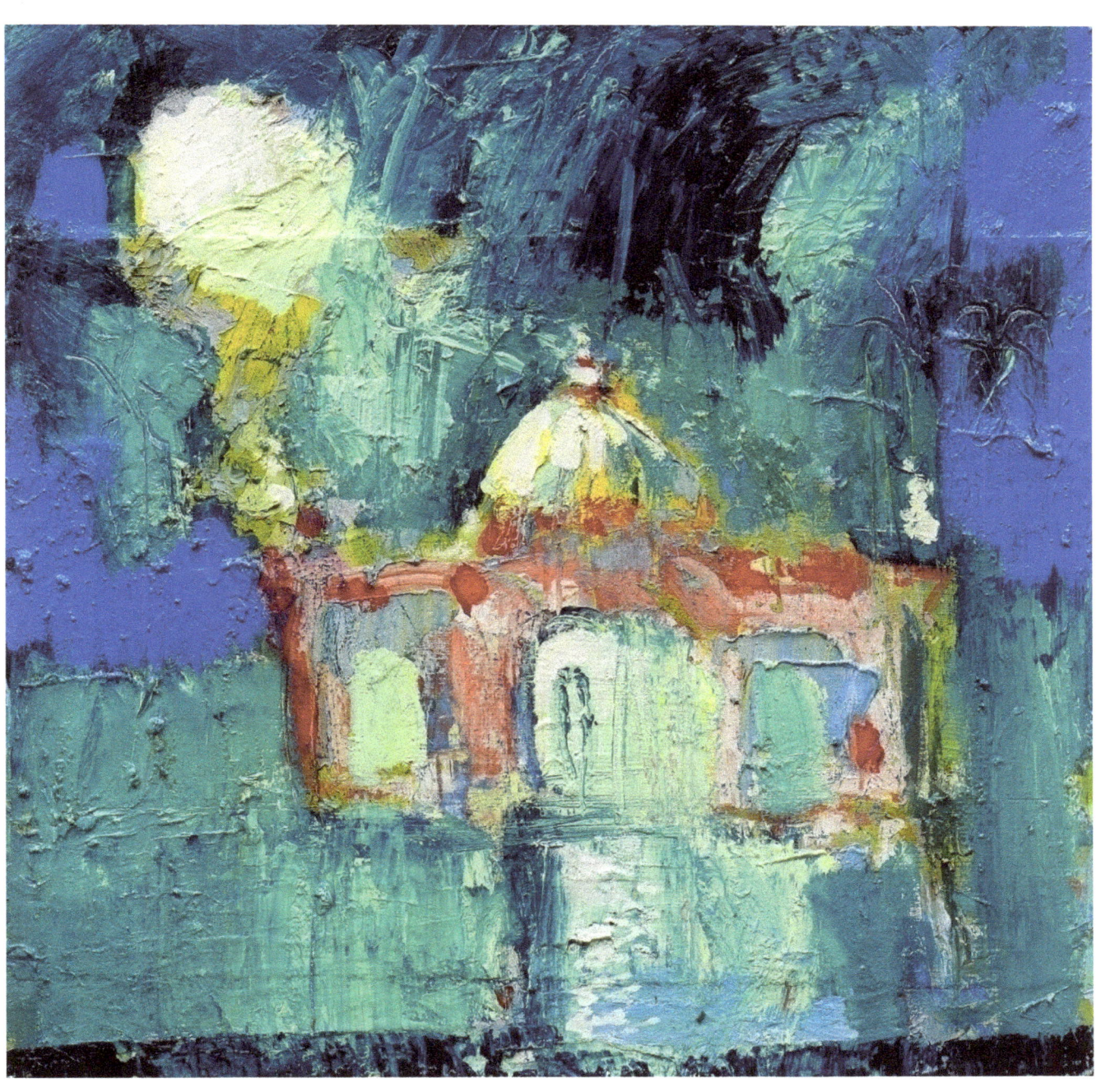

Title: Temple meeting

Size: 60x60cm

Stories From The Banyan Tree

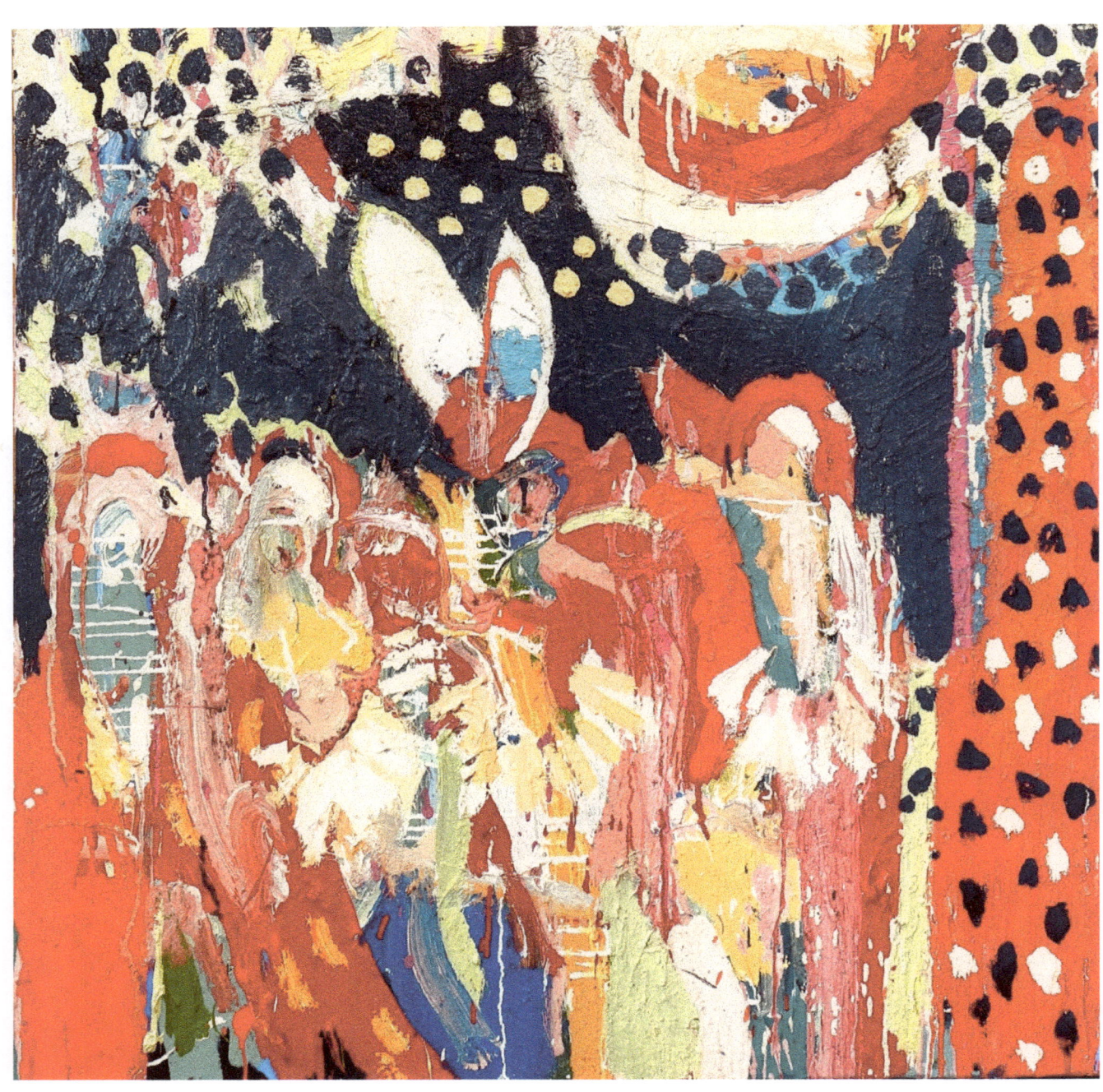

Title: The angels have a party
Size: 90x90cm

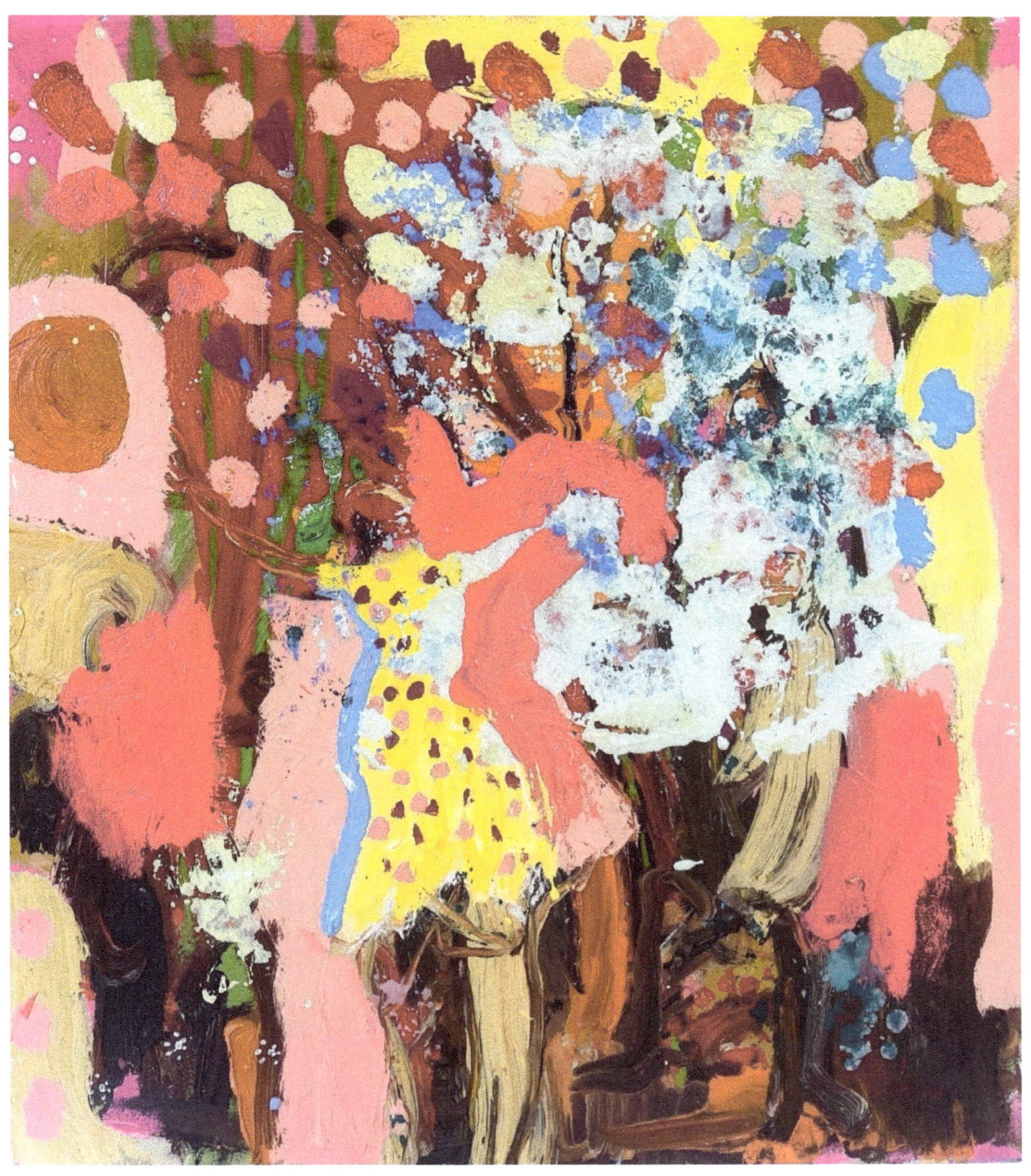

Title: The colour balloon seller

Size: 63x77cm

Stories From The Banyan Tree

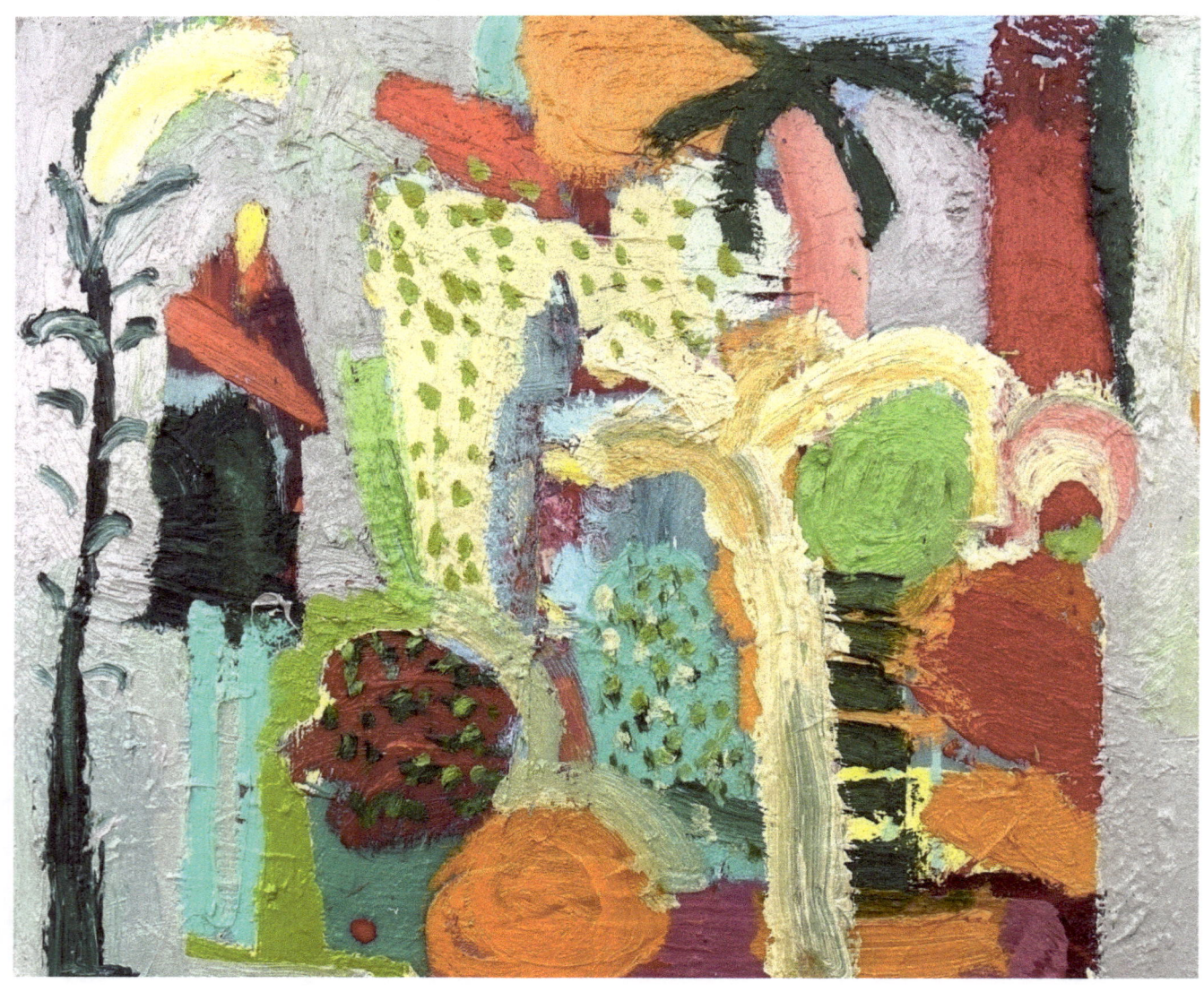

Title: The colour garden
Size: 63x77cm

Paul Wadsworth

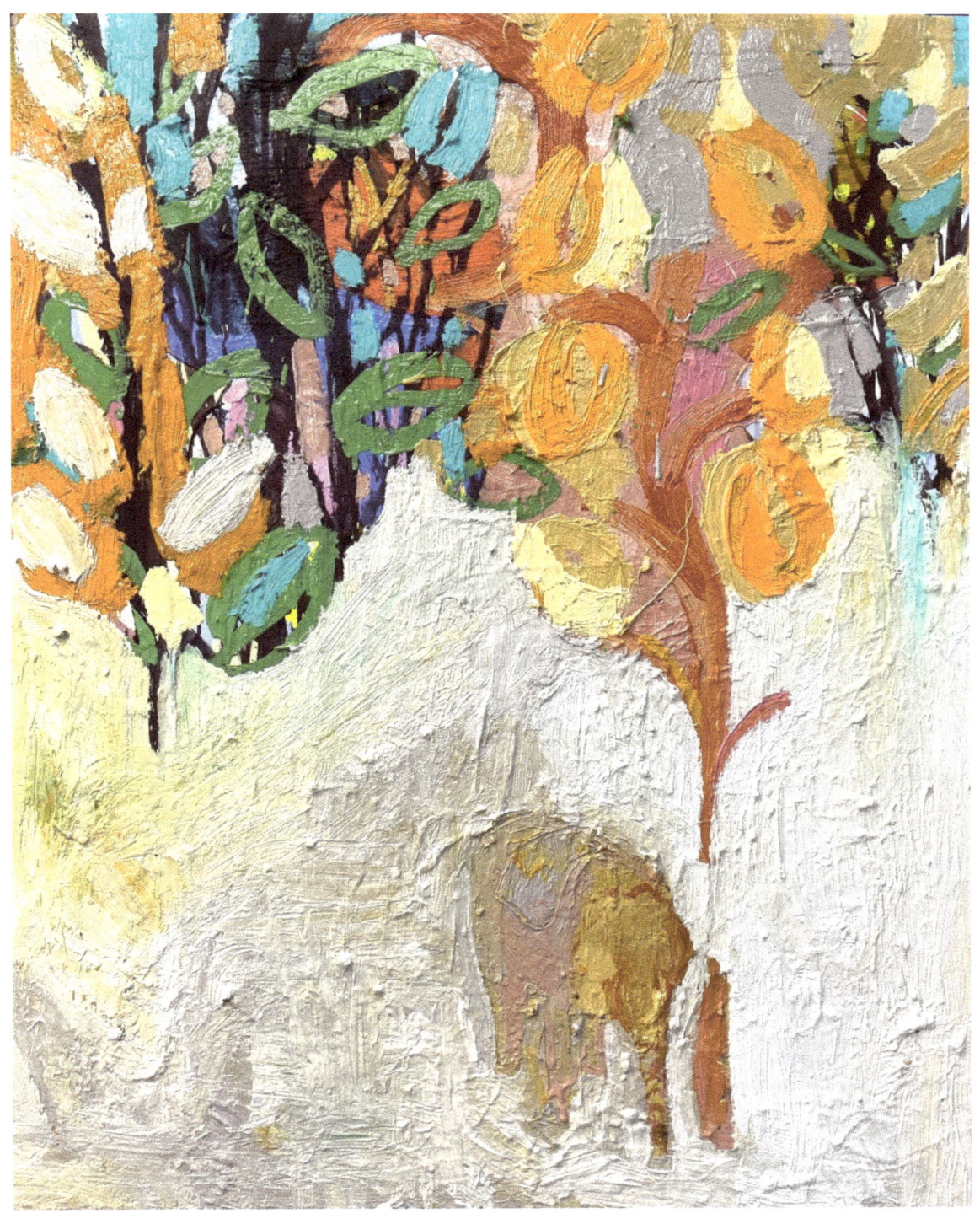

Title: The elephant friend
Size: 90x70cm

Stories From The Banyan Tree

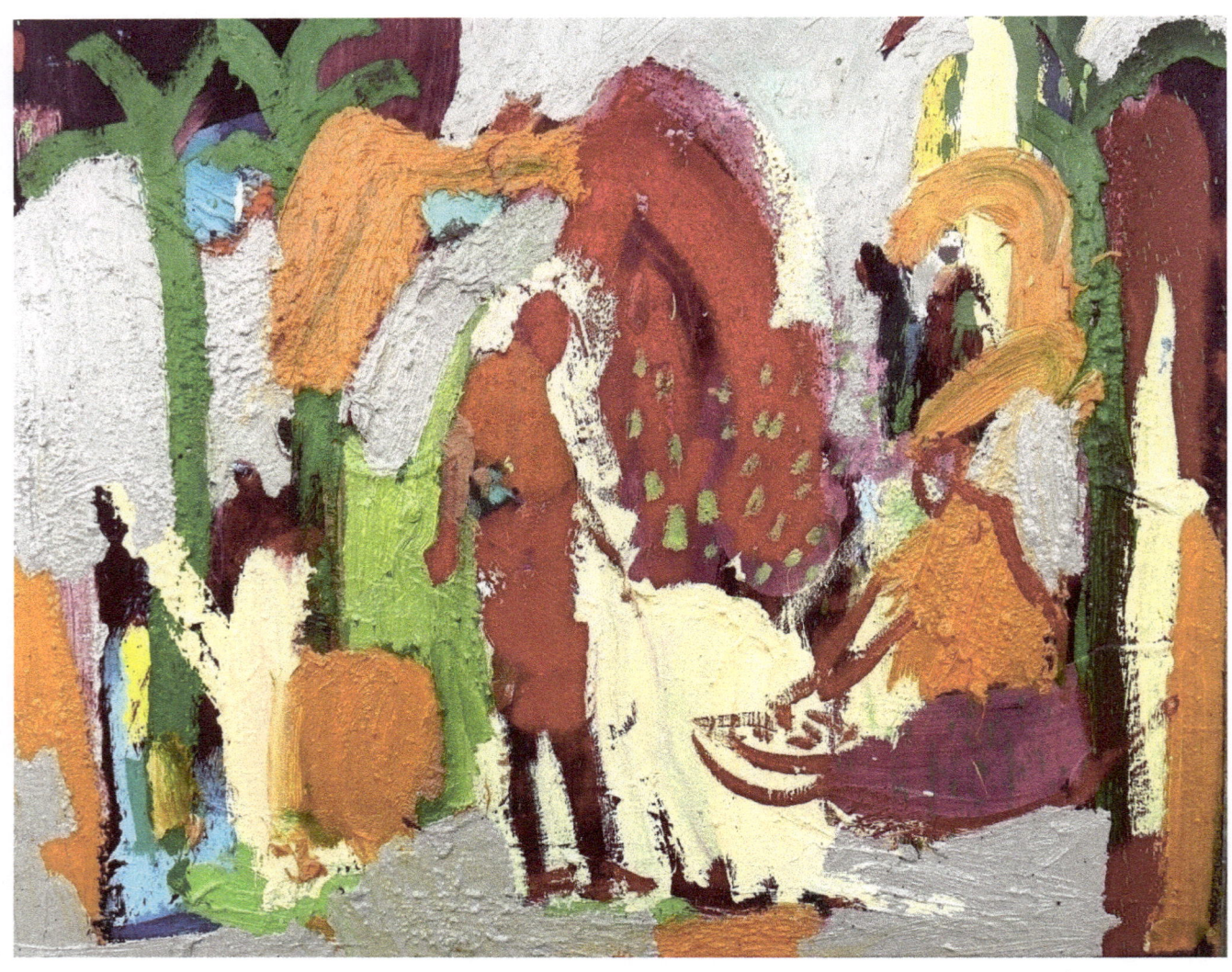

Title: The fish seller
Size:63x77cm

Paul Wadsworth

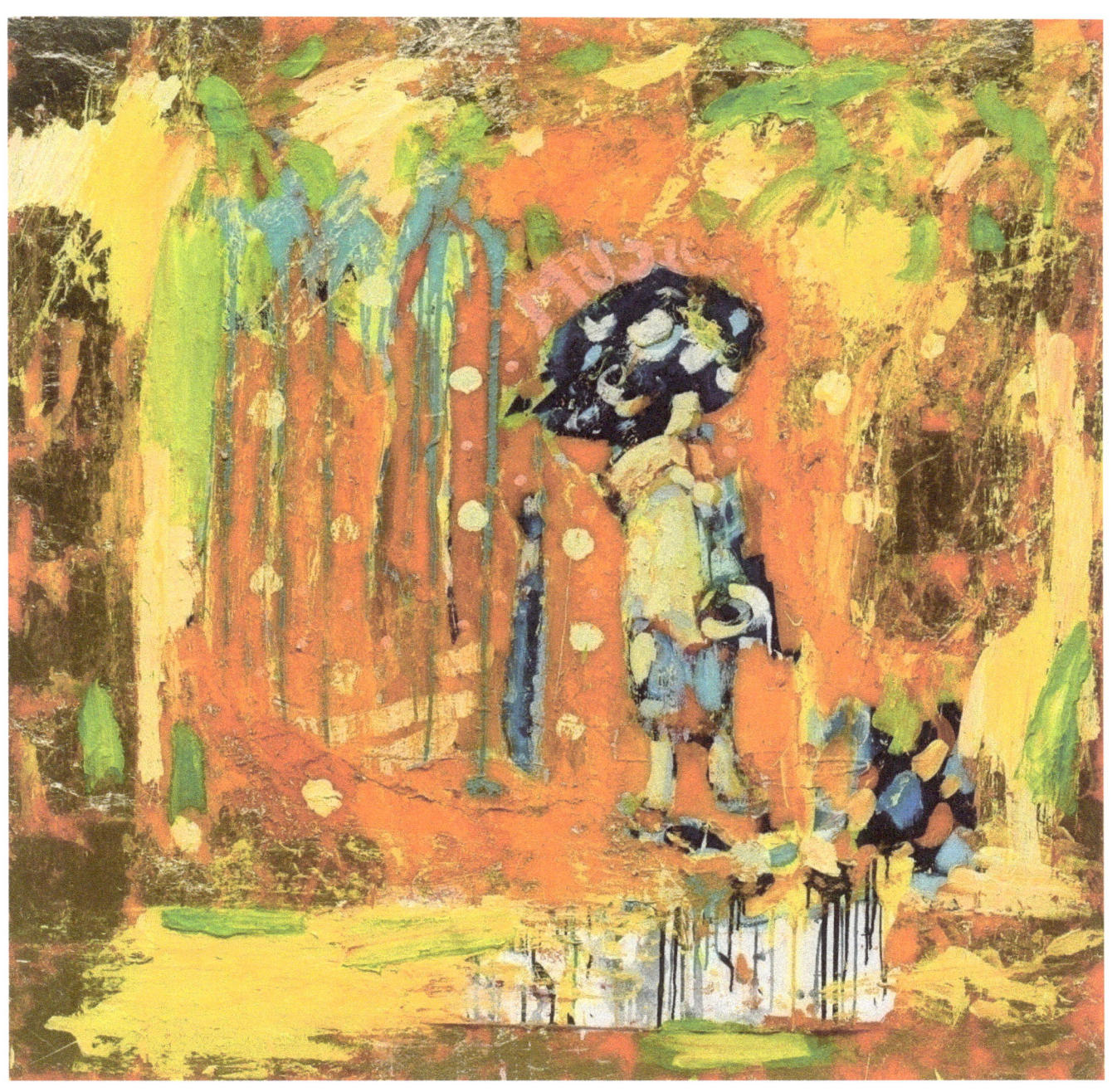

Title: The magic flute player
Size: 140x140cm

Stories From The Banyan Tree

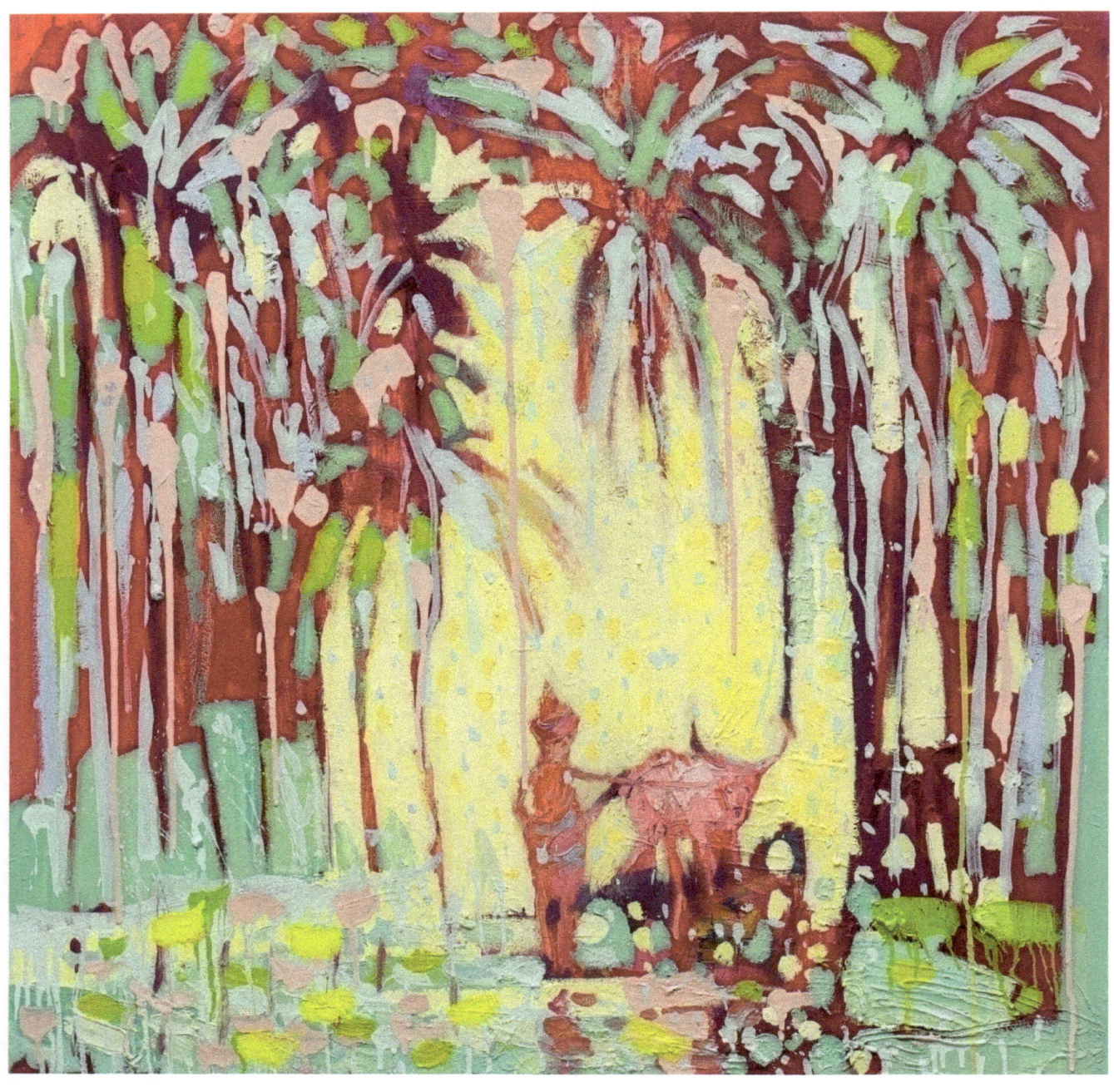

Title: The magician and the sacred cow

Size: 100x100cm

Paul Wadsworth

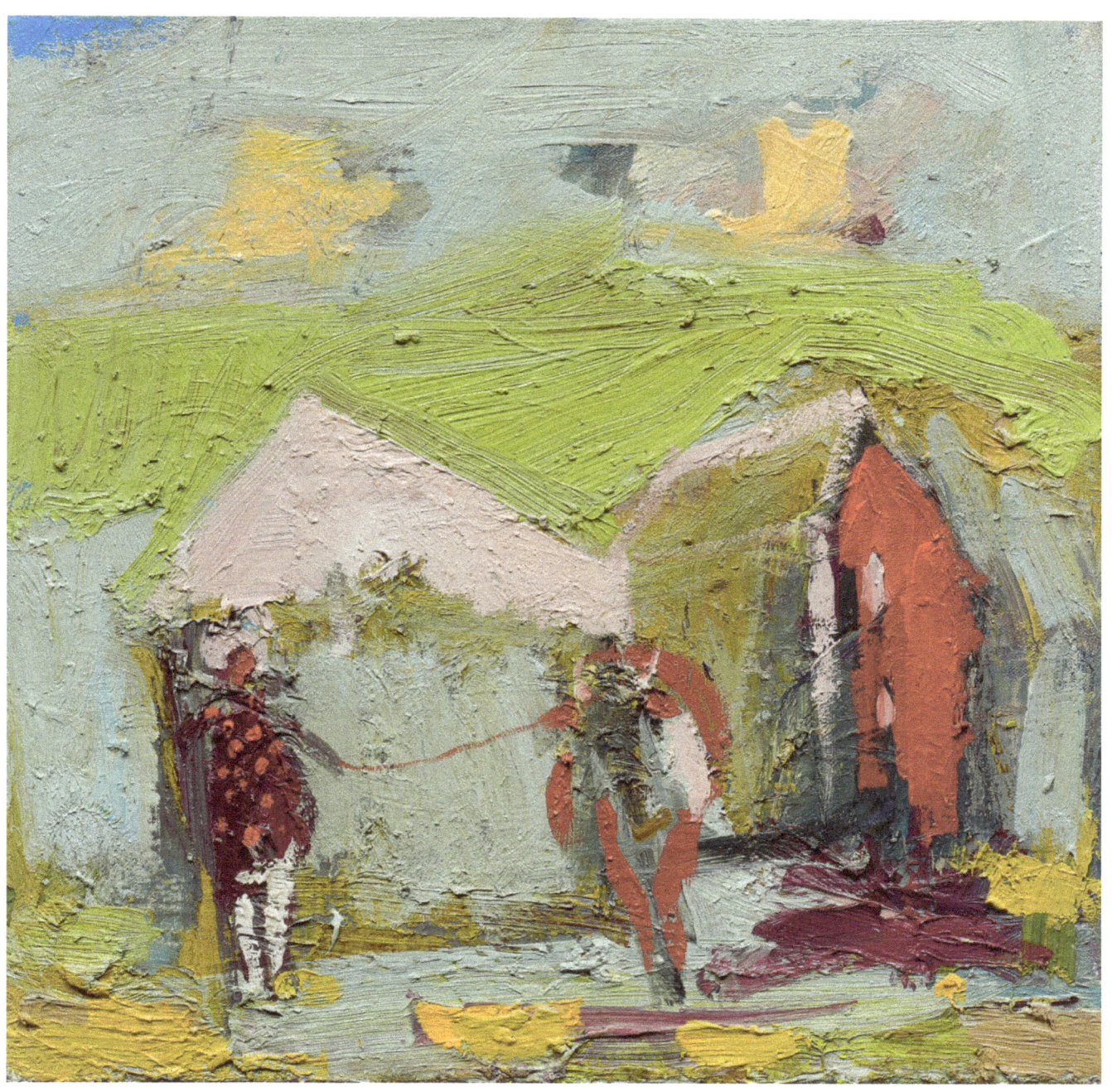

Title: The musician and his cow
Size: 50x50cm

Stories From The Banyan Tree

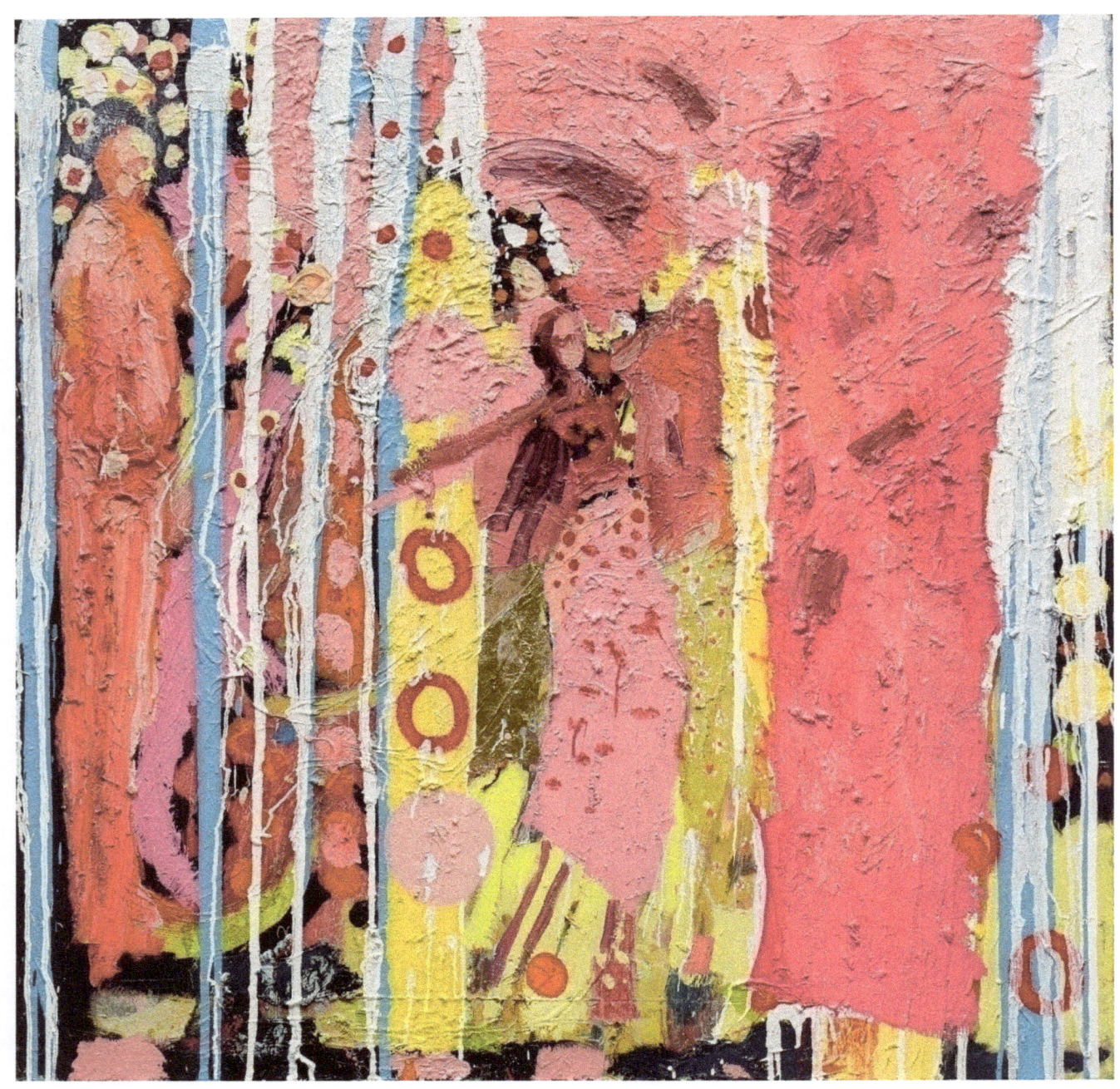

Title: The pink dancer

Size: 100x100cm

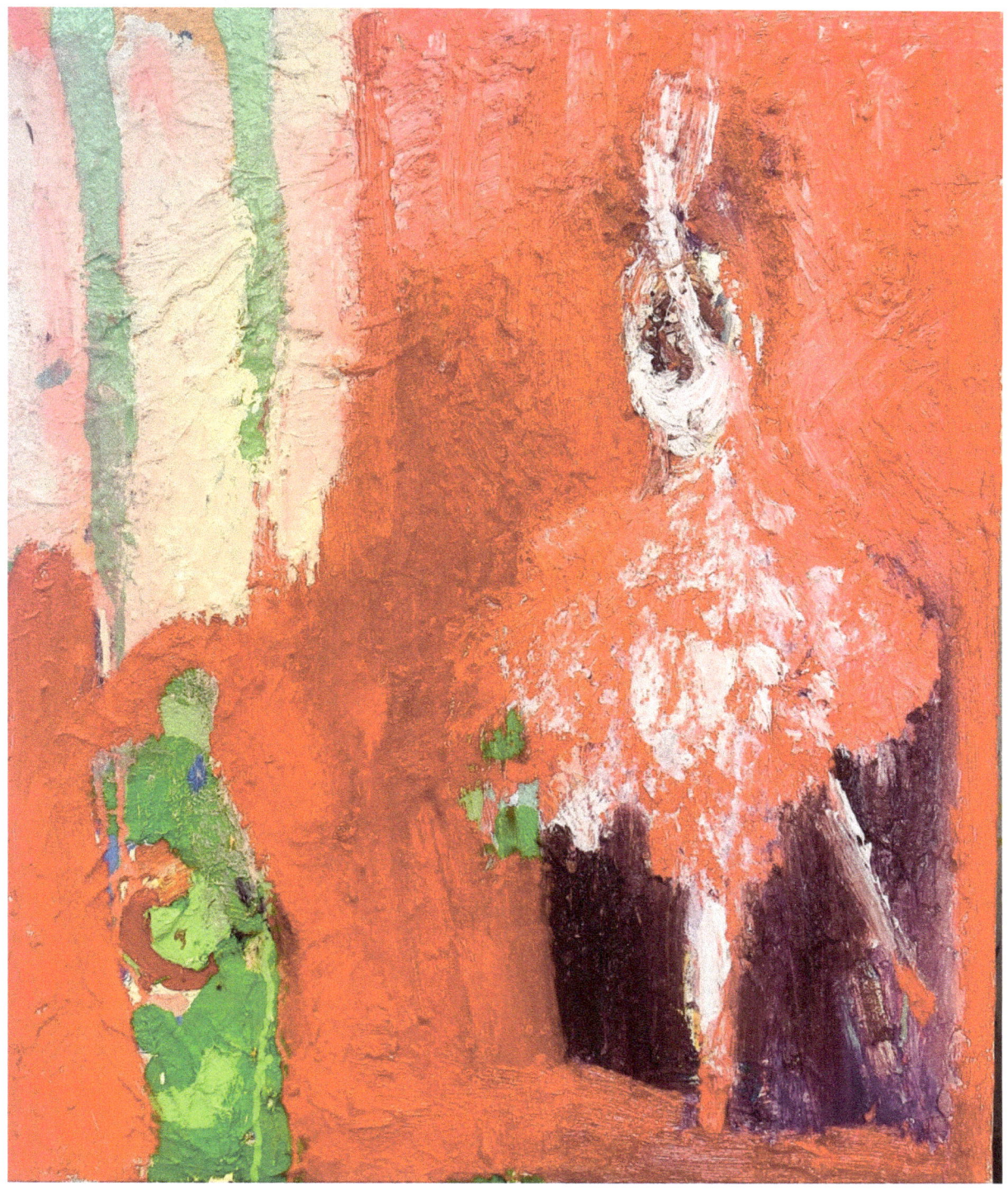

Title: The red Rajasthan dancer

Size: 70x60cm

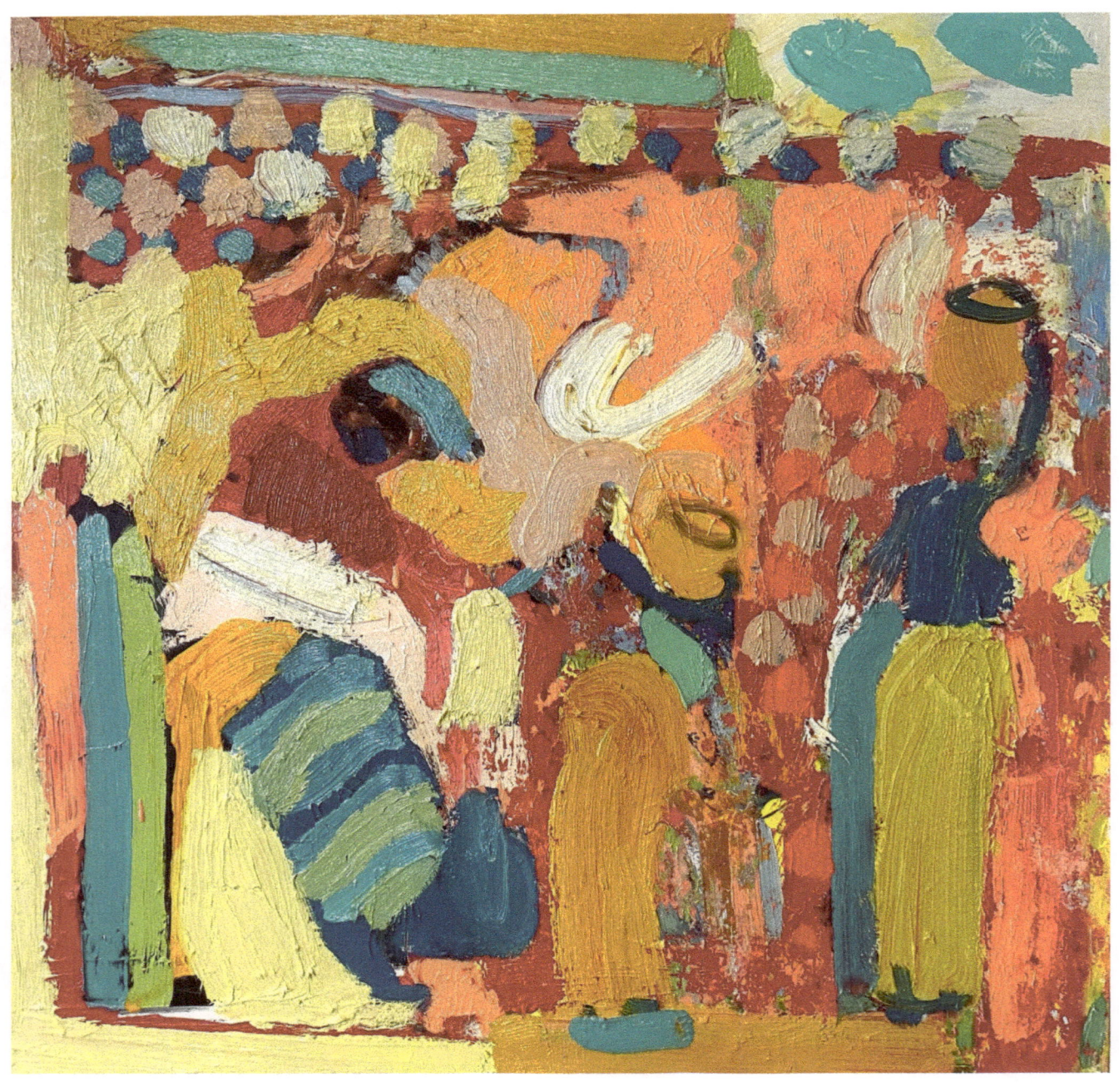

Title: The Taylor shop
Size: 90x90cm

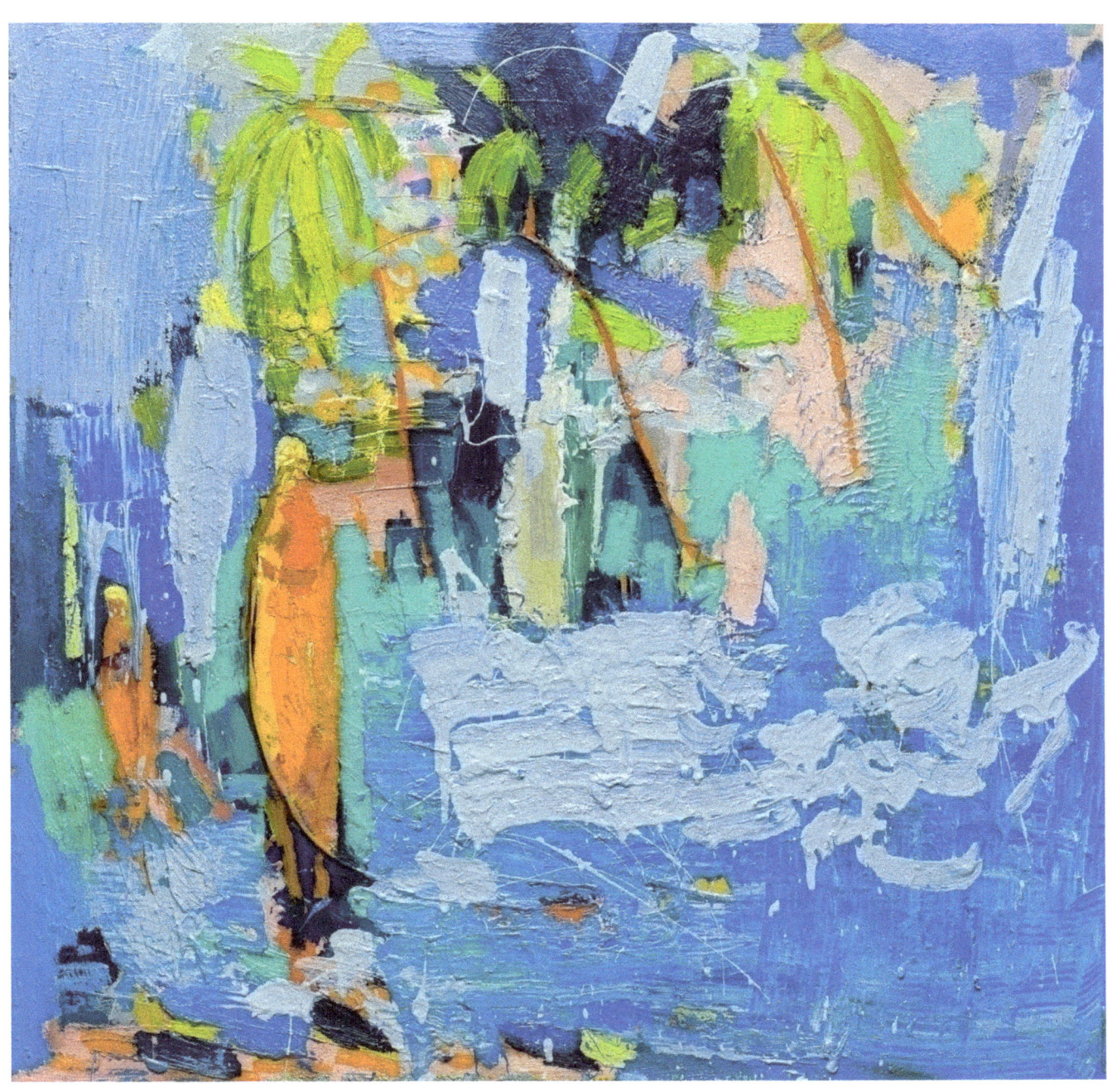

Title: The water garden

Size: 100x100cm

Stories From The Banyan Tree

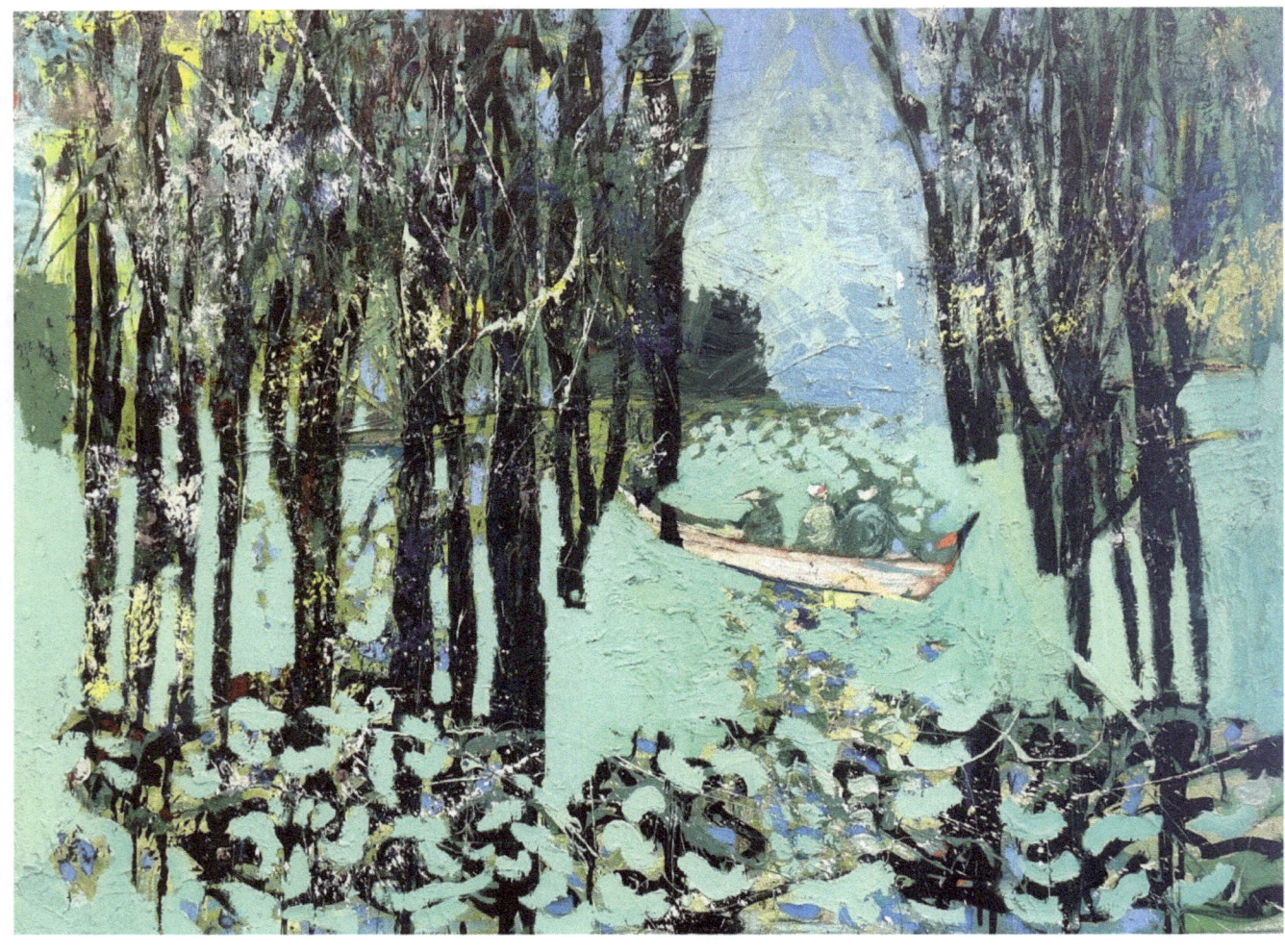

Title: Three men in a boat
Size: 110x165cm

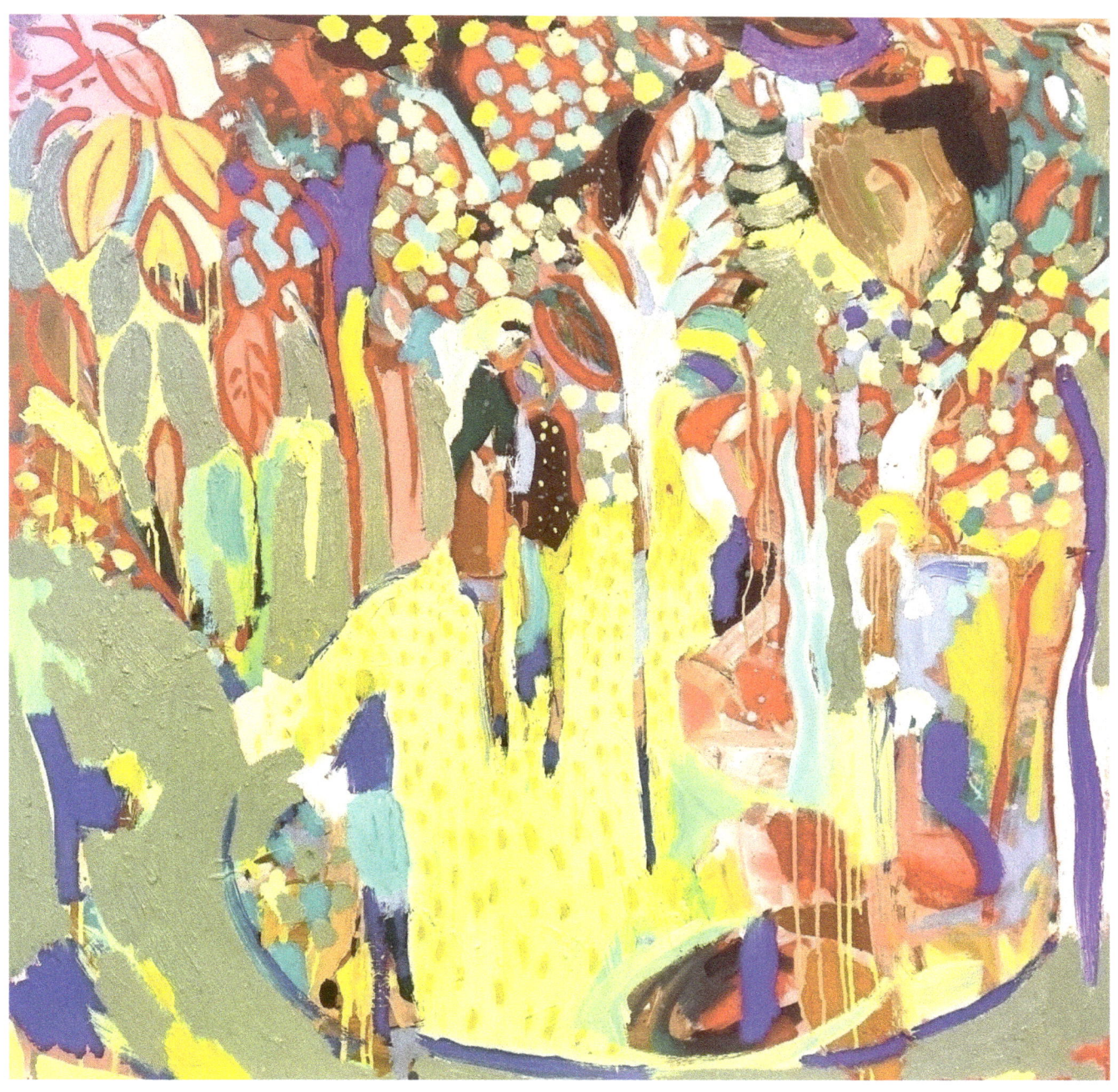

Title: Together in a forest of colour
Size: 120x120cm

Stories From The Banyan Tree

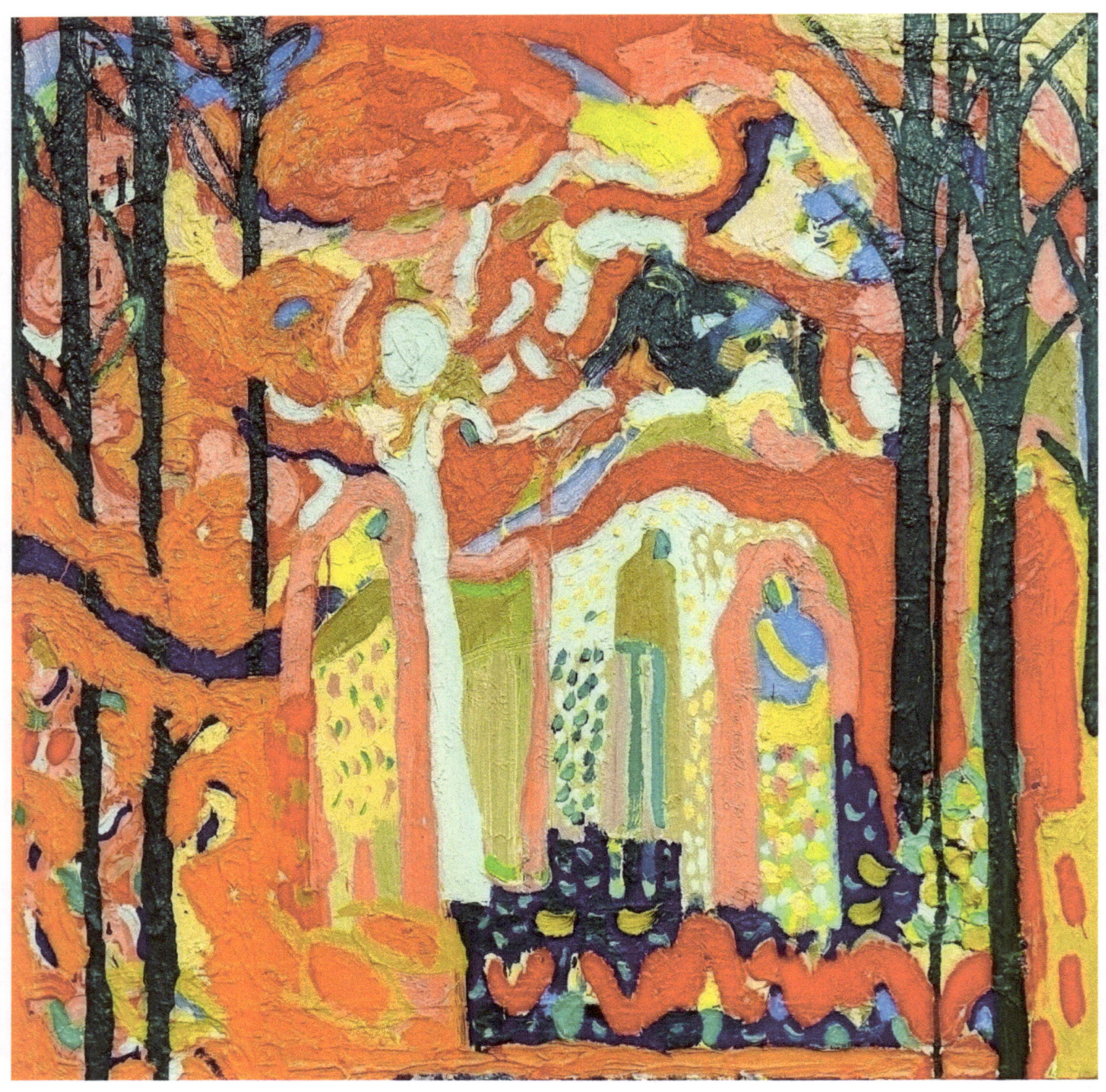

Title: Touching god
Size: 120x120cm

Paul Wadsworth

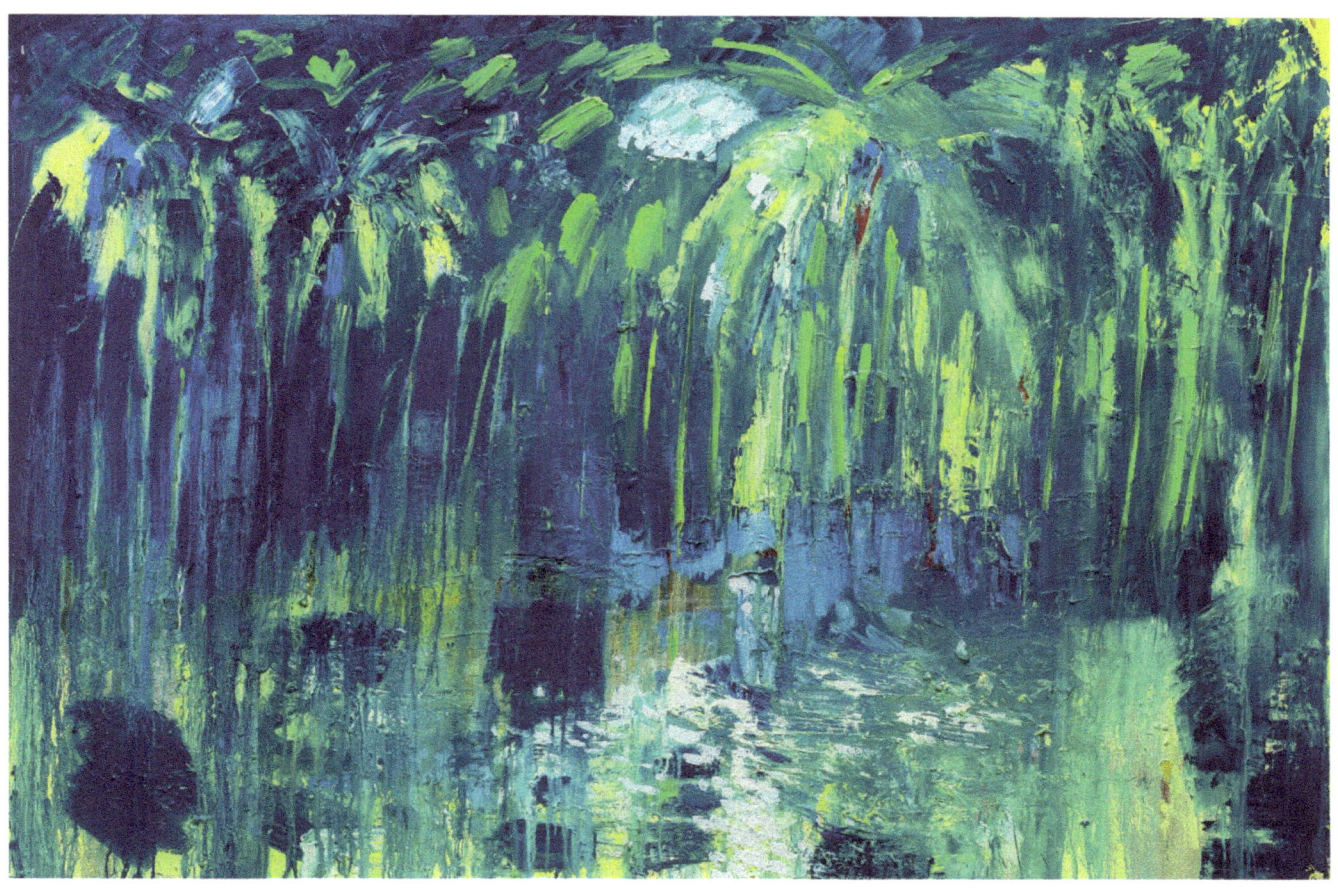

Title: Tranquility
Size: 120x180cm

Stories From The Banyan Tree

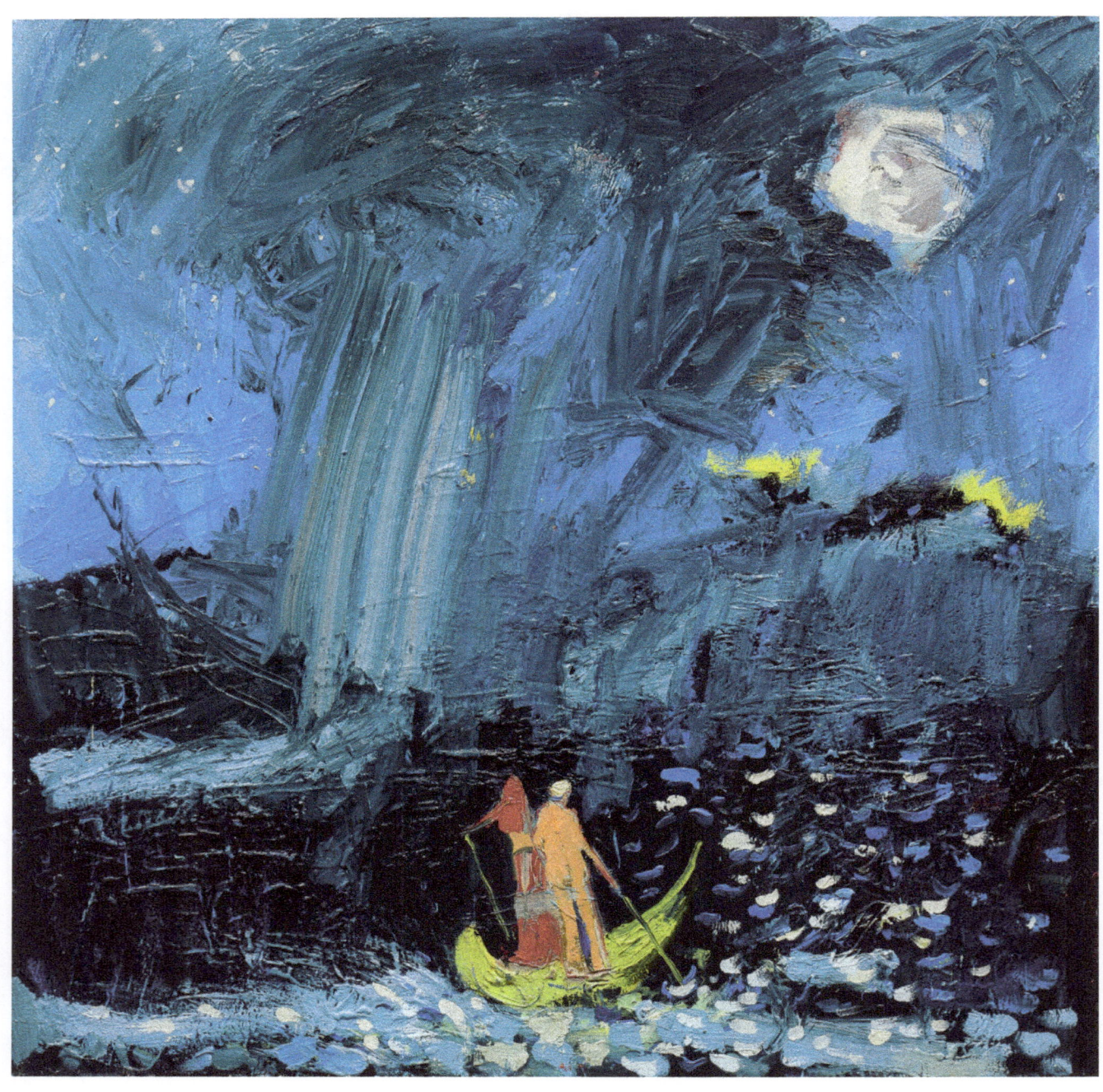

Title: Travellers by sea
Size: 100x100cm

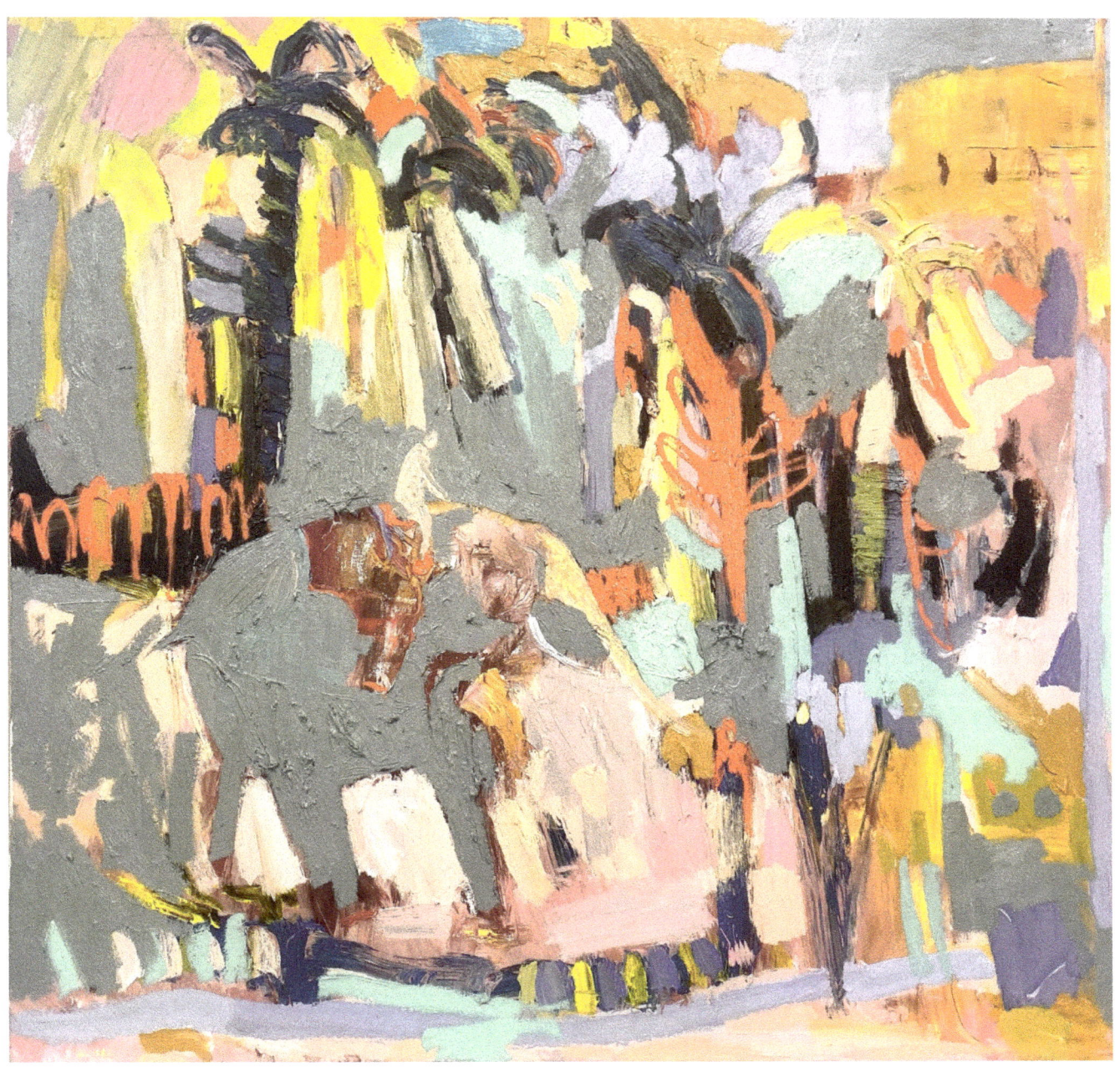

Title: Travelling together
Size: 120x120cm

Stories From The Banyan Tree

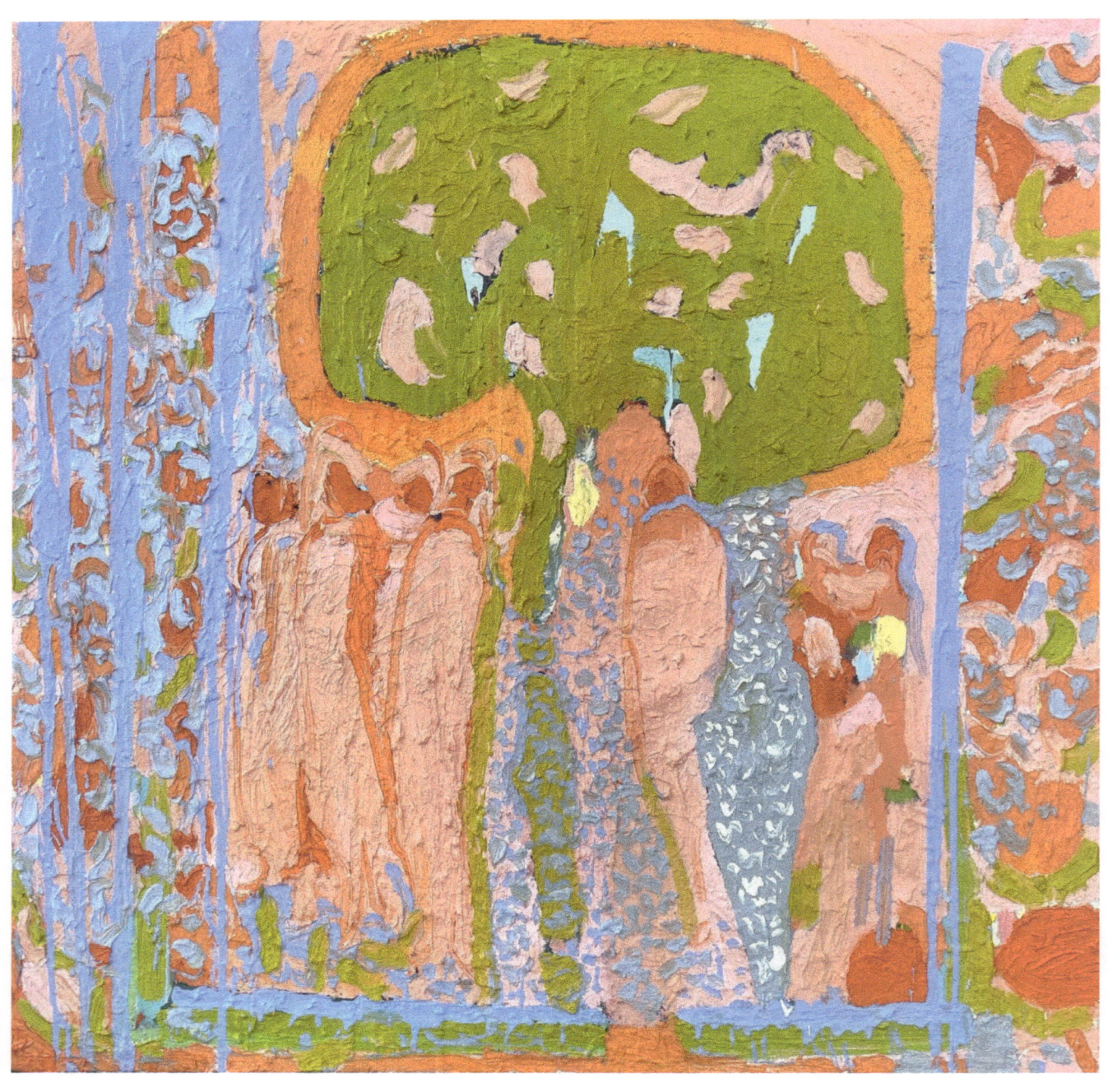

Title: Under the banyan tree

Size: 145x145cm

Paul Wadsworth

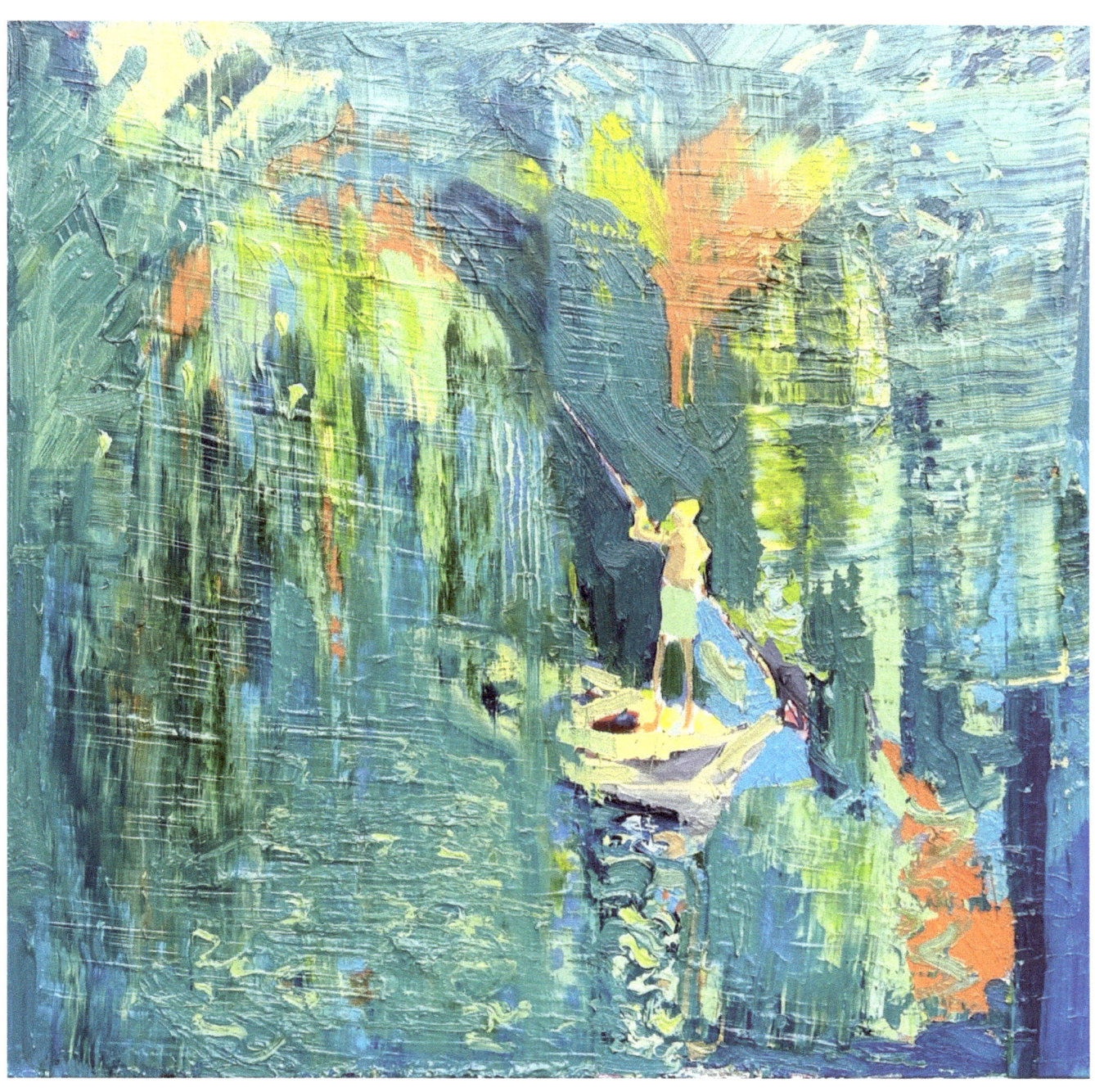

Title: Under the waterfall

Size: 120x120cm

Stories From The Banyan Tree

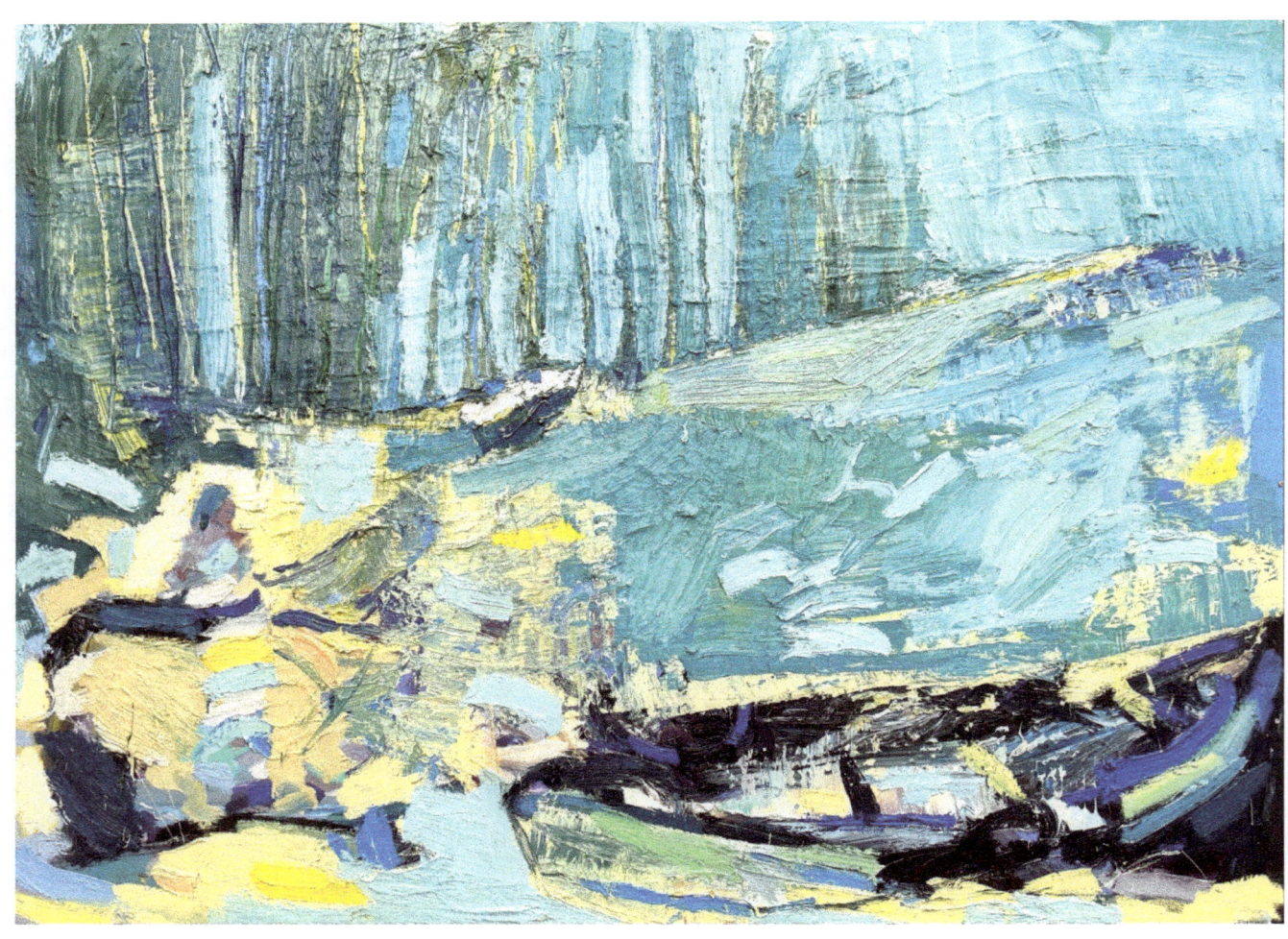

Title: Waiting
Size: 126x177cm

Paul Wadsworth

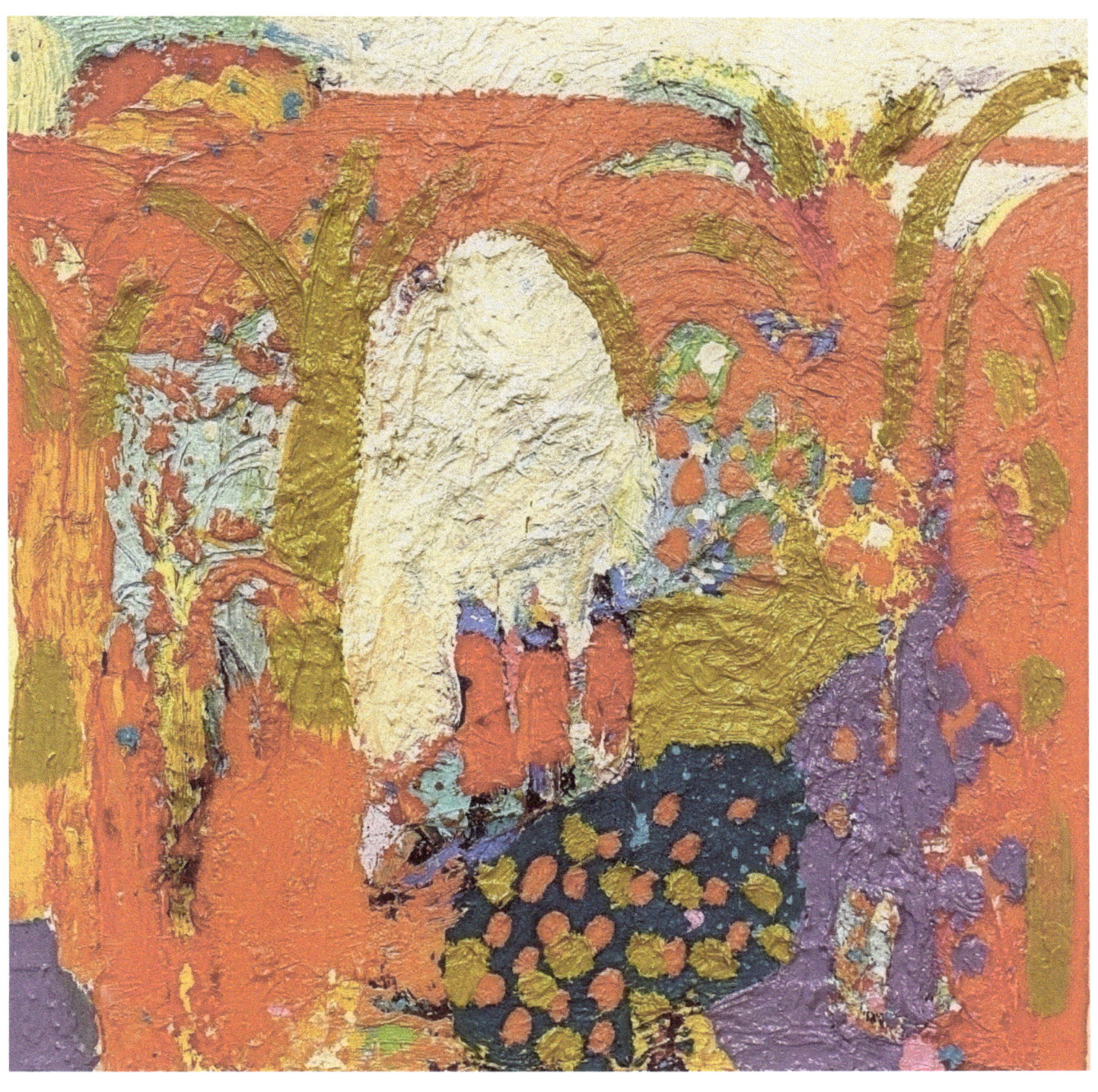

Title: Walking home after the festival

Size: 60x60cm

123

Stories From The Banyan Tree

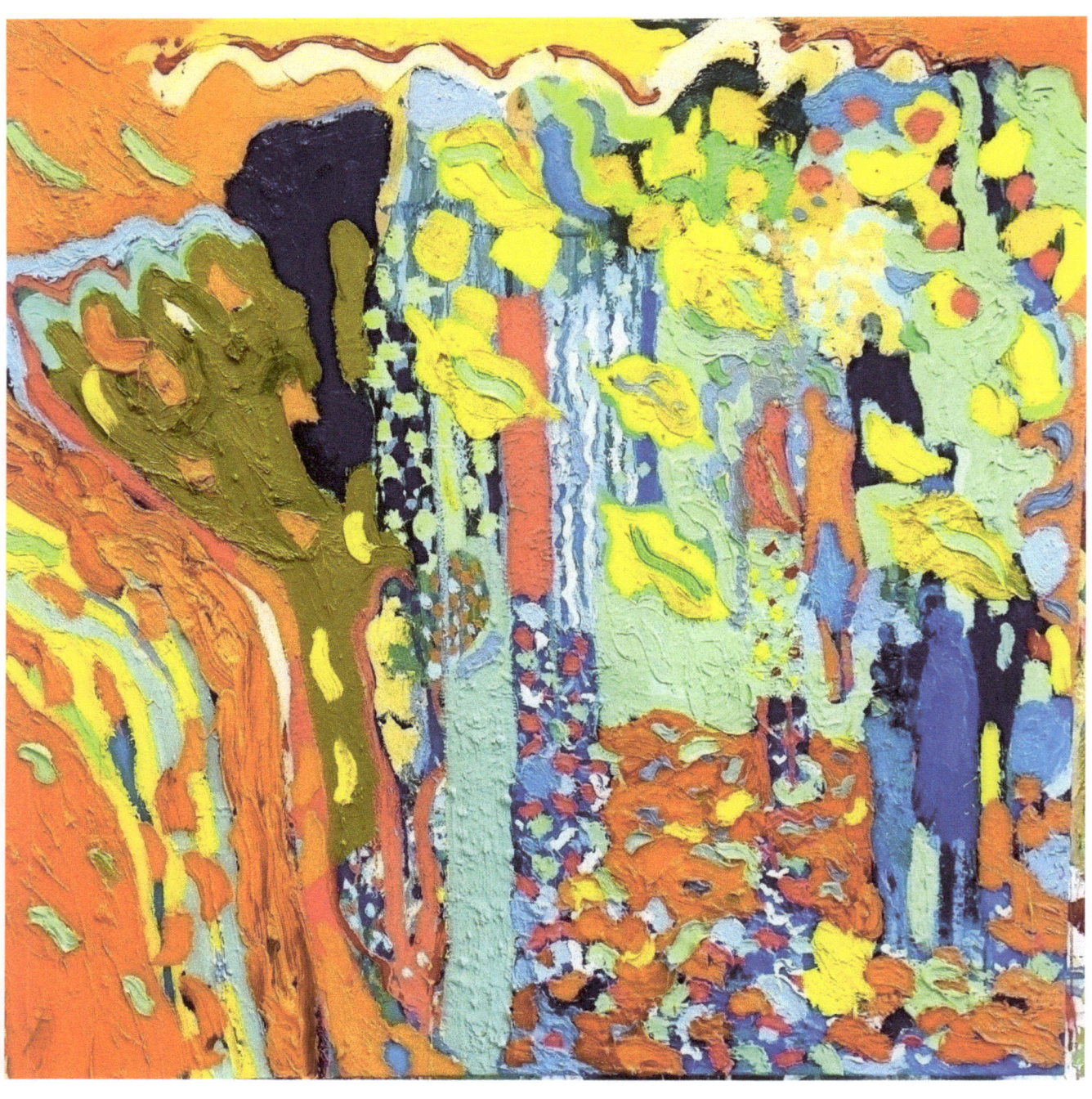

Title: Walking to the waterfall

Size: 120x120cm

Paul Wadsworth

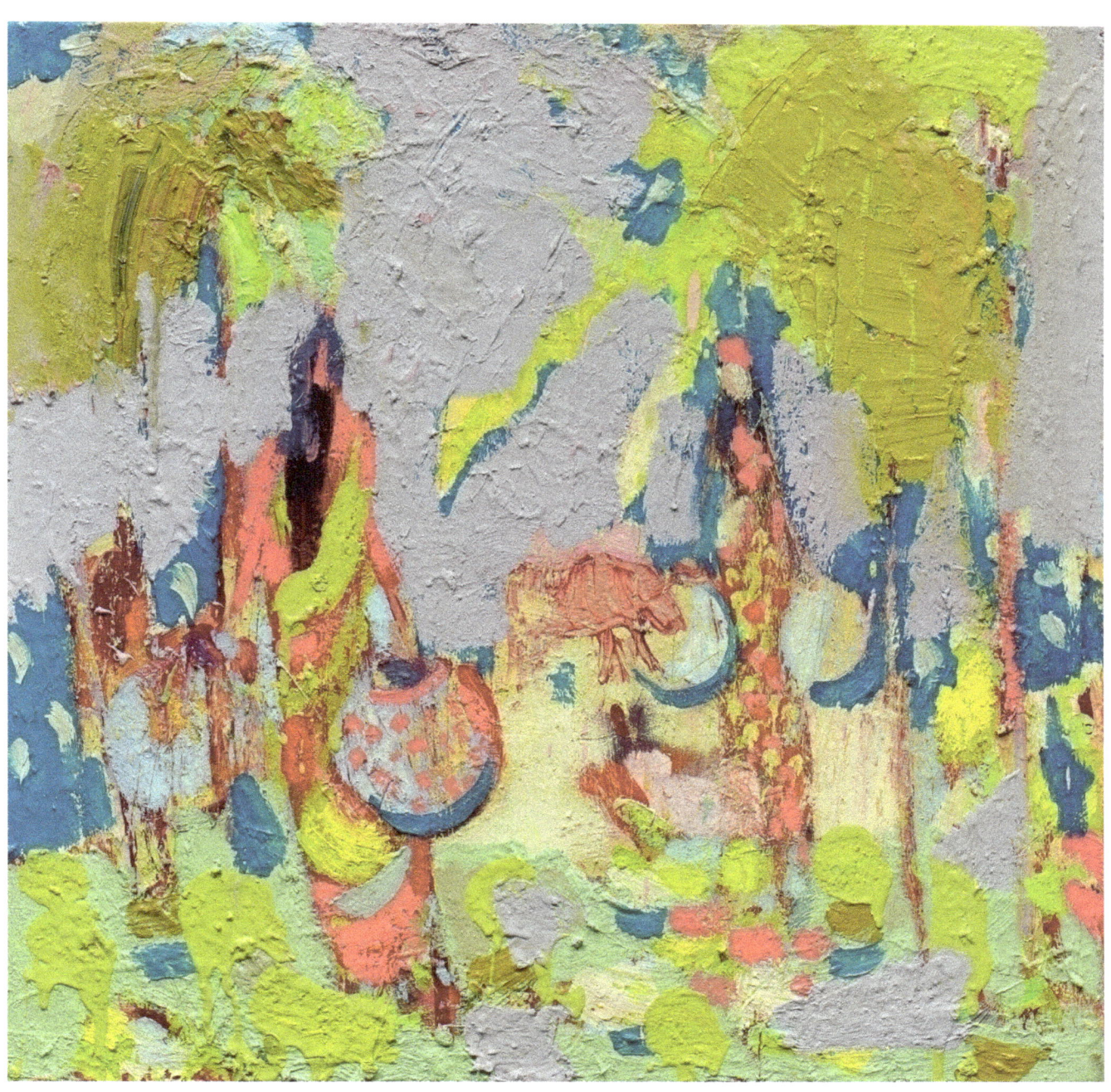

Title: Water carriers
Size: 60x60cm

Stories From The Banyan Tree

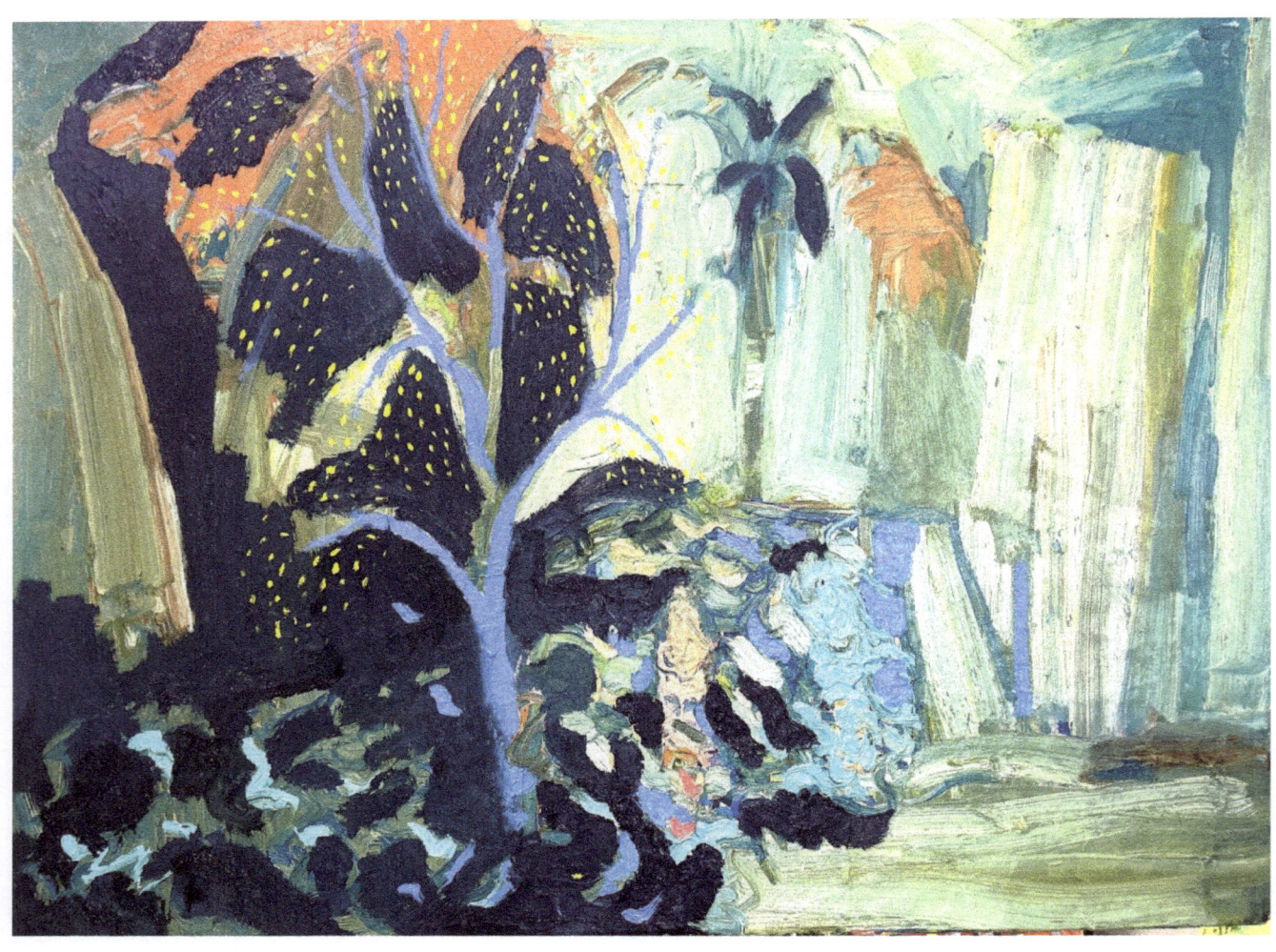

Title: Waterfall

Size: 130x177cm

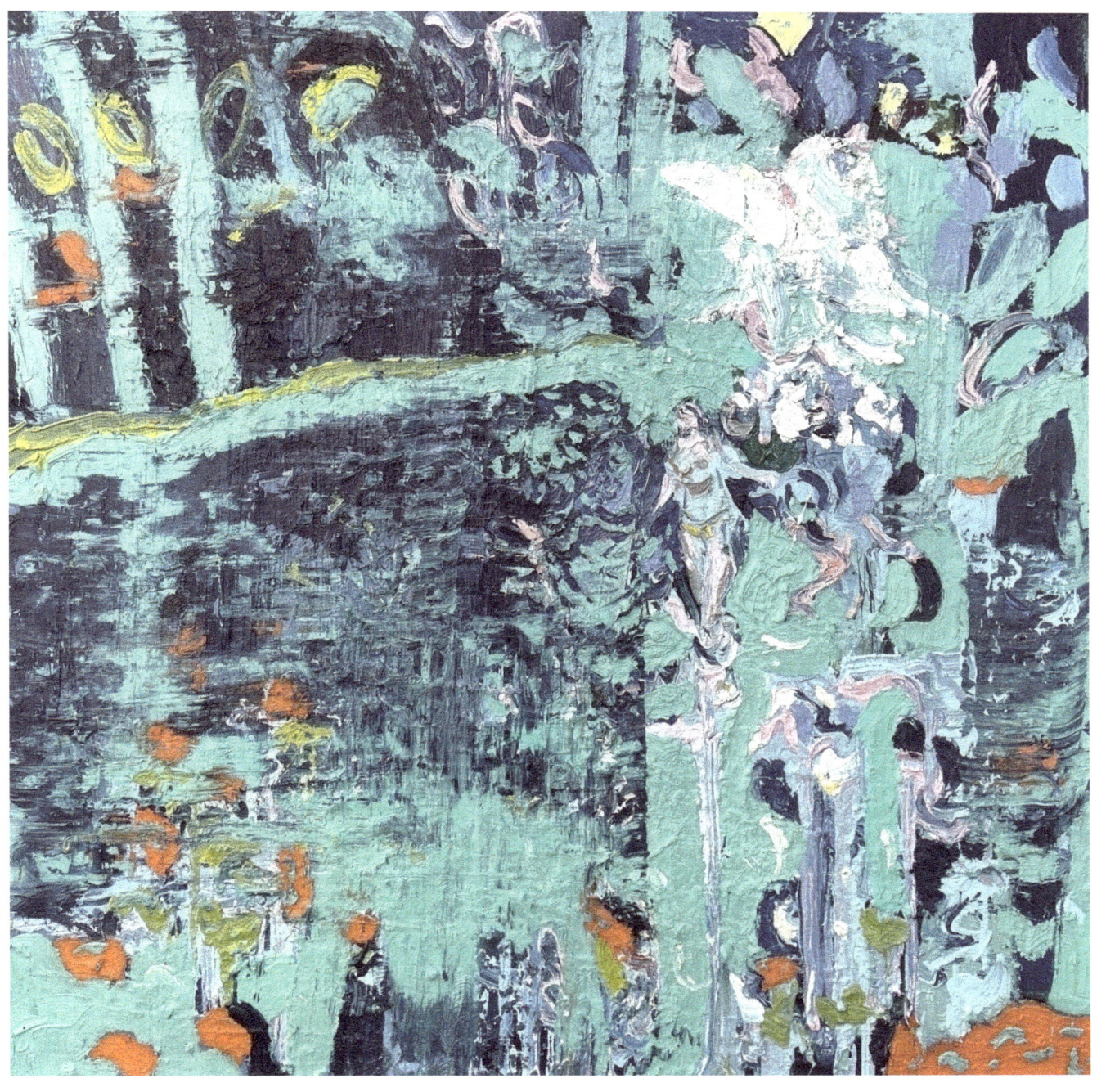

Title: White butterfly

Size: 120x120cm

Stories From The Banyan Tree

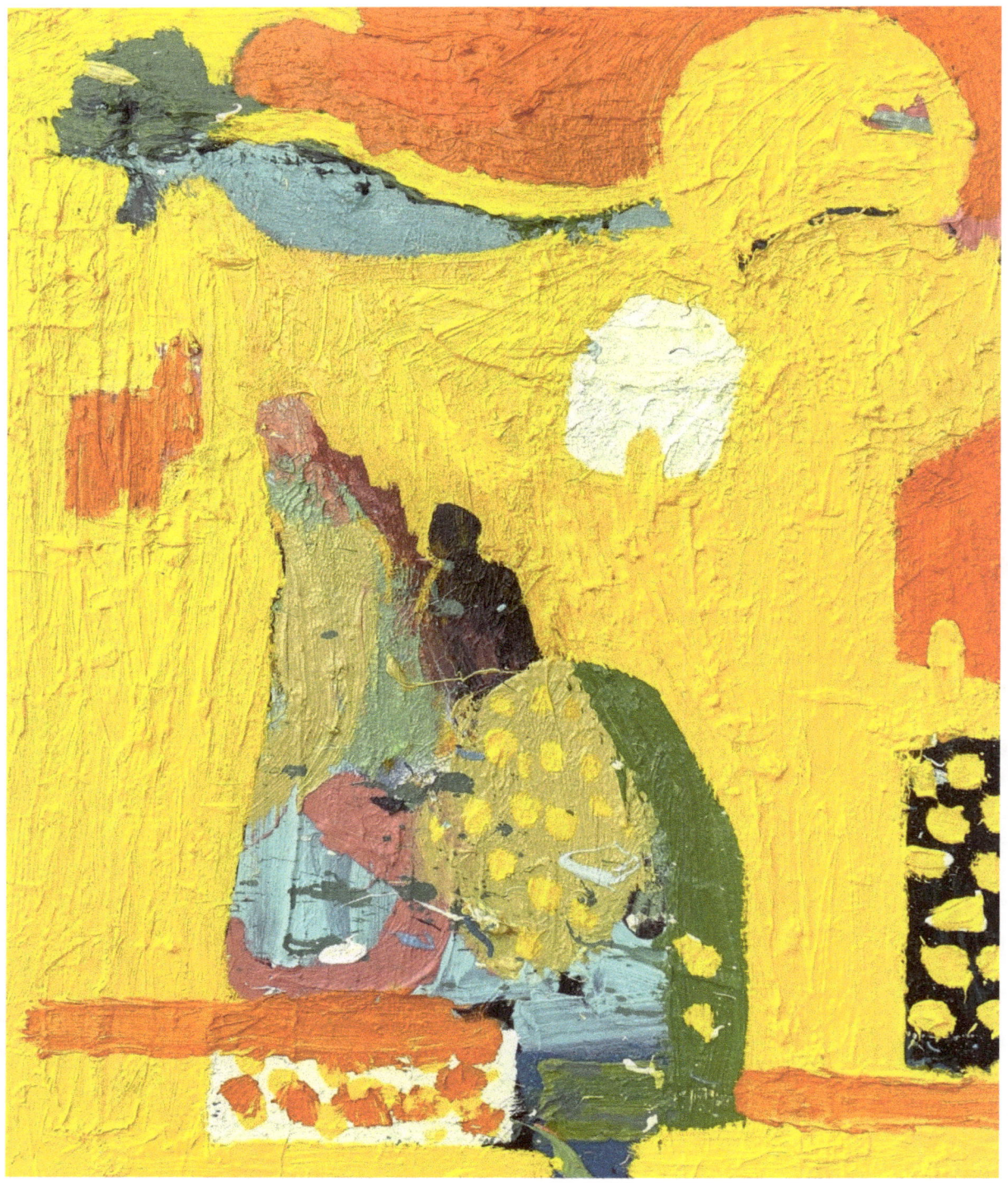

Title: Yellow desert
Size: 70x60cm

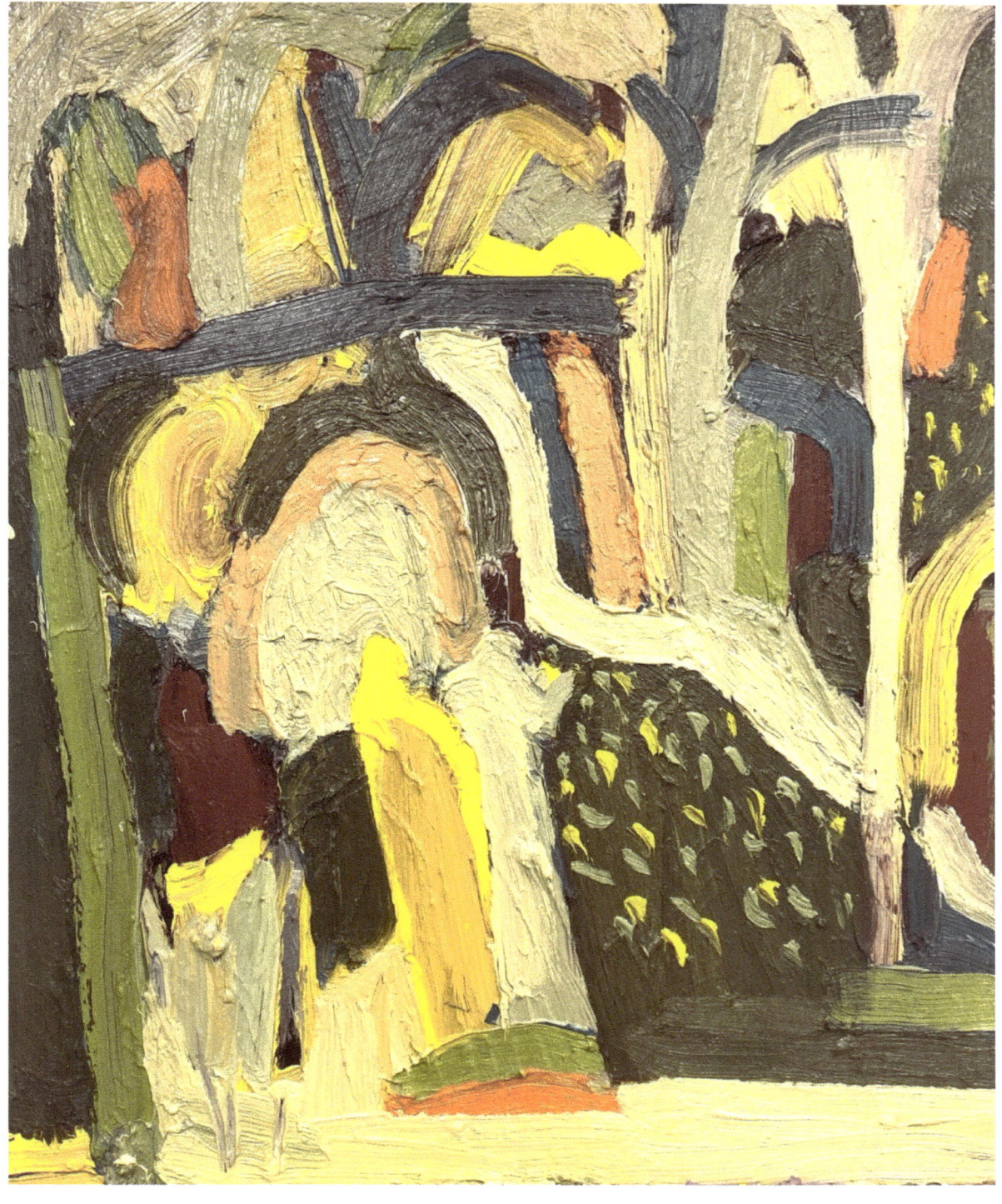

Title: Yellow sari

Size: 77x63cm

Stories From The Banyan Tree

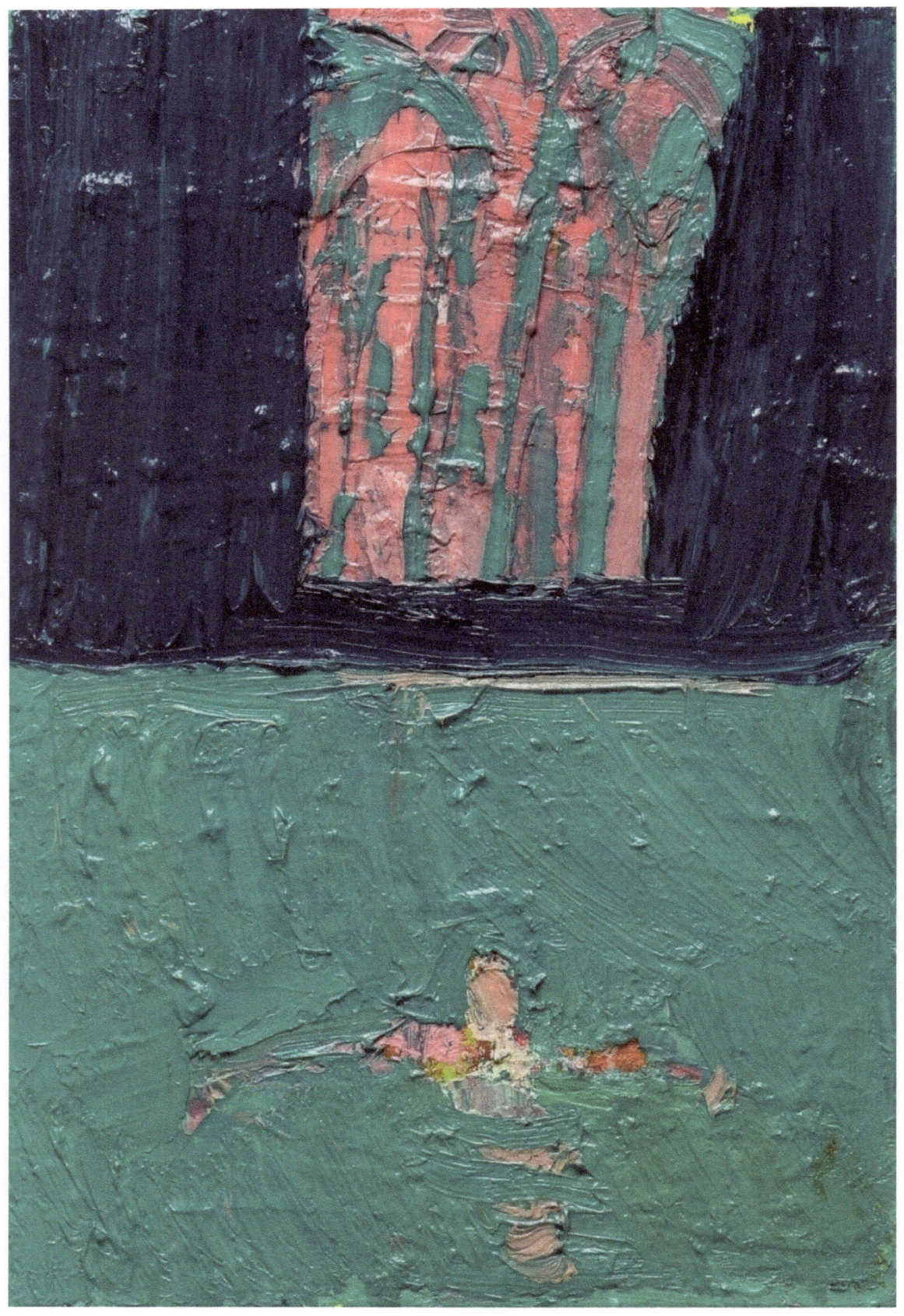

Title: Pink forest swimmer

Size: 60x40cm

Acrylic on Paper

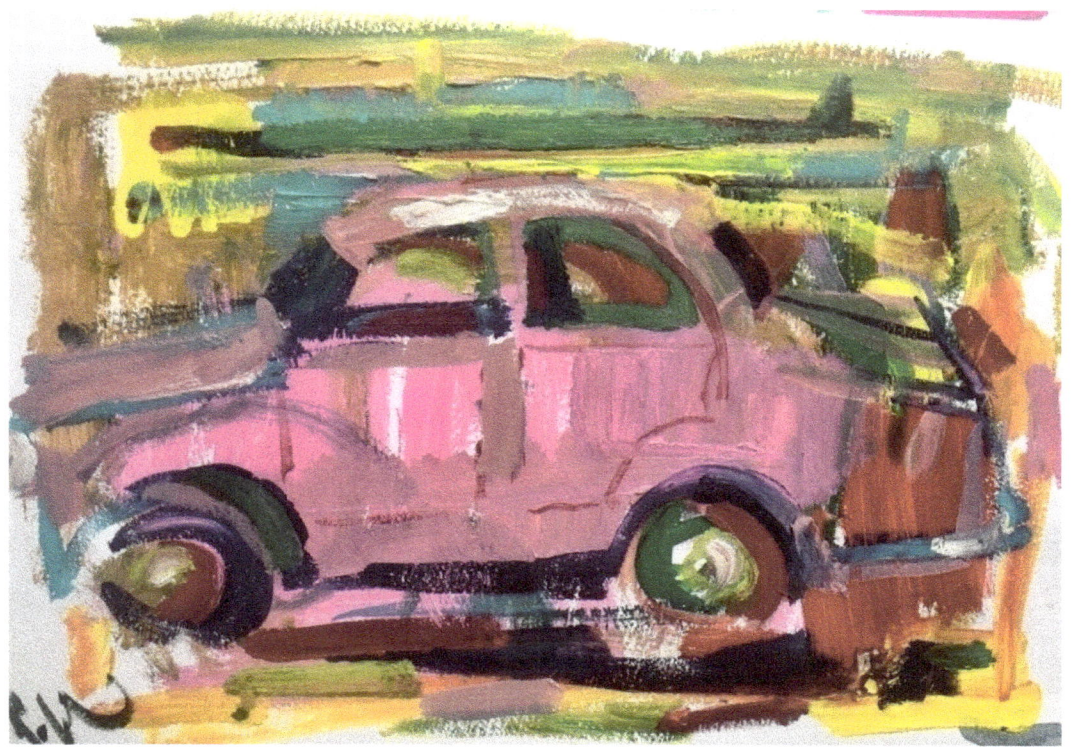

Title: Pink Ambassador

Size: 35x55cm

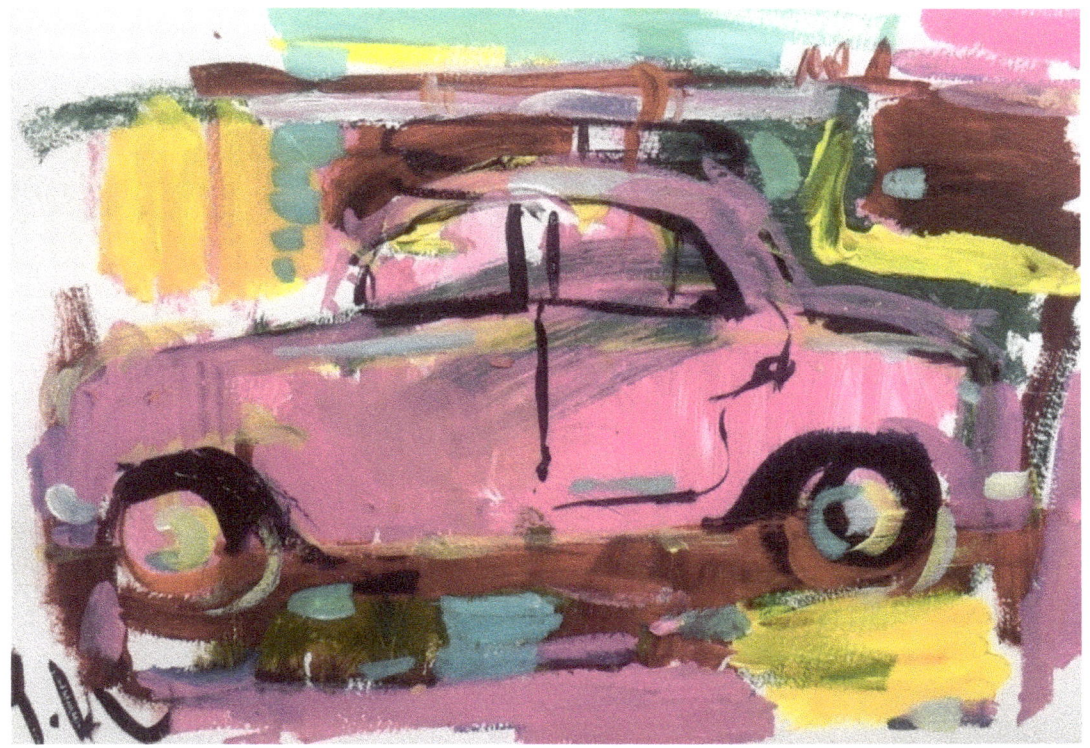

Title: Surf up

Size: 35x55cm

Stories From The Banyan Tree

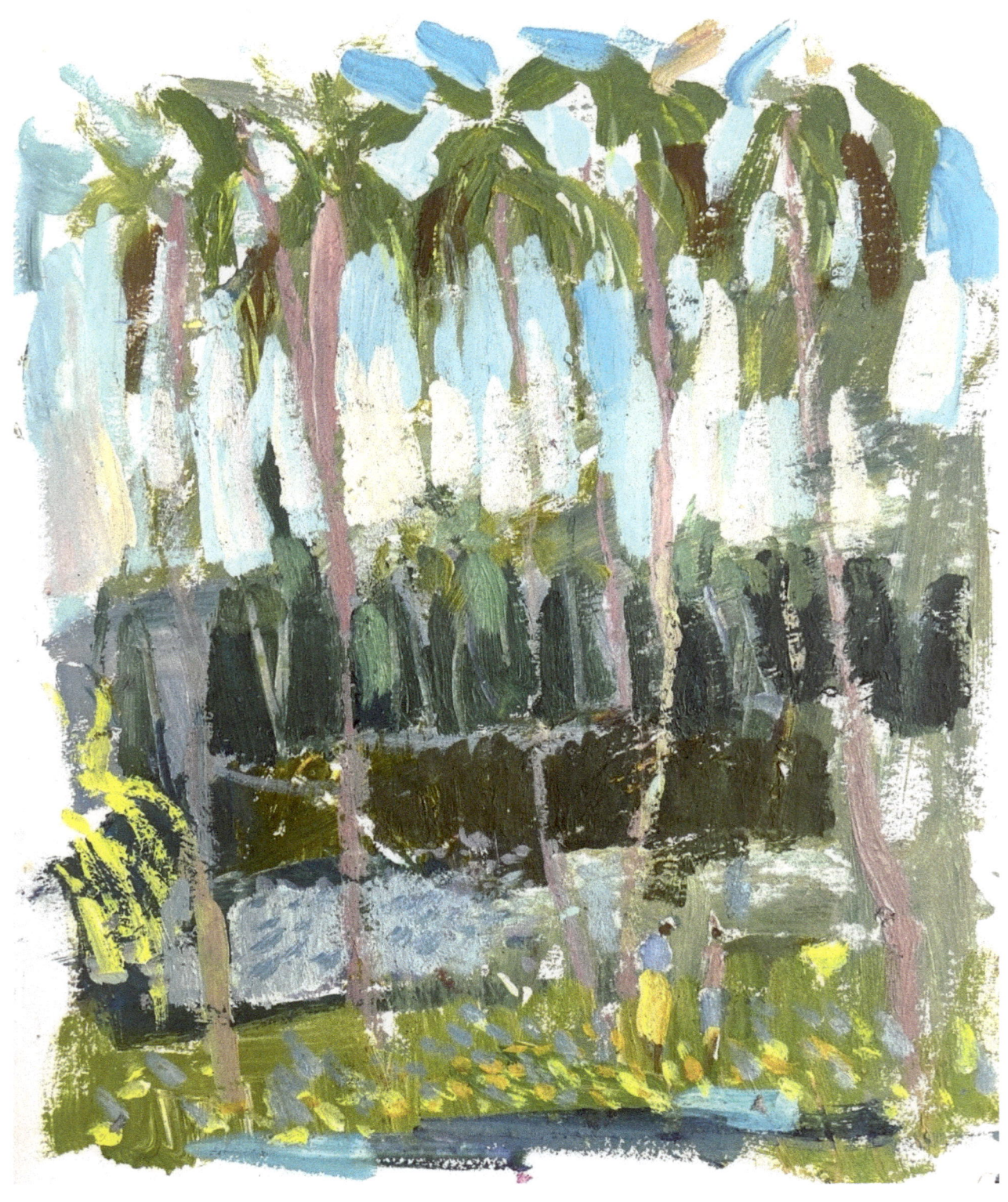

Title: A beautiful conversation

Size: 55x45cm

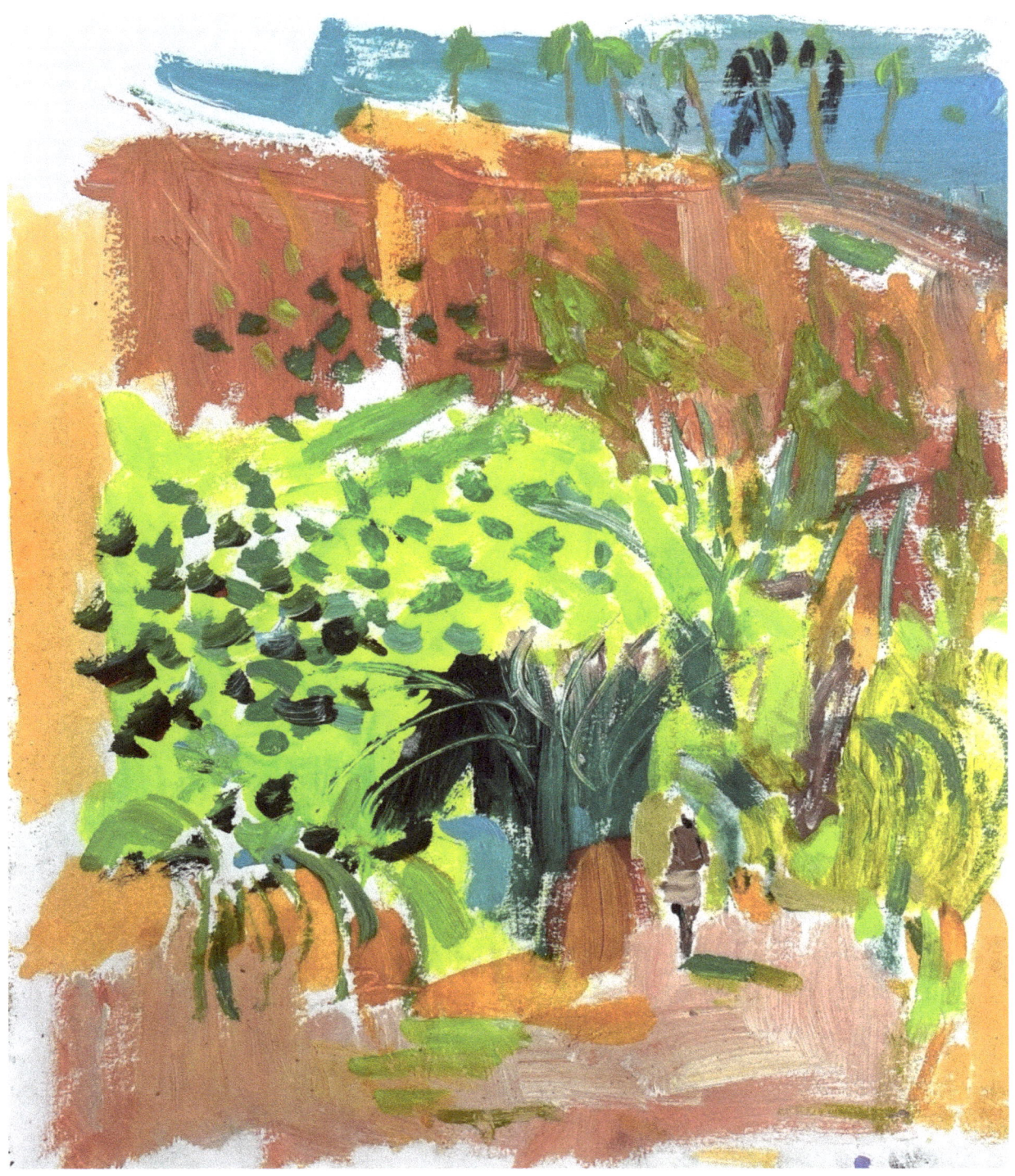

Title: Beach below the orange cliff

Size: 55x45cm

Stories From The Banyan Tree

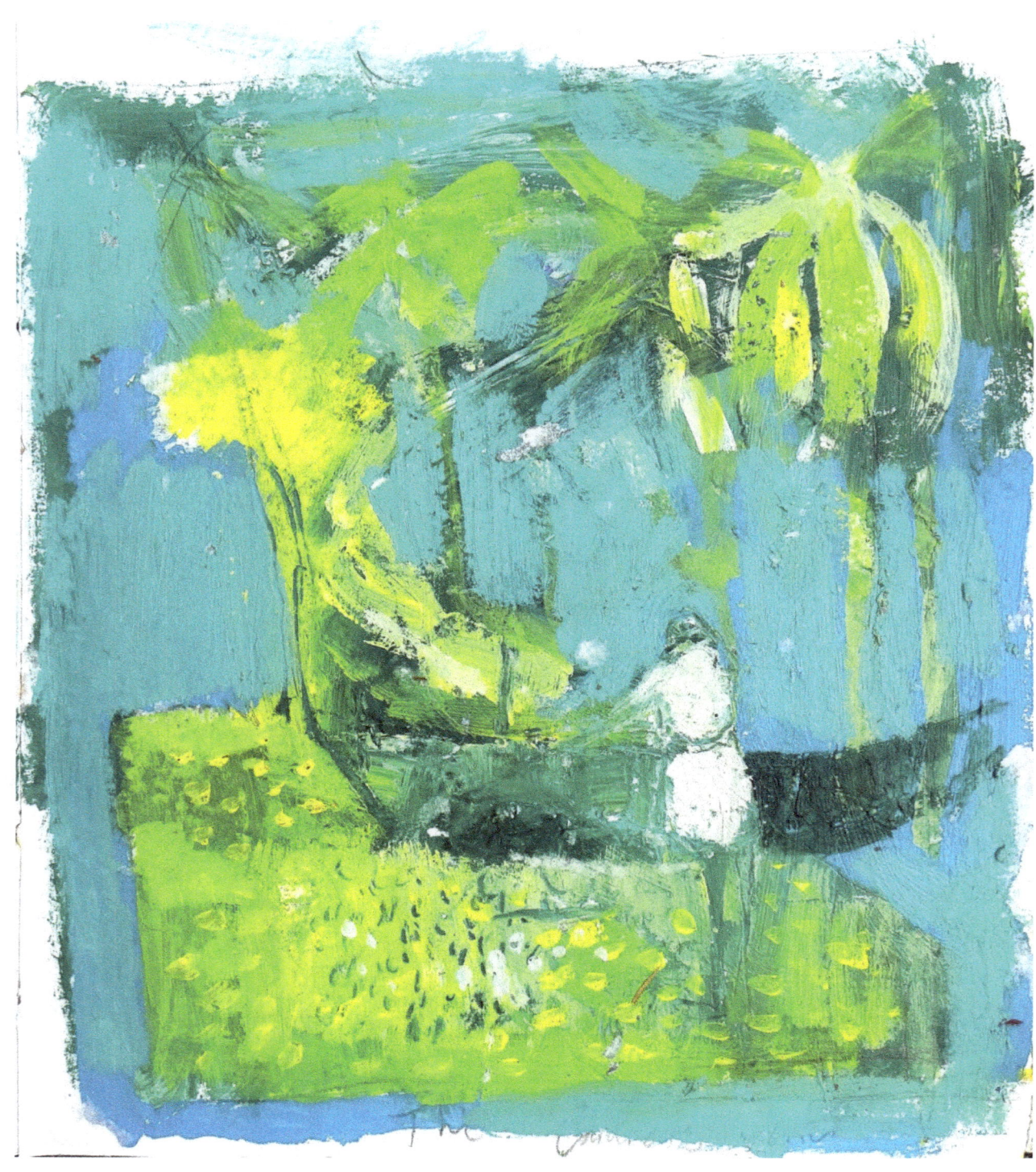

Title: Fisherman

Size: 55x45cm

Paul Wadsworth

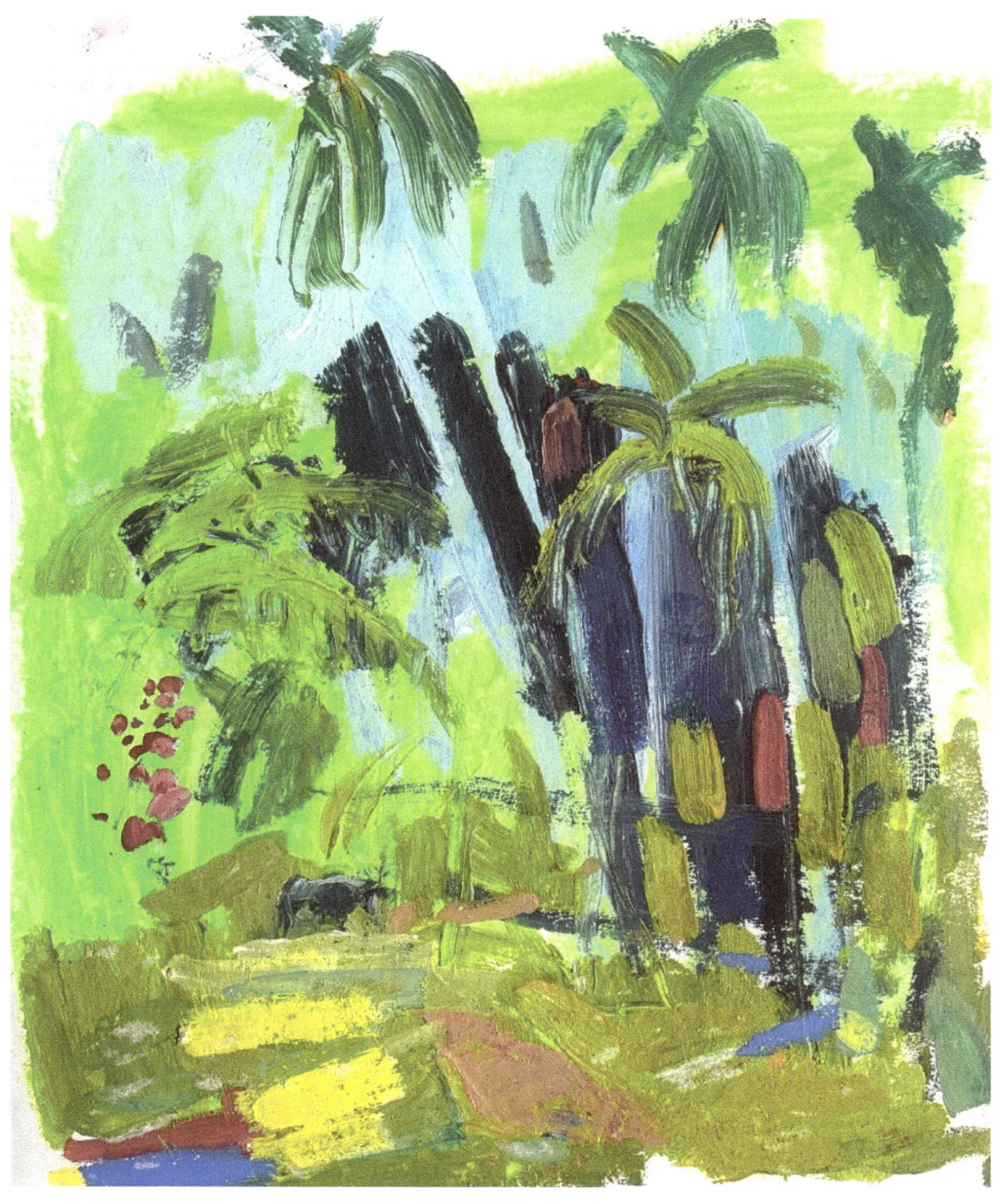

Title: Forest cow
Size: 55x45cm

Stories From The Banyan Tree

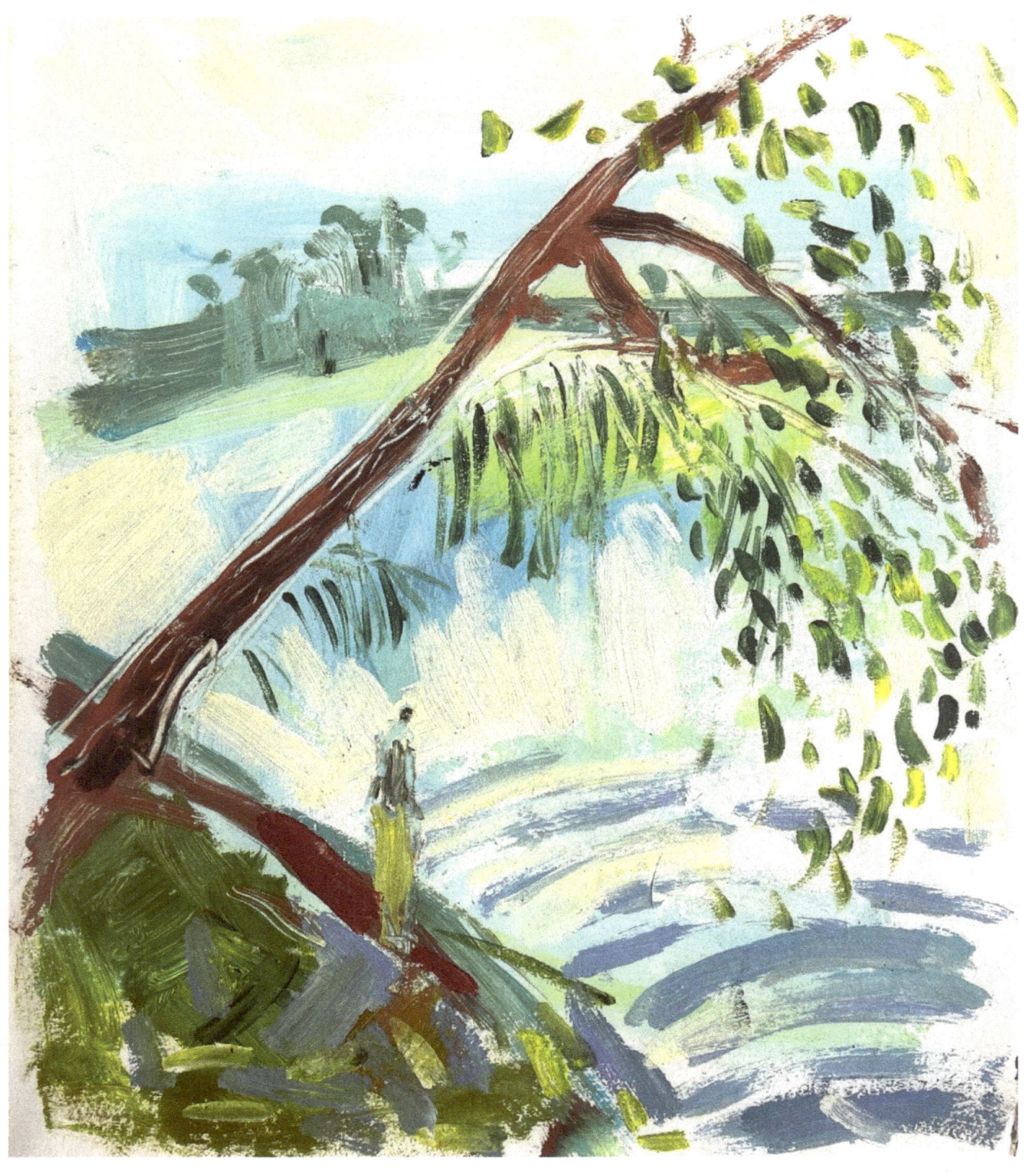

Title: Golden Island
Size: 55x45cm

Paul Wadsworth

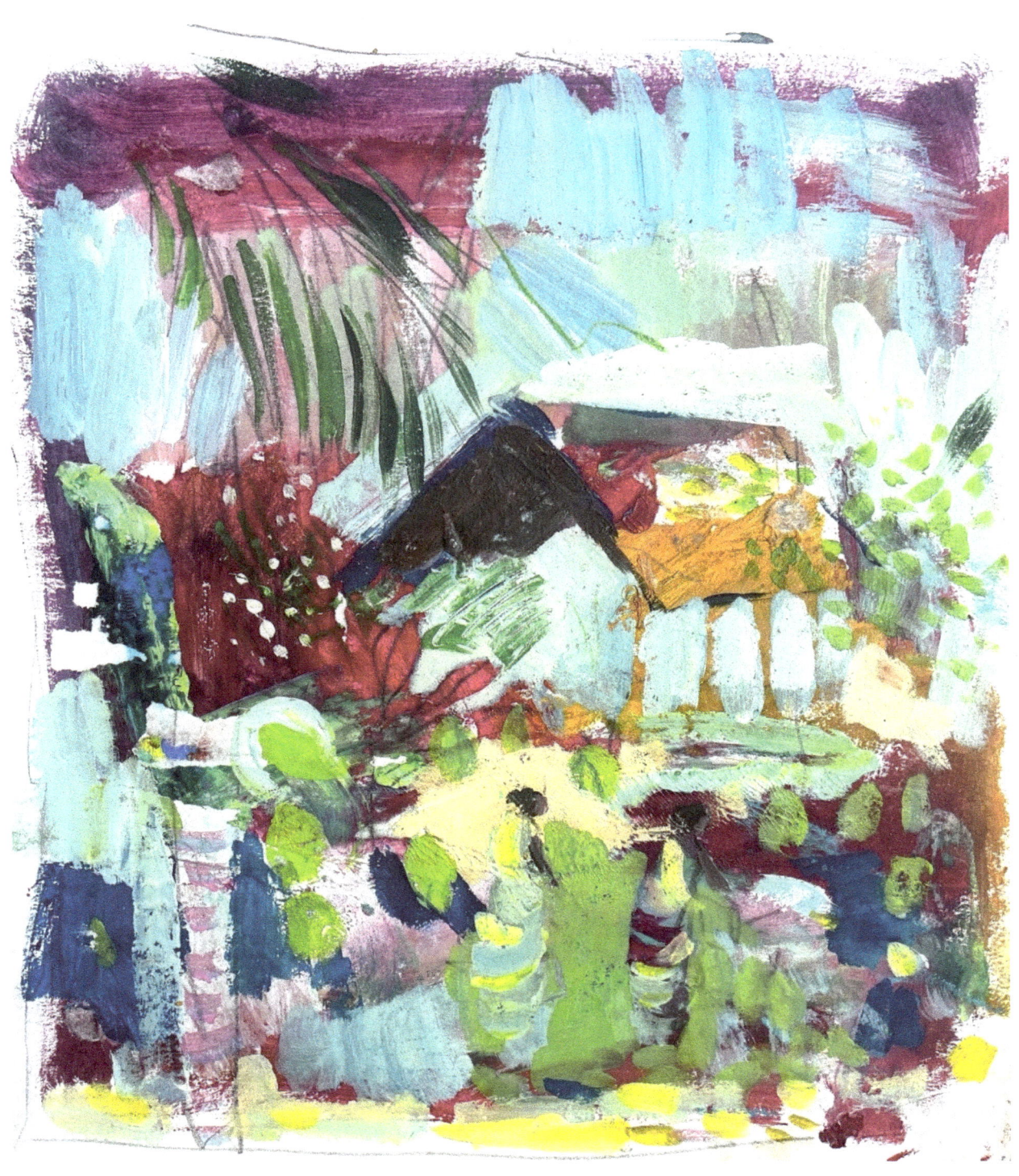

Title: Home by the sea

Size: 55x45cm

Stories From The Banyan Tree

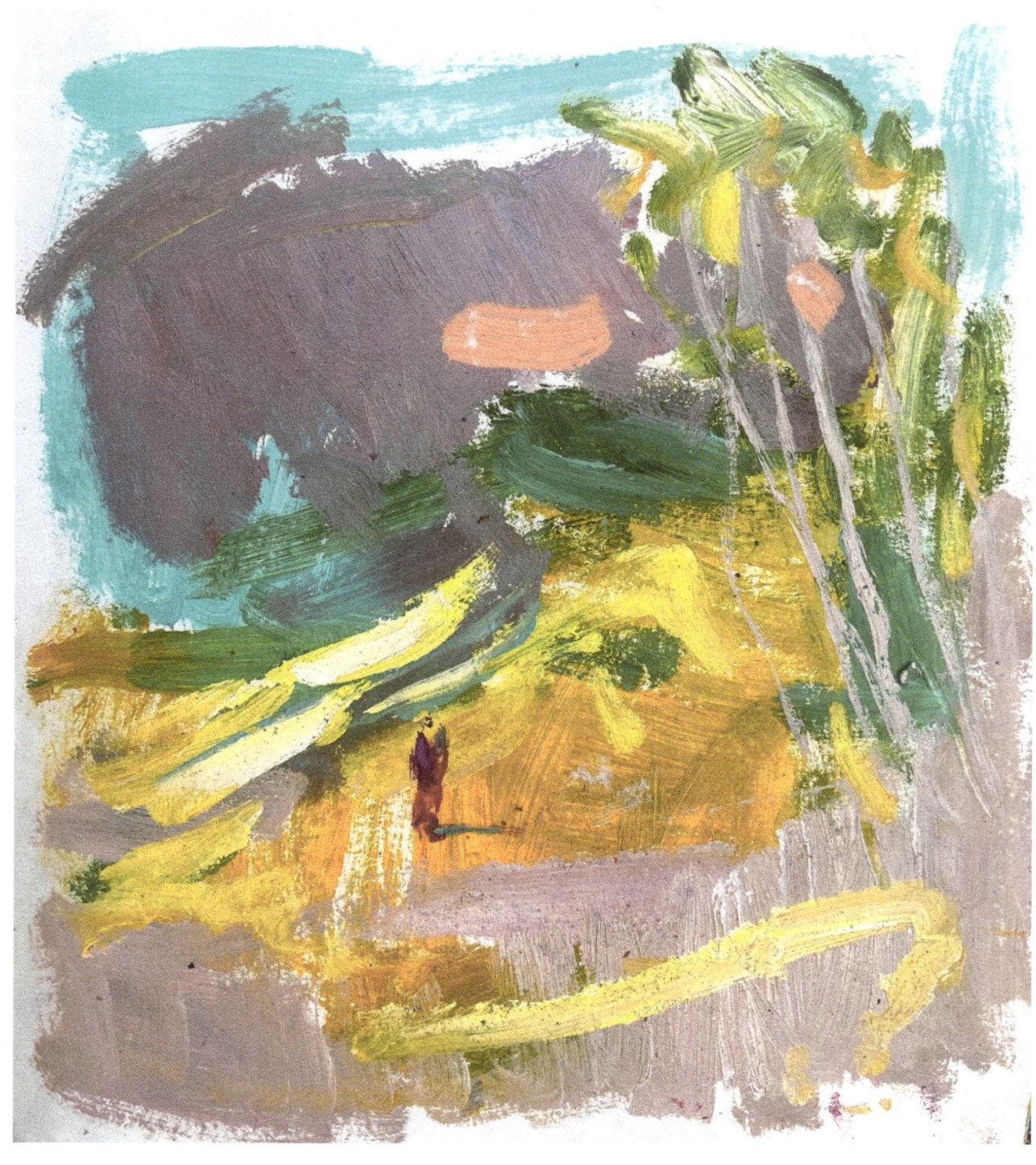

Title: Morning walk

Size: 55x45cm

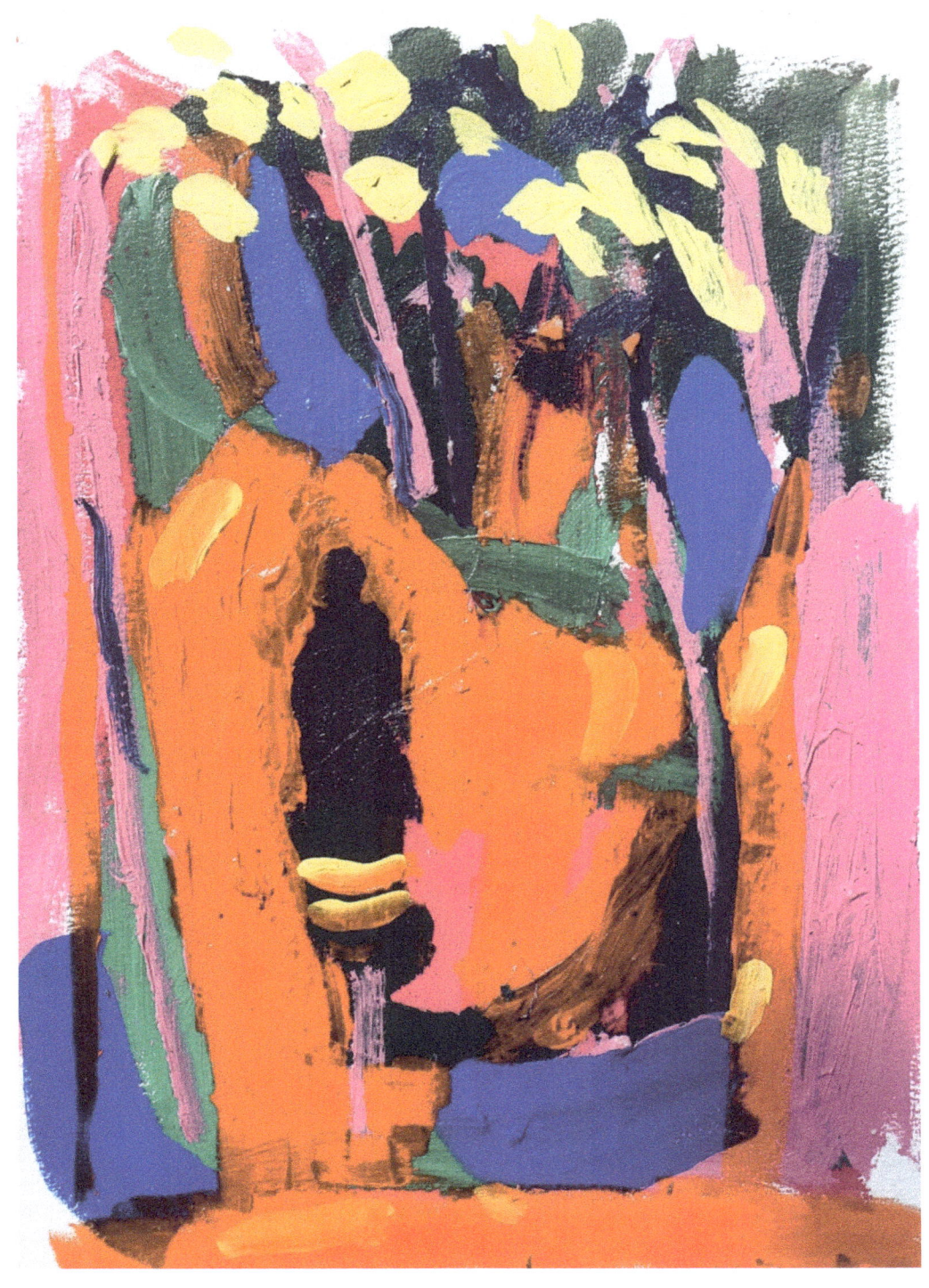

Title: Red forest

Size: 55x35cm

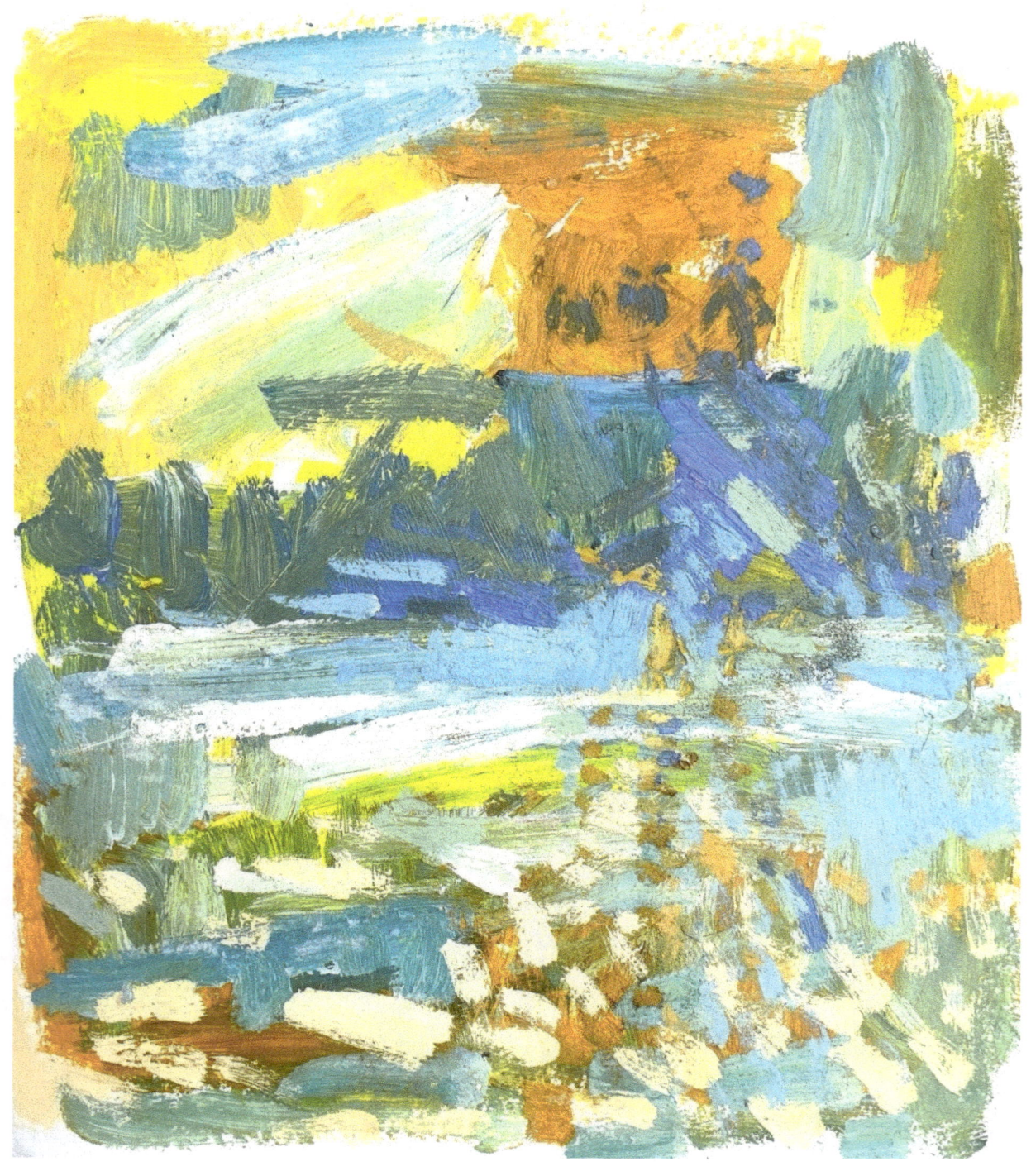

Title: Sun swimmers
Size: 55x45cm

Paul Wadsworth

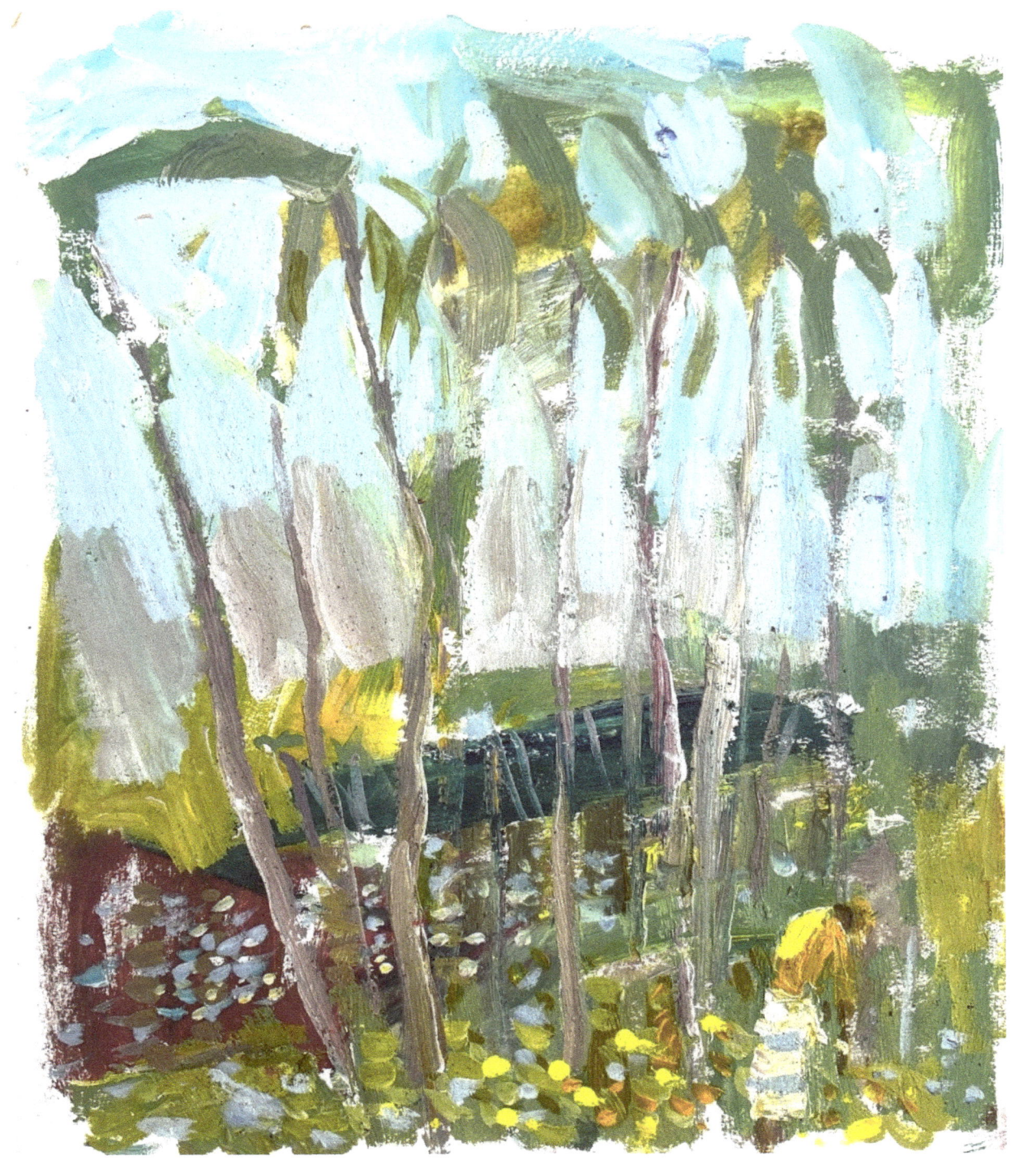

Title: Wood collector

Size: 55x45cm

Watercolours

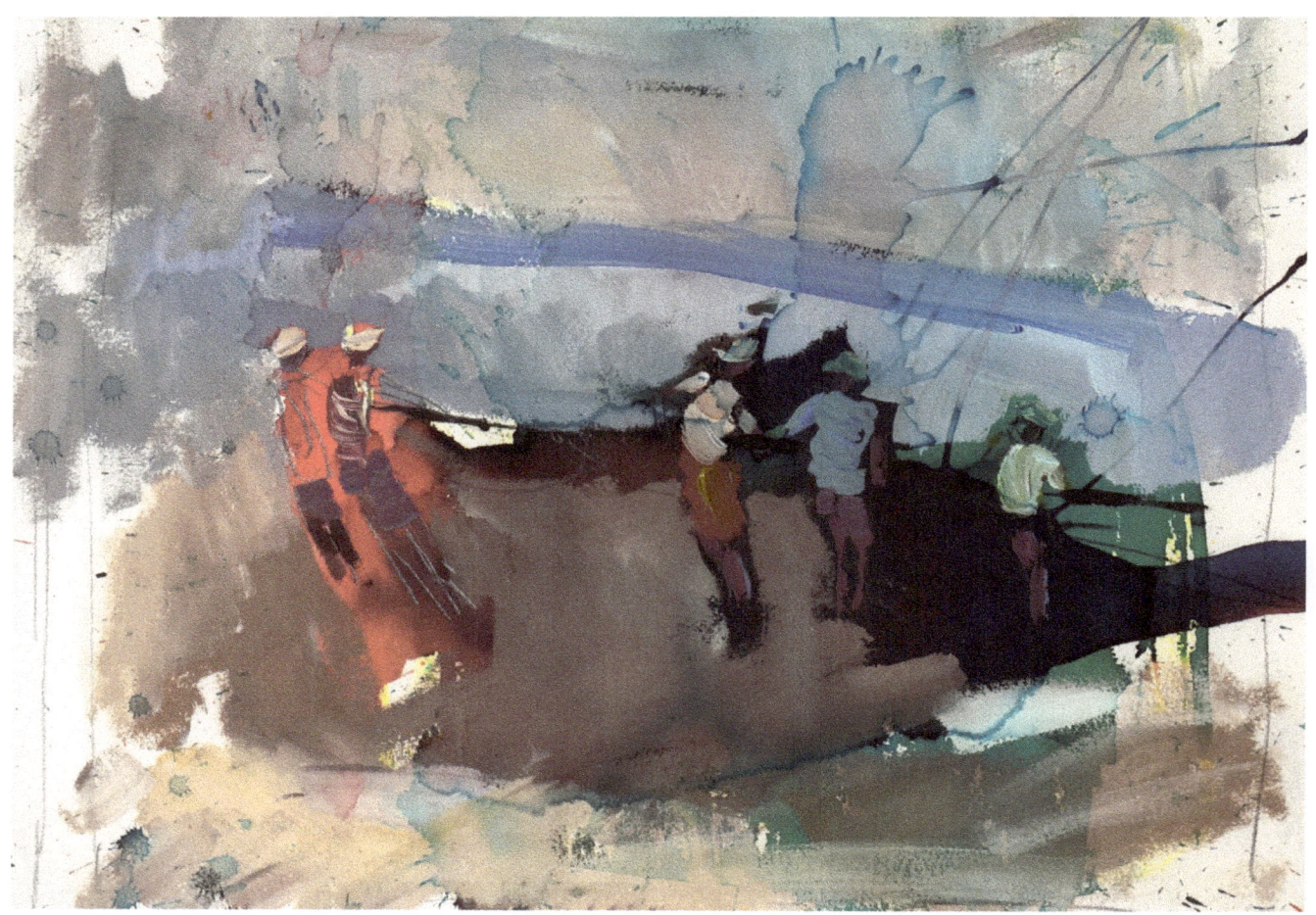

Title: Hauling the nets, Kerala

Size: 40x60cm

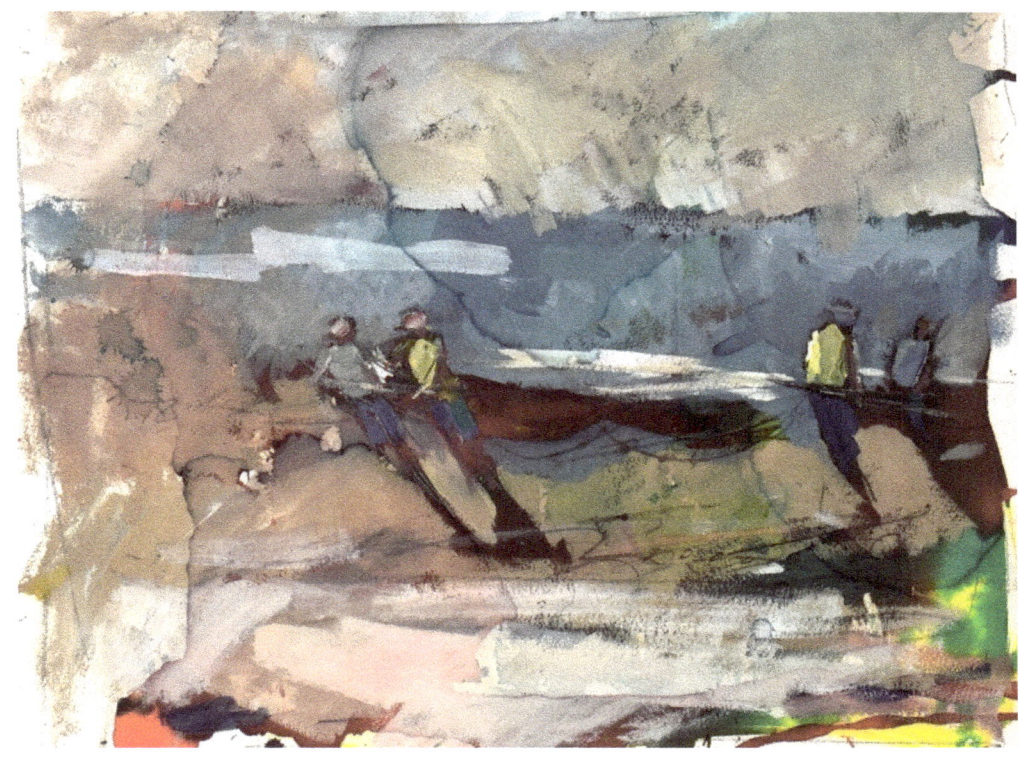

Title: Kerala fishermen

Size: 40x60cm

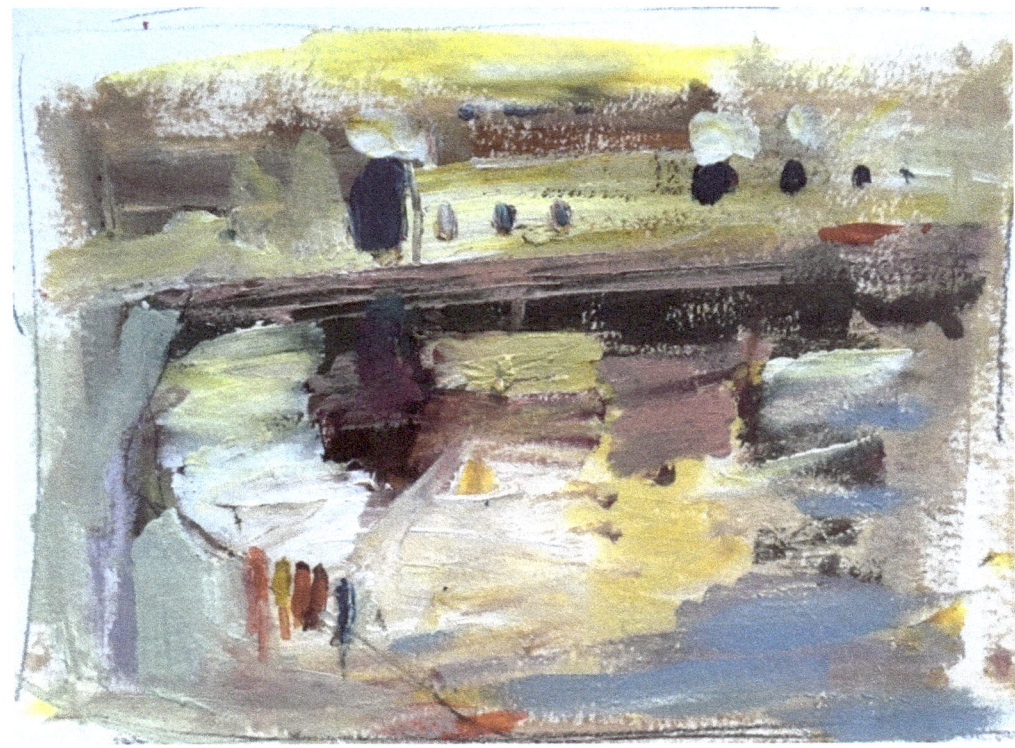

Title: Pilgrimage

Size: 40x60cm

Stories From The Banyan Tree

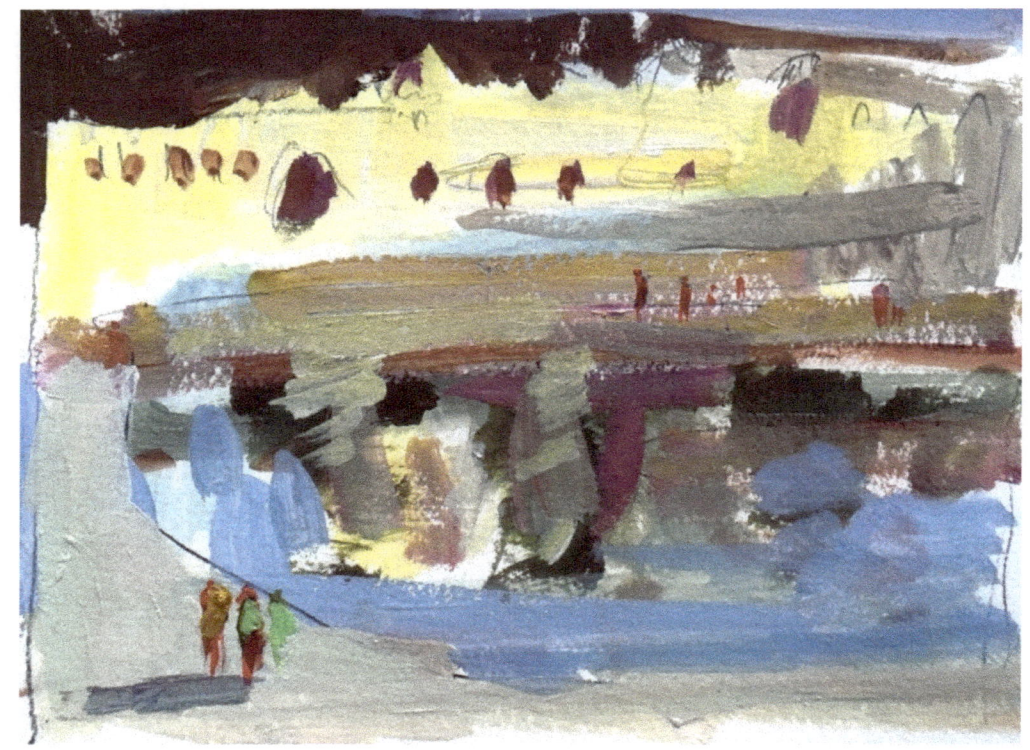

Title: Pushkar walk

Size: 40x60cm

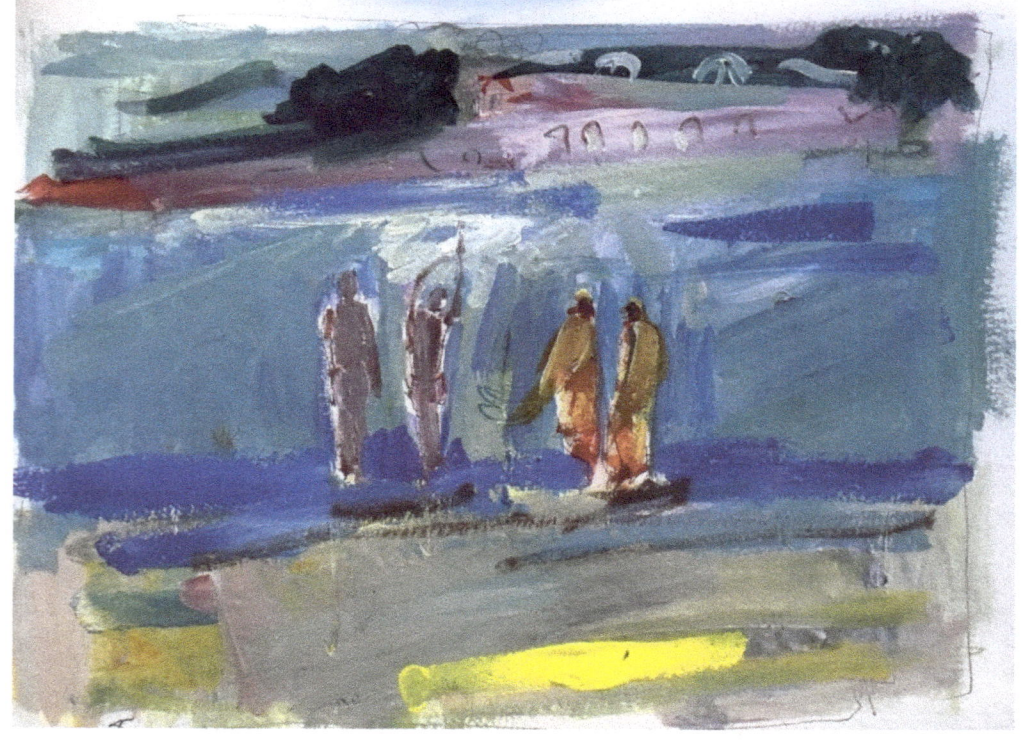

Title: Sacred swim

Size: 40x60cm

Paul Wadsworth

CV

1992-94 Ipswich College of Art and Design
1994-97 Falmouth College of Arts BA (Hons) Fine Art

Selected Exhibitions International:
2000 to 2010	Traveling	In the Middle East, Arab Emirates and Oman to paint and gather resource material.
2007	Stronarch Gallery, Ireland.	
2007	Bait Munza Gallery, Oman.	Abu Dhabi, Art Paris.
2007	Collection for Saudi Arabian investment bank.	
2008	Dubai	Residency Gulf art fair Dubai.
2010	Majlis Gallery, Dubai.	Book signing and print show from Arabian love story. Book goes to the Abu Dhabi Royal Family.
2010	Bait Munza Gallery Oman.	
2013	Travels	To Oman and Dubai.
2014	Majlis Gallery, Dubai	

International Solo Shows:
2001	Majlis Gallery, Dubai.	Residency and solo show.
2002	Majlis Gallery, Dubai.	2 month residency & solo show.
2003	Majlis Gallery, Dubai.	1 month residency & solo show.
2005	Majlis Gallery, Dubai.	solo show large mixed media pieces.
2006	Majlis Gallery, Dubai.	2 month residency painting. Dubai art fair.
2007	Majlis Gallery, Dubai.	Solo Show.
2009	Majlis Gallery, Dubai.	Solo show.
2011	Majlis Gallery, Dubai.	Solo show.
2012	Majlis Gallery, Dubai.	Solo show works from Oman over 3 months travel in the Country.
2016	Majlis Gallery, Dubai.	Solo show.

Selected Exhibitions UK based:
2002	Pilgrim Gallery, Holborn, London.	
2003	Gallery 27, Cork Street, London.	Joint show.
2003	Woolffe Gallery, London.	
2004	Anthony Hepworth Gallery, Bath.	
2005	Hunting art prize, London show.	
2005	Newlyn Gallery, Cornwall.	
2007	Campden Gallery.	Chipping Campden exploring images from the Middle East.
2007	Tresco Gallery, Isles of Scilly, Cornwall.	Large collection for Tresco estate.
2008	Black cloth project.	Working with the model.
2009	Barclays bank Dubai.	Collection of 80 originals.
2009	Working on book to be published.	Arabian Love Story.
2009	Janet Rady.	Fine art.
2010	Newlyn Gallery Cornwall.	Black cloth project video I was elected to be a Member of Newlyn Society of Artists.
2014	Hilton fine arts, Bath.	
2014	Beside The Wave Gallery, Falmouth, Cornwall.	
2015	Tresco Gallery, Isles of Scilly, Cornwall.	
2020	Chelsea, London.	Cricket fine art.

Solo shows:
2002	Badcocks Gallery, Newlyn, Cornwall.	Exploring the use of gold and mixed media in painting.
2002	Kings Road Gallery, London.	
2003	Kings Road Gallery, London.	"Eastern Jewels" exploring imagery from travel in the Middle East.
2004	Beside The Wave Gallery, Falmouth, Cornwall.	"Coast to Coast" 2005, Kings Road Gallery, London.
2005	Badcocks Gallery Newlyn, Cornwall.	
2005	Beside The Wave Gallery, Falmouth, Cornwall.	"Open Spaces,"
2006	Goldfish Contemporary, Cornwall.	
2008	Hilton -Young Gallery Penzance.	The sacred and profane.
2008	Campden Gallery.	
2009	Caxton Contemporary.	Drawings.

2011	Campden Gallery.	Arabian Love Story.
2011	Bo Hilton fine arts Bath.	
2012	Crypt Gallery, St Ives, Cornwall.	Black cloth project.
2012	Beside the Wave gallery Falmouth, Cornwall.	West to East. Paintings from Cornwall and Oman.
2013	Campden Gallery.	Stories from the cloth.
2015	Campden Gallery.	Travels in India stories from the banyan tree.
2015	Penwith Gallery, St Ives, Cornwall.	
2017	Campden Gallery.	India and performance.
2018	Chelsea, London.	Cricket fine art.
2018	Campden Gallery.	Circus.
2019	Crypt Gallery, St Ives, Cornwall.	
2019	Cornwall Contemporary, Penzance, Cornwall.	
2021	Campden Gallery.	Travels India.

Worked on large commission for Marks and Spencer's for outlet in Marble Arch, London and three hundred forty other stores in UK and Europe.

Collections:
- Tresco Estate
- Barclays Bank Dubai
- Saudi Arabian Investment Bank
- Marks and Spencer's

Publications:

2011	Campden Gallery	"Arabian Love Story"
2018	Campden Gallery	"Circus" 3-25 November exhibition, 28 Page catalogue, ISBN: 978-1908753-57-1
2018	Campden Gallery	"Winter Exhibition" 1 December – 31 January exhibition, 36 page catalogue, ISBN: 978-1-908753-58-8
2021	Campden Gallery	"India & Cornwall" 12 April - 9 May exhibition, 28 page catalogue, ISBN: 978-1-908753-68-7

www.ingramcontent.com/pod-product-compliance
Lightning Source LLC
Chambersburg PA
CBHW041546220526
45473CB00015B/2966